D1430392

# Christian Responses
## to the HOLOCAUST

*Religion, Theology, and the Holocaust*
Alan L. Berger, *Series Editor*

# Christian Responses
## to the HOLOCAUST

*Moral and Ethical Issues*

*Edited by*

DONALD J. DIETRICH

 Syracuse University Press

**Library of Congress Cataloging-in-Publication Data**

Christian responses to the Holocaust : moral and ethical issues / edited
by Donald J. Dietrich.— 1st ed.
p. cm.—(Religion, theology, and the Holocaust)
Includes bibliographical references and index.
ISBN 0–8156–3029–8 (pbk. : alk. paper)
1. Christianity and antisemitism—Germany—History—20th century. 2. National socialism
and religion. 3. Holocaust (Christian theology) 4.
Holocaust, Jewish (1939–1945) I. Dietrich, Donald J., 1941-II. Series.
BT93.C495 2003
261.8'73—dc21
2003002093

TO OUR GRANDCHILDREN

*Dana, Gage, Isabella, Layne, Liam, Nicholas, and Robin*

# Contents

# Acknowledgments

I WOULD LIKE TO THANK those who participated in the conference at Boston College for clarifying some of my own ideas on the Christian-Nazi encounter and for making their research available for publication. On behalf of the participants in this book, I would also like to thank Gloria Rufo for her work in editing the essays. Finally, I would like to thank my wife, Linda, for her patience as I edited this book. I would be remiss if I did not also thank Audrey, our miniature dachshund, for not eating the manuscript and for providing me with many amusing moments.

# Contributors

**Lawrence Baron** has served as the Nasatir Professor of Modern Jewish History and the director of the Lipinsky Institute for Judaic Studies at San Diego State University since 1988. He has coedited the anthologies *Embracing the Other: Philosophical, Psychological, and Historical Perspective on Altruism* (1992) and *Martin Buber and the Human Sciences* (1996). He currently is writing a book on thematic trends in recent Holocaust feature films.

**John S. Conway** is emeritus professor of history at the University of British Columbia, Vancouver, Canada. His study *The Nazi Persecution of the Churches 1933–1945* has recently been reissued. He is also the author of numerous articles on the role of the churches during the Holocaust.

**John J. Delaney** is an associate professor of history at Kutztown University in Pennsylvania. His research centers on rural Catholics, Polish workers, and Nazi racial policy in Bavaria, 1939–1945. It targets Nazi Germany's efforts to isolate, subjugate, and control Polish forced laborers in Germany's war economy. He is the author of "Racial Values vs. Religious Values: Clerical Opposition to Nazi Anti-Polish Racial Policy," *Church History* 70 (2001).

**Donald J. Dietrich,** professor of theology at Boston College, is the author of *Catholic Citizens in the Third Reich: Psycho-Social Principles and Moral Reasoning* (1988) and *God and Humanity in Auschwitz: Jewish-Christian Relations and Sanctioned Murder* (1995). He is currently writing a book on the emerging human rights conversation in the Catholic Church.

**Gershon Greenberg** is professor of religion and philosophy at American University and Visiting Professor of Jewish Philosophy at Bar Ilan University. His area of research is Jewish religious life and thought concerning the Holocaust, for which he recently completed a term as Fellow at the International Center for Holocaust Research at Yad Vashem. His latest publications include a three-volume annotated bibliography of religious responses through the catastrophe as it unfolded.

**Stephen R. Haynes** is associate professor in the Department of Religious Studies at Rhodes College, Memphis, Tennessee. He is the author of *Holocaust Education and the Church-Related College: Restoring Ruptured Traditions* (1997) and *The Death of God Movement and the Holocaust: Radical Theology Encounters the Shoah,* edited with John K. Roth (1999).

**Matthew D. Hockenos** is assistant professor of history at Skidmore College in Saratoga Springs, New York. He is completing a book-length manuscript entitled "Coming to Terms with the Past: The Protestant Church in Postwar Germany, 1945–50." He is currently conducting research on "The German Protestant Church and the Jewish Question" and has been a visiting scholar at the Institute for European History in Mainz.

**Kyle T. Jantzen** is assistant professor of church history and director of extension education at the Canadian Theological Seminary. He has written numerous articles and book chapters on the German Church Struggle and is currently working on a book dealing with the theological roots of pastors engaged in resisting Nazism.

**Robert A. Krieg** is professor of theology at the University of Notre Dame. He specializes in German historical theology in the modern period. He is the author of *Story-Shaped Christology* (1988), *Karl Adam: Catholicism in German Culture* (1992), and *Romano Guardini: A Precursor of Vatican II* (1997).

**John T. Pawlikowski, O.S.M** is professor of social ethics at the Catholic Theological Union in Chicago, where he also directs the Catholic-Jewish Studies Program in the school's Cardinal Joseph Bernardin Center. He has served by presidential appointment on the United States Holocaust Memorial Council since its inception in 1980. He is a member of the U.S. Catholic Bishops' Advisory Committee on Catholic-Jewish Relations and a vice president of the International Council of Christians & Jews. He is a coeditor and contributor to two recent volumes on the Holocaust: *Good and Evil After Auschwitz: Ethical Impli-*

*cations for Today* and *Ethics in the Shadow of the Holocaust: Christian and Jewish Perspectives.* He is currently completing a book on the non-Jewish victims of the Nazis.

**Michael Phayer** has written extensively on the German Catholic church under the Nazis and on the Holocaust, including *The Catholic Church and the Holocaust, 1935–1965* (2000). At the Center for Advanced Holocaust Studies (U.S. Holocaust Memorial Museum) he was a Fellow in 2001. Phayer is now working on a book on Vatican finances during the Holocaust.

**Thomas Ruster** is professor of systematic theology at the University of Dortmund/Germany. He has worked on Catholic theology in the Weimar Republic. He has written *Die verlorene Nützlickeit der Religion: Katholizismus und Moderne in der Weimarer Republik* (1994).

**Kevin P. Spicer, C.S.C.,** is assistant professor of history at Stonehill College, Easton, Massachusetts. Currently, he is writing a book on German Catholic priests who openly embraced National Socialism. His most recent articles are "Last Years of a Resister in the Diocese of Berlin: Berhnard Lichtenberg's Conflict with Karl Adam and His Fateful Imprisonment," in *Church History* 70 (2001) and "To Serve God or Hitler: Nazi Priests, a Preliminary Discussion," in *Remembering for the Future 2000, The Holocaust in an Age of Genocide,* (2001). Spicer is a member of the Church Relations Committee of the Center for Advanced Holocaust Studies, U.S. Holocaust Memorial Museum.

# Introduction

DONALD J. DIETRICH

1

ON SEPTEMBER 17–18, 1999, a conference organized around the theme "Christian Life and Thought: Confronting Authoritarianism/Totalitarianism in the Twentieth Century" was held at Boston College in Chestnut Hill, Massachusetts. Two dozen scholars gathered to discuss their previously distributed papers. Their contributions addressed the phenomenon of both Nazi and non-Nazi oppression in the twentieth century. The essays selected for this volume focus on the Christian responses to Nazi political and racial assaults on human dignity.

The Nazi experience itself may be concluded, but Hitler and his policies have framed some of the seminal questions that we continue asking as we try to understand the dynamics still operating in contemporary systematic attacks that have dehumanized persons in the decades after World War II. From 1933 to 1945, Christians all too often betrayed their heritage by failing to "love their neighbors" (Ericksen and Heschel 1999). This commandment was, of course, the very essence of the charism at the root of their faith and the theological basis for the human rights discourse today (Besier et al. 1986; Besier et al. 1999). But the response of Christians was more complex and ambivalent than Ericksen and Heschel have shown in their collection of essays focused on recounting the lack of courage and of insight into the sinister Nazi agenda that inhibited churchgoing men and women. In fact, Christians frequently seemed to have only a murky understanding of the meaning of _neighbor._ Nationalism also constricted the meaning of _inclusivity_ for Christians in Germany. Along with historians, theologians have also wrestled with the roles that their churches played or should have played in the public arena of the Reich. We are still asking, not surprisingly, how religion has historically managed to ameliorate brutality (Appleby 2000).

The parts played by the churches and by the individual faithful still raise haunting concerns, because of the accommodation and adaptation techniques that Christians employed to fulfill their national aspirations as well as because of the all too rare examples of heroic resistance. How, for example, could Christianity, rooted in such values as love, compassion, and solidarity with victims (Lamb 1982) have become so entwined with the nationalistic and racist emphases of their culture? Is there a fatal flaw in Christianity itself that makes it so vulnerable to virtually any and all political impulses (Lächele 1994; Metz 1979; Littell 1975)? How can Christians, nurtured in particular cultures, define their faith commitment in a way that resonates with the words of Jesus Christ?

The conference participants spent hours grappling with the tensions that seem to erupt when faith engages culture. Their varied approaches to issues of personal and class resistance as well as adaptation, which are sketched in these essays, again call to mind the complexity of the human condition under pressure and help to explicate the sociopolitical dynamics that seem to affect the moral reasoning of men and women (Wickert 1995; Kaiser 1985) in totalitarian states (Dietrich 1988). How do ordinary people struggle with extraordinary evil? And why do they capitulate or oppose political force?

Historians and social scientists continue to debate the role that religion does or even should play in modern societies (Hering 1990; Lächele 1994), and arguments continue to swirl around whether religion should be marginalized, a viewpoint stemming from the Enlightenment, or whether it should enter the public arena (Casanova 1994). The essays collected here explore the notion that religion embodies values and seems to have a public role. They point out that historically, for better or worse, moral and political values as they were articulated by individual Germans under the pressure of the Hitler regime helped shape their personal attitudes as well as their behavioral patterns in response to Nazi intrusions into their private lives.

For decades, scholars have analyzed the nuanced forms of opposition to the regime (Broszat 1981), as Germans individually and collectively experienced the totalitarian impulses of their Nazi rulers. The experiences of the men and women described in the following essays can help shed some light on the humane visions that at least some courageous people had during this dark period and can help us comprehend the adaptive tactics and rationales that less courageous Christians employed. Their words and deeds remind us of the fragility that accompanies human communal bonding. As individuals and as members of social groups, many of the protagonists in these essays explored the meaning of justice and liberty often at peril to their own lives. Their visions may have been personal and restricted to the possibilities available to them, but they gained a powerful hold over the individuals involved and even today deserve to be explored. Of course, some did not act so heroically. This volume tries to examine the spectrum of responses, which includes endorsement, accommodation, disapproval, nonconformity, dissent, loyal reluctance, and resistance (Geyer and Boyer 1994; Broszat 1981; Tenfelde 1985; Kershaw 1985; Mallmann and Paul 1993). In hindsight, those who opposed the corrupting evil of Hitler's Reich were struggling to reestablish the viability of the human community in light of the violence nourished by anti-Semitism, racism, and the brutalization that has plagued us since World War I. Resistance in most cases in this book was not a continuing permanent state, but a daily changing and probably fragile behavioral pattern that again and again moved back to conformity as many of our actors tried to negotiate their paths through this complex era. Mallmann and Paul have labeled such opposition "loyal reluctance" and have asserted that the acts of resistance that were actually the most long-lived were those brought into play by the Nazi leaders themselves as they competed for power within the apparatus of party and state. But, of course, one should probably not refer to National Socialist bureaucrats as resisters.

2

The anti-Semitic marginalization issues that had to be negotiated spring from the cancerous growth of this bias during the last two millennia (Ruether 1974; Katz 1980; Flannery 1985). This anti-Semitism had Christian origins; was propelled into the popular mind by stereotypes as well as by political, social, and economic fantasies; and was given concrete life through the needs of men and women down through the ages. Religious anti-Semitism relied on conversion to resolve the issues that impacted European Christian culture. The lethal metamorphosis that led to the death camps of the Third Reich occurred after the French Revolution in the age of scientific secularism (Dietrich 1995, chapter 3). During this one and one-half century, racist axioms rooted in Social Darwinism, eugenics, and anthropology lent respectability and scientific legitimacy to categorization and marginalization techniques. When science was joined to religious and popular anti-Semitism, the brew became even more potent. From 1870 until 1945, many of the sociopolitical elite in European countries and the United States became convinced that the biopolitical issues that they faced could only be resolved through the partial or total elimination of inferior "races" and ethnic groups, including the Jews, through restricting immigration, encouraging emigration, legalizing sterilization and euthanasia, and finally, in Germany, by implementing extermination processes (Friedlander 1995). This is the continuum of destruction that Ervin Staub (1989) has so carefully analyzed. Anti-Semitism as a virulent political tool could be accepted even by "normal" Europeans whose consciences had been softened by centuries of culturally learning to marginalize minorities (Dietrich 1988, chapter 7). For many, anti-Semitism was a tool that could be used to address the stresses and strains of modernization itself.

Part of the historical context that also nourished Nazism was created by the murderous exercise of power in World War I, which began to unpack some of the brutalizing horrors that would shape the twentieth century (Rubenstein 1983). Subsequently, the Versailles Treaty aggravated anger in a Germany that had lost the war. The fragility of the interwar democracies and the rise of Bolshevism, which some attributed to the alleged Jewish Conspiracy, also made Germans desperate for the implementation of the sociopolitical promises made by Hitler (Hamilton 1982). Nazism, then, blossomed as an ideology that promised national renewal and assured Germans that their country could be mended through a vigorous opposition to liberalism and democracy along with the values at the base of these ideologies. The ensuing Second World War proved that these were fallacious assertions. The opposition to Nazism during this period has helped recenter moral values since then as men and women have sought to uncover the needed community bonds that can support human dignity.

Throughout this chaotic period (1933–45) the Christian churches and their members had to discern the paths to be followed within the context of the anti-Semitism that they themselves had helped to spawn (Forstman 1992; Scholder 1988; Conway 1968; Ericksen 1985; Tal 1975). By 1945, it was clear that institutional Christianity had failed in its task of confronting Nazism and that it had played a degrading role while the Nazis perpetrated their atrocities (Ericksen and Heschel 1999). The historically developed essence of Christianity itself as a religion stressing the community of humanity, therefore, had to be questioned. Another theme that has emerged from these essays revolves around the problem of creating a sense of communal solidarity frequently through exclusionary policies, an issue that has been ongoing in modern history and remains as current as our daily newspapers (Baranowski 1986; Gerlach 2000; Barnett 1992).

## 3

Acts of resistance and adaptation were nurtured in the political, social, and cultural environment of Nazi Germany. Accordingly, these essays have focused on probing how individuals handled living in an intrusive state and how they formed their responses to the everyday denigration of human dignity that they experienced. The authors have reinforced the contributions made by those engaged in stressing the importance of *Alltagsgeschichte,* because personal acts do seem crucial in understanding how social and political dynamics play out in policies. These essays add to the growing list of scholarly works focusing on average Germans trying to navigate through the terrain created by twentieth-century dictatorships powered by ideologies of terror.

Two decades ago Broszat (1981) helped turn our attention toward *Alltagsgeschichte* and away from the principal leaders to the individuals, who had to live out a "normal" daily existence in the Reich. The extent of the German population's anti-Semitism as depicted in Kershaw's analysis (Kershaw 1983) has also helped us in understanding local and personal opinion formation in the Third Reich and has reminded scholars to focus on issues of daily compliance and nonconformity. Following in the same vein, although engaged in controversy, Goldhagen (1996) and Browning (1998) have likewise moved attention in their analyses to the followers.

The works of both Eric Johnson (1999) and Robert Gellately (1990) have helped crystallize our understanding that individual Germans living out their hopes, fears, and, frequently, petty jealousies made operant the ideological and physical terror that empowered Nazi oppression. The Gestapo and courts, of course, formally carried out the brutalization of society. The government itself, however, was assisted by countless Germans, who fulfilled the Nazi agenda by pursuing their own personal goals.

The Gestapo was relatively small in comparison to the size of the population that had to be shaped ideologically and controlled. To concretize the power of the regime, Johnson and Gellately have found, citizens in their everyday lives, and frequently for their own personal advantages, monitored their fellow citizens. These scholars have found that Nazi oppression was certainly initiated by the state. Normal citizens, however, became dynamically involved in oppressing one another. Petty fears and jealousies as well as the desire for ideological consonance with the regime's anti-Semitic and national renewal policies breathed life into the bureaucratic oppression of those Germans directly implementing genocidal public policy.

Studies on resistance and adaptive responses have moved from the macro to the micro level, that is, to the more intimate lives of individuals facing an oppressive system that was rooted in the unique features of the regime that perpetrated the Shoah. Social welfare, medicine, and ordinary neighborly relations were enacted within a Germany and later a Europe that was dominated by a regime devoted to murder as a solution to biopolitical, social, and economic issues. In local communities living in terror, even normal activities could present moral dilemmas as well as opportunities to oppose the types of control that the regime was trying to establish. What were the motivations of those engaged in adaptation and outright resistance or nonconformity or dissent? How did they concretize their values? Under the pervasive terror thriving in the Third Reich, dissent and even nonconformity seem to have been more dangerous than earlier scholars of resistance have suggested (Hoffmann 1988; Nicosia and Stokes 1990), because even minimal refusal to adhere to the regime's ideological impetus through stressing personal or even professional independence could have serious repercussions, given the pervasive influence of the Gestapo and its desire to control all civil and cultural life. Reflecting on the experiences of those who resisted and who adapted can assist us in understanding the dynamics at work in destroying as well as in constructing the civil life necessary for our communal and individual activities.

**4**

John S. Conway's keynote address helped establish the parameters for the discussion, by reminding all of us that the religious tradition nurtured by ambivalent Christian principles had been ruptured by Nazi strategies and tactics, which attacked both ecclesial institutions and personal values. The Third Reich illustrates how the dynamic fervor of ideological politics mobilized the nation and attempted to restrict resistance. Contemporary Christians have now been compelled, he asserted, to reexamine their faith and to ask why it proved so impotent. Politics and personal ethics along with Nazi totalitarianism and German theological responses interacted in profoundly subtle and surprising ways that have affected our lives ever since. Conway ended his presentation by laying out the institutional and private issues present in contemporary challenges, which bear a remarkable resemblance to the task that the churches failed to perform from 1933 to 1945. Christian failures in the Third Reich have taught us much about the theological questions that we should be asking.

## 5

How did the churches and their theologians, for example, react to Hitler's rise to power in 1933? Thomas Ruster, Robert Krieg, and Kevin Spicer show that, at least theologically, the churches could and did adapt quite easily to the nationalistic impulses, even if not totally to the racist incitement ideologically driving the Nazi Party. The theological responses to Nazism reflect this ambivalence. In their hour of need Christian theologians saw in Hitler an ordained leader, maybe even a savior, who could heroically lead Germany out of the Weimar chaos splintered by interest-driven political parties. The führer promised national renewal, anti-bolshevism, and a unity that would abolish a political culture splintered by democratic ideals. Such myopic hopes inspired Catholics to seek a Concordat and Protestants to align their faith with the cultural principles that served as the foundation for the ethnocentric *Volk*.

Ruster has offered a discouraging account of how such prominent theologians as Karl Adam and Michael Schmaus constructed an instrumentalized theology that could respond positively to the political impulses of the Party. Ruster has highlighted how the Catholic concept of "nature-supernature," for example, became susceptible to such a profound misunderstanding that religious faith could actually lose its primary meaning when facing the political juggernaut that was threatening personal freedom and dignity. When nature was identified with the Nazi state, he has concluded, grace would almost inevitably suffer.

While Ruster points out the dangers to which theology was susceptible in 1933, Krieg and Spicer indicate that the theological betrayal of the Christian tradition was not the entire story because some Catholics did not adapt. Krieg has analyzed the correlation that Engelbert Krebs devised to relate ecclesiology to politics. In Krebs's view, German Catholicism was obliged publicly to engage the intellectual, cultural, and political life of society. Theology, therefore, found its relevance by constructively responding to the policies of the Third Reich. Krebs did not succeed and finally became a target when he disagreed with

Archbishop Gröber, the "brown bishop," on ecclesial policies. Finally, in 1943 he contended that Germans should certainly fight their nation's enemies, but should not hate them. In the process of living in Hitler's Germany, Krebs helped shape a hermeneutical tool that has gained prominence in post-1945 Christian theology, when he analyzed how the history of humanity was to be delineated as an historical interaction among humanity, Christ, and the church. To be meaningful, Krebs felt, theology has to be historically grounded and be open to the world in which it lives.

Spicer has shown the more subtle role that resistance could play among some clergy by selecting as his focus Father Albert Coppenrath, a parish priest. Coppenrath provides an interesting case study that helps illuminate how some Catholics tried to balance their patriotism with their own faith. How, such men as Coppenrath asked, can Christians be men and women of faith as well as citizens in a highly charged political milieu? How can they limit the encroachment of the state into church life? Coppenrath used his pulpit reports to inform his congregation about the inconsistencies that emerged when Nazi actions collided with Catholic principles. In light of Nazism's anti-Semitic foundation, Coppenrath courageously maintained that the church had to be open to all men and women without any distinction of race, although distinctions of religion were not so easily tolerated.

The essays of Ruster, Krieg, and Spicer all draw attention to the danger of religiously legitimating political ideologies as well as illustrate the difficulties of balancing dual loyalties in a totalitarian state. Indeed, they explicate the problems faced by theologians and clergy under pressure in any society. The Catholic clergy discussed in these essays tried to be true to their religious traditions and simultaneously to engage the culture of the Third Reich. Their successes and failures suggest that Christian theology was hard-pressed then, and even now, some would add, to critique fundamentally the political policies dominant in any historically bound culture. Is resistance to a specific policy in the same league as resistance to a weltanschauung, that is, to an ideologically driven political system? What must churches do structurally to encapsulate a critical stance?

Kyle Jantzen and John Delaney offer essays that suggest the complexity involved in resistance and adaptation on the local levels of German society. Both Jantzen and Delaney maintain that the nonconformist behavior displayed by church members and their dissent have to be seen as a type of resistance. A great deal of ink has been spilled over the issue of what constitutes resistance.

Bomb-throwing and assassination attempts certainly qualify as courageous acts and so do the statements of such figures as Bernard Lichtenberg, who condemned the Nazis for their oppression of the Jews. More ambiguous, but yet more normal, are the activities of those Christians studied by Jantzen and Delaney.

German Protestants were shocked by defeat in World War I and shattered by the lack of vitality manifest in the divisive political atmosphere of Weimar democratic politics. In response to the horrors of World War I, Karl Barth had responded by attacking liberal Protestantism, namely, hyphenated Christianity, which he thought had overly adapted to the culture (Fangmeier and Stoevesandt 1981). In a more political response to the times, some Protestant leaders during the Weimar and Nazi eras developed a conservative nationalist attitude with which they could critique their fragmented culture. Most German Protestants seemed predisposed to welcome Hitler's advance to power despite his anti-Semitism (Hamilton 1982), which never enjoyed the degree of support that such scholars as Goldhagen (1996) have assumed. They found that they could support Hitler's stress on national renewal as well as his anti-liberalism, anti-democracy, and anti-bolshevism. For his study, Jantzen has selected the town of Nauen, which experienced a bitter struggle over the appointment of German Christian pastors to vacant parishes. Jantzen effectively has delineated how Nazi politics of "coordination" profoundly influenced German Protestants, who initially may have formed an electoral and ideological mainstay for the Party prior to 1933, but who ultimately reacted in their parishes to the behemoth that they had helped create. Nazi totalitarianism was not as awesome as some of the Party leaders thought it was, because Protestant resistance seemingly could be very effective on the local level through delay and bureaucratic manipulation.

Delaney's paper on clerical opposition among Catholics also highlights the clay feet of totalitarianism by investigating how parish priests opposed the Nazi anti-Polish racial policy that was aimed at Bavarian peasants during World War II. Lacking institutional leadership, local priests found that they had to fend for themselves. While opposing the central government, they did not aggressively and ideologically confront it. Delaney has assiduously explicated the complexities of attitudes and behavioral patterns of resistance in the countryside. Although nominally almost slave labor from the Nazi racist perspective, Poles were made welcome at Mass by both pastors and parishioners in Bavaria. Given the Nazi efforts to marginalize Jews and other non-Aryans to the boundaries, if not beyond, of their political communities, it may seem surprising that these foreign laborers were treated as human beings. In the minds of the Bavarians, however, co-religionists were not to be treated as subhuman. This acceptance of Polish workers, Delaney insists, was not the result of some abstruse psychological dynamic. Poles were Catholic, and in Bavaria this religious affiliation counted. The covert activity of priests supporting human interaction yielded noncompliance with Nazi ethnic policy.

Jantzen and Delaney have pointed out that Nazi authorities had a constant suspicion of institutional Protestantism and Catholicism, which they felt could potentially engage in politically deviant behavior. As in so many other attempts to control social and cultural enclaves, Nazi political power for a variety of local reasons could not impregnate the entire society. Protestants and Catholics remained loyal Germans, even when disobeying the Nazis in specific acts centering on life in their villages. How they handled the dissonance between being loyal citizens and opposing the Nazi Party makes the story of their parishes and opposition intriguing. They certainly did not consider themselves part of any resistance movement, and they clearly were not trying to overthrow the regime. These Christians, however, do highlight in depth the weakness and the lack of control of Nazi totalitarianism as well as indicate the maneuverability that Germans had when they wanted to derail the dictates of the Nazi regime.

The power of such local opposition again raises questions about the lack of meaningful ecclesial resistance. If peasants could say "no" to Nazism, could not institutional churches have been more courageous? Jantzen and Delaney point up the ambiguity surrounding the opposition of these "Germans in the street" and ask how they and others like them can be categorized in relation to the regime. Many average rural Germans may have opposed Nazism just as they probably would have opposed any intrusive act, even one instigated by a democratic regime, because they resented outside interference. That resentment alone should suggest that a totalitarian system may have built-in weaknesses because of its emphasis on centralized control. Christians could be and were anti-Semitic as well as nationalistic, and so questions about the legitimacy of Catholic resistance in Germany, for example, have rightfully been raised by such contemporary scholars as Oded Heilbronner (1998). Can nonconformity and dissent on one level exist with support for the regime's goals on another? Individuals engaged in opposing the regime actually seemed able to maintain a surprising degree of cognitive dissonance in their daily lives.

The unavoidable theme that continues to emerge when reflecting on

Christian life and Nazism is the response of the churches to anti-Semitism. For decades now churches and their representatives have tried to understand the roots of Christian anti-Semitism and how these self-perpetuating values, even if innocently begotten, formed attitudes that subsequently helped support murderous patterns of behavior (Flannery 1985; Dietrich 1995). The relationship between Christian theology and lived experience, which helped produce the virulent anti-Semitism of the Third Reich, is complex and has resulted in a gigantic output of historical literature. Scholars are also still exploring the nuances and permutations of Christian anti-Semitism as it played out during these years of the Third Reich. The contributions to this discussion presented by Michael Phayer, Stephen Haynes, Lawrence Baron, and Gershon Greenberg have very creatively probed the issue of Christianity and its anti-Semitic weltanschauung.

Michael Phayer has explicitly addressed the debate that has continued bubbling around the role of Pius XII (Cornwell 1999), who is still being considered for canonization. Phayer has long been acknowledged as a specialist on the intentions and behavior of Pius XII, a pope who preferred to deal with Nazism through the diplomatic offices of the Vatican. As Phayer indicates, Pius had three defensive goals: safeguarding Europe from Communism, avoiding a showdown with Nazism, and protecting Rome from bombardment. Countering genocide was not a primary priority. Phayer's analysis explicates the motivations behind Pius's behavior toward Jewish and Polish issues and seems to bear out that the pope was neither saint nor demon. Pius was a man rooted in his ecclesial and diplomatic culture, who had priorities that were not the post-1945 agenda items of Christianity. Still, the question lingers concerning how Christianity can measure up to its own standards. Had Pius reacted to the Nazi Polish policy as explicitly as Delaney's German peasants did, historians might have evaluated this pope differently. Did the ecclesial behavior of Pius diminish the role that Christianity, even in Nazi-occupied Europe, should have played in politics? Should we realistically expect churches to do what political governments do not? What are the roles of churches in contemporary societies (Goldhagen 2002)? Cornwell has stressed that modern popes have pressed institutional ambitions and have tried to center the Vatican's control of local churches in their own persons. Phayer relies on the motivation of Pius XII less than Cornwell and highlights the more immediate ecclesial goals of this pope.

When theologians reflect on saintly behavior during this dark period, invariably the name of Dietrich Bonhoeffer surfaces. Stephen Haynes offers here a nuanced corrective to the assumption that Bonhoeffer had a consistent pro-Jewish stance. Bonhoeffer's resistance to Nazi totalitarianism emerged, Haynes has reminded us, only after a long struggle. The early Bonhoeffer, a bystander to the growing assault against German Jews, ultimately would seem to be a man whose personal behavior toward his Jewish in-laws was better than his early theology, which dealt more abstractly with understanding the religious and historical interactions of Judaism and Christianity. Haynes portrays Bonhoeffer as a theologian who overcame his own anti-Semitic and cultural heritage as he worked to explicate a more authentic meaning of the Christian story. In a manner similar to that of Krebs, Bonhoeffer seemed to feel that history had to speak to theology so that Christian religious ideals could adequately respond to the world of marching soldiers.

Popes and theologians, of course, are not the only representatives of the Christian faith. Both Lawrence Baron and Gershon Greenberg have presented Christian women who had to face anti-Semitism as they tried to navigate through the Nazi world. Given the social location of women during this era, Greenberg's and Baron's essays suggest that perhaps women, especially sensitive to marginalization issues, found anti-Semitism particularly noxious. Such a reaction on the part of these women should not be surprising, when we recall that the Huguenots of Le Chambon, as a community that had been historically marginalized, found that under the charismatic leadership of André Trocmé it wanted to rescue Jews and successfully did so (Hallie 1979). Baron has offered a vivid portrait of Corrie ten Boom, one of the most widely known righteous gentiles of the Holocaust era. *The Hiding Place* is her account of how her family helped Jews in wartime Holland and then how they themselves experienced betrayal and internment in concentration camps. Corrie ten Boom's life and work reinforces the reason for this volume. Non-nuanced reflections and research do not capture the complex world of the Third Reich, with its challenges and the opportunities that Christians confronted and handled, sometimes well and sometimes less than appropriately.

Theologians have almost unequivocally maintained that the root of religious, that is, theological, anti-Semitism has been supersessionism. Their insistence on this point is nearly a dogmatic truism in virtually every work that deals with the Jewish-Christian relationship. Corrie ten Boom warns us not to feel comfortable even with what might seem to be obvious and never to assume that even statements concerning anti-Semitism are universally "true". Her own supersessionism, for example, cannot really be equated with malevolent anti-

Semitism, even though we may now see how dangerous such triumphalism really is. Corrie's life affirms that Jews and non-Jews can dialogue with one another, even though the latter may hope for the conversion of the former. The key point seems to be that Christians should not attempt to enforce a spiritual metamorphosis, that is, conversion, with rancor and persecution. We may not accept such a view today, but Baron's essay serves to point out the fundamental difference between religious and racial anti-Semitism. Baron's study reminds us that human complexity is at the heart of historical events and so must be respected by scholars, even though their own professional ethos may be to attempt to smooth historical idiosyncrasies into a conceptual model to eliminate the "rough edges" of the concrete world. How can scholars today classify such a supersessionist righteous gentile as Corrie ten Boom? Baron's contribution suggests that Jewish-Christian dialogue itself should not fear the lack of conceptual clarity that reminds us of the danger of reductionism. Jews and Christians should be ready to meet the challenges that inevitably will emerge as they speak to one another and address the fundamental issues of exclusion and marginalization.

Gershon Greensburg has offered a provocative study of Irene Harand, a Viennese journalist who wrote in support of the Jews, who she saw were being persecuted. Harand reminds us that Christians, even after nineteen centuries, had still failed to delineate the scriptural meaning of *Nächstenliebe* (love of neighbor), which in theory should have helped determine even their political policies. Harand herself managed to use the humanistic principles of Catholicism to avoid any adaptation to the theological and sociopolitical elements that grew out of religious anti-Semitism. Harand was also one of the few who seemed to see that anti-Semitism undermined Christianity along with its Judaic conversation partner, something that many Christians seemed to miss at that time. In particular, Harand's life and work pointed up that people's lives will be endangered when they are not treated as neighbors, and inevitably they will be marginalized to the fringes of or excluded from their communities. Her life and work serve to remind Christians that they have to work out the concrete meanings of the injunction "love thy neighbor."

Postwar ecclesial commentators have tended to overlook such Christians as Irene Harand and Corrie ten Boom as they seek less complex portrayals of Christian life, which frequently fail to reveal the real world in which Europeans were struggling. The Christian behavior of ten Boom and Harand should compel prelates and theologians to examine their own Christian attitudes that are brought to the public square. The personal responses of ten Boom and Harand to Nazism as well as the reactions of the local priests, pastors, and parishioners depicted in the essays of Haynes, Delaney, and Jantzen remind us of the difficulties with which scholars must wrestle in trying to categorize Christian responses to Nazism. Germans of all socioeconomic classes, religious persuasions, and both genders could and did find a home in Nazism, and so it is not surprising that the resistance or nonconformity or dissent efforts of individuals varied as they tried to remain Christian and patriotic. People voted for and resisted Nazism for very specific, personal reasons. They negotiated personal paths through twelve years of brutal rule. It remains the task of scholars to try to unravel the complexities of these human dramas.

As scholars struggle to offer a coherent narrative that can embrace the confusing facticity of real life from 1933 to 1945, those interested in the theological dimensions of these issues for postwar Christians have been trying to realign Christian values along an axis that can support human dignity so that future genocides can be prevented. Their goal has been to instrumentalize pro-life values into our culture. Two participants—Matthew Hockenos and John Pawlikowski—addressed the issues confronting post-1945 theology and culture.

Hockenos provides a very finely honed study intent on understanding the interactions among the major German Protestant leaders in 1945, who were attempting to re-read history in order to position their church for the future. The responses of such Protestant leaders as Martin Niemöller and Karl Barth to their past was a mixture of self-pity, self-praise, and criticism. Hockenos has unraveled the intensity of the struggle among the Confessing church leaders to construct an interpretation of the past that would allow them to devise strategies that would mandate how the church's future was to be shaped. Hockenos unfolds a story that is nearly Orwellian. History for these men was perceived as a tool to reconcile the disparate Protestant responses emerging from their shattered world as they tried to envision their future. Such attempts by Protestant theologians to establish a viable postwar foundation again points to one of the fundamental issues confronting Christianity. How can Christianity develop an ability to engage in as well as to critique its culture? How can the Christian churches develop mechanisms for self-critique?

Finally, John Pawlikowski's essay shows why it is important to establish a paradigm for a renewed theology that will reflect on the role of the oppressor in order to produce a liturgy that can support human dignity. This renewed theology should be capable of nurturing a moral sensitivity already apparent in those who opposed Nazism in some fashion. Such a sensitivity seems an indispensable prelude to moral reasoning. The value of a person, he insists, cannot be taught solely within the context of a philosophical proof. Human value and dignity can only be subjectively revealed and appreciated by appealing to our affective natures. That said, he has focused on the vitality of liturgy. What humans create to support dignity is sacred and belongs properly to some dimension of liturgy in which God and humans confront one another. Humans and God, he contends, have a co-creational responsibility for the earth and its creatures. This means that God and humanity will each have to surrender sole responsibility for political acts, since both now will mutually have to make creation work for humanity. Creation thus becomes the product of human and divine activity, which would mean that we all have to assume the responsibility to protect the dignity of men and women. Only liturgy, Pawlikowski insists, can capture God's and humanity's relational dependence and vulnerability, which should be portrayed in the public arena as our mutual commitment toward one another, that is, a dialogical covenant (Eckardt 1986; Littell 1975; Rubenstein 1966). Liturgy is instrumental in creating a sense of the God-human relationship that can help shape a legitimate moral sensibility designed to assist humanity in avoiding any future holocaust. Theology without an emotive, affective, and personal dimension will not help protect the marginalized. Reliance on universal moral norms and national dictates did not prevent the Shoah. In fact, as Ruster has shown, conceptual theological models could pave the way for adaptation.

## 6

The essays included in this volume explore some examples of adaptive mechanisms, but mostly focus on varied levels of resistance. The authors are really delving into moral history (Geyer in Geyer and Boyer 1994, 325–50) by unpacking the vision of humanity that was offered by resisters, nonconformists, and dissenters. Through reflecting on those whose response was adaptation, they have gone to the heart of the insidious corruption that powered the Third Reich. The men and women portrayed in these essays, who opposed at least some aspects of the regime, however, developed a very concrete sense of the justice and freedom that was rooted in the transformative values needed to support human dignity. Some men and women very courageously saw the need to go beyond the seemingly harmless realm of abstract reflection into the

world of brutal oppression. Their visions of moral order and of human responsibilities, even if only concerned with their private lives, their understanding of
the significance of community, and their reflections on human dignity directed
their questioning of and their critical reactions to the Nazi leviathan. Their personal acts of resistance or dissent or nonconformity required choices in their
everyday lives through overt actions, where even if only subtly they opposed
the exclusion of persons and collectivities from their communities. Both explicitly and implicitly those who opposed and those who adapted had to ask
what it concretely means to be human.

Resistance against the Third Reich offers to us an intimate look into what
Dietrich Bonhoeffer has labeled "a world come of age," that is, a world in which
we must assume responsibility. How can we wrest civil society from the reins of
totalizing institutional power? How can we sculpt relations that leave space for
the humanity of others? How can we rejoice in the identity of the others (Geyer
in Geyer and Boyer 1994, 340–50)? Churches themselves offered very little
heroic sustenance to their members (Dietrich 1988, 294–308), but instead
seemed to be satisfied with a very unfortunate, self-centered resistance, bent on
their own survival as institutions. Fortunately for Christianity as an ongoing
religious tradition, individuals seemed to do better than institutions in safeguarding the meaning of "person" against Hitler's diabolical agenda.

Nazi ideology itself was a secularized doctrine of salvation, that is, a political theology, and insisted that it possessed a divine warrant that legitimated its
manipulation of public opinion by means of lies. In fact, it thrived by offering a
sweeping simplification of complex realities (Bracher 1983, 1–24; Lease 1995;
Burleigh 2000). Behind the mystic feeling generated by the vision of a *Gemeinschaft* that supported national renewal existed a tyranny that imposed political
and spiritual oppression. Nazi ideology targeted both the political self-restraint
that has supported democracy as a source for the renewal of the human spirit
in modern times and assaulted the religious kingdom, which ideally, at least in
Christianity, was meant to shape the unfolding of the potential possessed by
men and women as God's images. The ideological, pseudoreligious qualities of
Nazism made it attractive during the Weimar years and dangerous until the
Third Reich could be defeated in war.

In the final analysis, the sustained existence of humanistic and Christian
values (reason, culture, humanity, dignity of the person) during this period
helped clear the way for the emergence of our current focus on the dignity of
the person as the necessary foundation for any discourse on human rights. This

return to the scriptural insight that all humans are the images of God, which can initially be found in Genesis and was then reiterated at the founding of the Christian faith, has proved to be important for the continued mending of the fractured humanity that remained after the Nazi oppression (Bonhoeffer 1965a, 55 ff). This ethical recentering away from an atomistic individualism or a brutalizing collectivity to an inclusionary notion that can support the integrity of the person has been crucial in the post-1945 attempts to respond to the incidents of sanctioned murder that have continued up to our time. The resistance during the Third Reich has helped us, at least ideologically, develop a significant nexus between democracy and Christianity as systems of value that can limit power. Significantly, Christianity and democracy urge restraint in the quest for perfection on this earth (Von Klemperer in Chandler 1998, 54–56). Finally, the religious and human experiences found present in acts of resistance and missing from moments of adaptation during the Third Reich have shown that both passion and compassion are necessary for healthy political systems and, indeed, for the growth of the spirit.

Those opposed to Nazism, portrayed in the essays in this volume, can be viewed from the perspective of a "crisis theology" that stresses that religion is no longer felt to be tangential, but rather is to be perceived as a resource for sustaining human dignity in a world seemingly bereft of spiritual values. These men and women risked their lives to plant the seeds for the future renewal of the Christian faith so battered in these times. At least from hindsight, these essays seem to insist that Christians should unceasingly question the traditional modes of adaptation that their churches have historically practiced.

What seemed to have moved persons in Hitler's Reich to deeds of courage, to a refusal to accept state intrusion, and to compassion was a realization of their connection to one another (Gushee 1994). John Donne has written that no man is an island, entire unto himself. His words may sound simple, but Donne was describing, as Victoria Barnett (1999) suggests, a complex ecology in which each person's actions and beliefs significantly and directly affect the present and the future. These essays teach us that life in any society should never be perceived as disposable, but rather should always be viewed as precious. The creation of an ideologically controlled "Brave New World" is what even the most mundane acts of resistance, nonconformity, and dissent opposed. These essays help reveal that the consciences and acts of ordinary men and women can have the power to reach far beyond the private struggle that each resister endured. Those who rejected the Nazi weltanschauung helped create a new web of relationships, a renewed human identity, that has resonated into our own era and has helped us move beyond the Third Reich into an ongoing discernment of the meaning of human rights and responsibilities.

The prosocial behaviors at every level of human discourse that are documented in these studies should be applauded just as we condemn the Nazi ones. These essays can help deepen our understanding of why and how at least some men and women responded to Nazism by trying to reassert communal bonds. Only through understanding the historical intricacies and surprising contradictions of this era as well as the human attempts to struggle through the pitfalls constructed by a regime bent on exclusion and then on genocide can we begin to critique and reorganize our own sociopolitical systems in a way designed to support the values that will be necessary in dealing with the future barbarities waiting to happen in the twenty-first century. The complex historical and theological issues that the essays in this volume have probed can also help us discern more carefully the political and cultural challenges that have pounded human culture unnecessarily since 1945.

Christian Responses
to the HOLOCAUST

# 1

# Totalitarianism and Theology

JOHN S. CONWAY

A PARTICULARLY DISTURBING FACT for a civilization ostensibly based on Judaeo-Christian principles is that such principles were not sturdy enough to forestall or curtail the disasters of Nazi totalitarian rule, including the Holocaust. Though the Nazis themselves were decidedly anti-Christian, Germany had been a Christian region, with Christian traditions, for centuries. What had then happened to the long-established moral behavioral patterns of the German nation? Over the past fifty years, the political factors that led to the overthrow of the Weimar Republic and the triumph of Hitler's dictatorship have been extensively described. So too have the military events surrounding the astounding and ambitious Nazi plans to rule the globe. But far fewer have been the attempts to explain the dynamic of the ideological fanaticism, which, surely, was the crucial and singular characteristic of Nazi Germany (Besier 1995; Brunotte and Wolf 1965). Even fewer have been the works that seek to record the paucity of resistance and/or opposition on the part of the established churches to the Nazis' overthrow of long-established moral norms, as could be found in their racial obsessions, especially against the Jews. This fundamental rupture of tradition, I would like to suggest, is possibly the most fateful legacy of the whole Nazi experience. I would like to share some thoughts about the relationship between politics and ethics, between Nazi totalitarianism and German theology, and to examine the question of whether this was a peculiar one-time phenomenon or whether this case study can and should be instructive for the future.

In 1945 Germany lay physically ruined and morally discredited. In the immediate aftermath of the war, there was no impetus to analyze the extent of the Nazis' crimes, and indeed several years were to elapse before this task was attempted. The vast majority of Germans sought to avoid any mention of the regime to which they had earlier and so fervently given their enthusiastic loyalty. They adopted a convenient unrepentant amnesia, unwilling to acknowledge the extent of their previous participation or to admit their complicity in the Nazi crimes that bit by bit were revealed to the world.

Such reluctance to come to terms with the past—the technical term is *Vergangenheitsbewältigung*—was compounded by the new political thrust of the postwar years. In West Germany, Chancellor Adenauer shrewdly calculated that any successful construction of a new democratic order required the integration of those citizens compromised by their beliefs and actions during the Third Reich (Spotts 1973). The price to be paid was silence about the crimes of that period. The rapid shift from de-Nazification to cold war anti-Communism only lent impetus to this process.

The same response was to be found in the churches. To be sure, a few sensitive leaders in the Protestant German Evangelical church at a meeting in Stuttgart in October 1945 had recognized the need to issue a Declaration of Guilt for their failure to witness against Nazism more ardently. But even this declaration was very general in scope and said nothing at all about the persecution and mass murder of the Jews. It was also widely regarded as a betrayal of the nation's interests or as an unwanted attempt to arouse moral concerns that would be better forgotten or concealed.

It was not, therefore, until the end of the 1950s that a new and more critical climate arose, in which the actual Nazi policies and the responses to them by established institutions could be examined. Much of the scholarly work was in fact done by foreigners, and an undeniable impetus was given by the Eichmann trial from 1961 onwards. As the record of Nazi totalitarian rule was gradually outlined in detail, so too was the picture of the ineffectiveness of those forces that sought to prevent the worst excesses of this monstrous ideology. The German churches had for centuries seen themselves as the moral guardians of the state and the defenders of Germany's national and Christian identity. For them, therefore, the question was all the more burning: Why did the churches not display a more forceful and effective resistance by seeking to prevent or at least to mitigate the Nazis' criminal acts, their military aggressions, or their racial policies of genocide? The seeming failure of the churches to live up to their own standards of moral responsibility when faced with this onslaught was, and indeed still is, a major issue for the current life and witness of the churches today.

Two major explanations have been given by historians. First, some have rightly pointed out that the Nazi regime was a terroristic dictatorship, which was unrestrained in the repression of perceived enemies. The threat of being taken off to a concentration camp operated already in the beginning of 1933 and served to create an all-pervasive fear and caution sufficient to deter most people from challenging the regime in any way. The notorious reputation of the Gestapo only increased throughout the Nazi years. And its activities were only enhanced by the widespread practice of the denunciation of any suspect dissident for whatever reason. The clergy were in a particularly exposed position. Their professional lives made them highly visible personalities. They now found themselves subject to greater and ever more hostile scrutiny. It was not long before the fact was widely known that an agent of the Gestapo, or an informer, would be found taking notes of every weekly sermon. The already overdeveloped German habit of social control could readily enough be applied to any church member believed to be in any way lacking in loyalty to the regime or its policies. There was a real smell of fear, the dread of denunciation, and the fright occasioned by the dire consequences suffered by the victims of Nazi repression. Church members who sought to uphold their personal institutional traditions were indeed intimidated and often paid the price of their defiance of the regime.

The record of those who sacrificed liberty and sometimes life for their resistance is impressive. Alongside such revered figures as Martin Niemöller, Dietrich Bonhoeffer, Father Lichtenberg, and Father Alfred Delp and his Munich Jesuits, we should also remember priests, pastors, and laypeople, such as, for example, the two thousand Jehovah's Witnesses who died in captivity. Their willingness to face official disgrace and the ruin of their public careers for the sake of their convictions was exemplary. While Pastor Niemöller was awaiting trial in a Berlin prison, for example, he was visited by the prison chaplain, who asked him in astonishment: "But Brother Martin! What brings you here? Why are you in prison?" To which Niemöller replied: "And Brother, why are you not in prison?" For the Catholics, one estimate is that approximately one-third of the priests endured some form of reprisal during the Third Reich. In Dachau there were no fewer than 2,771 priests, the majority of them Polish, but including some 400 German Catholic priests and 35 Evangelical pastors. Virtually all were sent there for political reasons.

Other historians, however, have suggested a much less favorable explanation for the lack of resistance among both the clergy and the laity of the Christian churches. There is overwhelming evidence that in the heady days of 1933 a very large proportion of both was swept up by the expectations for national renewal and regeneration offered by Nazi propagandists. The euphoria of those early months was unparalleled since the similar enthusiasm of August 1914 and was reflected in the high percentage of Evangelical pastors who set an example to their flocks by taking out membership in the Nazi Party.

Even when later in 1933 the scales began to fall from the church leaders' eyes, their opposition to the Nazi totalitarian ambitions was bifurcated (Siegele and Wenschkewitz 1974). Their theologically-based dissent from the Nazis' church policies could often enough be combined with fervent approval of the regime's more secular goals, for instance those in the field of foreign policy.

Even more significant was the readiness of the Catholic leaders to sign a concordat with the Nazi government in July 1933 (Albrecht 1976; Volk 1987; Zahn 1962), indulging in highly erroneous illusions that this agreement would enhance their position and at the same time oblige the Nazis to uphold the Catholics' standards of political behavior. In retrospect we can see that the concordat was to have fateful consequences for the mobilization of Catholic resistance. At no time were the bishops prepared to admit their mistake. Nor were German Catholics at any time during the whole Nazi era taught to recognize the demonic character of the regime. And even when the courageous bishop of Münster, Count Galen, raised his voice publicly in 1941 to denounce the iniquitous policies of the SS (*Schutzstaffel*) and Gestapo in the so-called "euthanasia" program, this protest was not designed to signal resistance against all aspects of Nazi policy. It is not recorded that Galen ever made any pronouncement about the terrible fate of the Jews.

Both historically and theologically the German churches were conditioned to regard themselves as upholders of traditional national and ecclesial values. As a result, they were soon alarmed by the Nazis' attempts to interfere with their established institutions and practices. Similarly, virtually all Catholics and a strong minority of Protestants in the Confessing church vigorously refused to condone the Nazi ideological attempts to pervert the truths of the Christian gospel. But such protests were still predicated on the idea that these noxious policies were only incidental. Anyone reading the archives must be struck by the frequency with which church members complained and even openly protested about specific aspects of the regime's persecution, but constantly attributed these to the work of underlings. Such errors, they went on believing right to the end, would be put right if only Hitler got to know about them. "*Wenn der Führer nur wusste*" was the expression of a mentality shared by many other sections of the community. All too often church members yearned to maintain an atmosphere of legality and were, therefore, unprepared to dispute or challenge the regime's political legitimacy. On May 1, 1945, on learning the news of Hitler's suicide, Cardinal Bertram drew up plans for a nationwide requiem service for the deceased head of state.

Resistance in the Nazi era was, therefore, a highly ambivalent matter. Some scholars have correctly characterized the churches' stance as one of *Widerstand wider Willen,* or reluctant resistance. The high degree of congruence between the church members' views and Hitler's secular goals is striking. With their hatred of Communism, their support for a nationalist and expansionist foreign policy, their disdain for the Jewish people, and their approval of the overthrow of parliamentary democracy, the churches were highly susceptible to accepting the Nazis' loudly proclaimed goals and failed to recognize the implicitly revolutionary character of Nazi totalitarianism.

Only when the Nazi attack directly affected their own institutions, practices, and doctrines did the Catholic and Protestant church leaders seek to mobilize their respective milieus in favor of the traditional order. These were defensive tactics—a raising of the drawbridge against a radical challenge from outside—but only accentuated their reluctance to oppose the regime on issues beyond the immediate church struggle. Such a concentration on their own concerns, though in the end relatively successful, in fact contributed to the separation of these protesting churchmen from other groups in society who might have been expected to join them.

More farsighted and ecumenically-minded theologians, such as Karl Barth or Dietrich Bonhoeffer, early on recognized these deficiencies. Above all, they were right to draw attention to the churches' lack of any adequate prophylactic against the nationalist, authoritarian, anti-Semitic, and militaristic conditioning of the German people. The German churches did not possess the kind of theology adequate to sustain any type of critical attack on the actions of their political rulers. Nor had the years since the downfall of the Wilhelmine Empire allowed any consensus to be developed, especially among the Protestants, as to the kind of government and political structures that the churches could accept as replacements appropriate for the changed circumstances brought about by Germany's defeat in 1918. The overthrow of the Hohenzollern dynasty and the introduction of the secular Weimar Republic had left many of them still nostalgically longing for the return of the securities of the old order.

In this confusion, it was hardly surprising that some of the younger, more radical Evangelical pastors, who combined theological superficiality with avid careerist ambitions, should have jumped on the Nazi bandwagon. They called themselves the Faith Movement of Christians, and in July 1933 with the aid of the Nazi Party they captured control of large sections of the church bureaucracy. This politically opportunistic seizure of power prevented any subsequent chance of the church's adopting a united stand on political affairs. Instead, these "German Christians," who saw Hitler as representing the messianic hope of the German nation, were able to portray themselves as the church's avantgarde. They claimed that their advocacy of a racist-positive Christianity was the wave of the future, which would revitalize German church life. By abandoning the outdated doctrines of the past, and by championing an exclusively German church, they would march step-by-step with the new Nazi order.

Such views, however, aroused widespread opposition within the more traditional church ranks, which was mobilized by such men as Martin Niemöller (Bentley 1984), Karl Barth (Barth and Hamel 1959), and Dietrich Bonhoeffer. But in 1935 Barth was expelled from Germany, in 1937 Niemöller was arrested and banished to a concentration camp for the following eight years, and Bonhoeffer was forced into clandestine activity. He was in fact the only theologian who saw that resistance had to involve more than mere theological dissent and so joined with other members of his family in a conspiracy that sought to overthrow Hitler's regime, if necessary by violence. This recognition that Nazi totalitarianism and aggression were incompatible with his Christian theology led him to note perceptively as the war clouds loomed over Europe in the summer of 1939 that Christians in Germany would have to face the terrible alternative of either willing the defeat of their nation in order that Christian civilization might survive, or willing the victory of their nation and thereby destroying civilization. But the majority of his less clear-sighted colleagues failed to recognize this terrible choice. As staunch nationalists, they accepted the Nazi propaganda version of the war's origins and willingly enough supported Hitler's expansionist goals. They still continued to believe that they could be good Nazis and good Christians at the same time and refused to accept the fact that the two faiths were incompatible. They clung to this view despite the Nazis' open persecution of the church and clergy as well as despite the growing evidence of wartime atrocities. The illusion that Hitler could do no wrong only faded when events in the last year of the war forced all Germans to see that their idol had feet of clay. This factor was really the core reason why so little resistance was raised against the brutal transgressions of the totalitarian regime. At no point can it be said that resistance from the churches endangered the regime from within. Even where the pastors and priests after 1939 were increasingly discomfited by the Nazis' ever-escalating persecution and oppression, they remained loyal to the nation and concentrated their activities on their pastoral tasks, now in wartime more necessary than ever.

It must in all fairness also be said that these theologians and church leaders, like their counterparts in other professions, were confronting a radical challenge both unprecedented and unwelcome. They were trying to restore and maintain their institutions and values after years of war and violence. By contrast, the Nazis sought to expunge all such traces of tradition in order to secure the victory of their new ideological vision of the racial *Volksgemeinschaft.* The National Socialist movement saw its strength in its novelty, energy, and mobility, refusing to be tied down by the moral or legal conventions of the past. Its essence, as Hannah Arendt noted, was "motion implemented by terror." Like a tornado, Nazi totalitarianism gained impetus and virulence by its ever-escalating radicalization and its ability to strike with devastating force against all barriers or obstacles, sweeping across the frontiers of the continent and wreaking catastrophic destruction in the killing fields of eastern Europe. This was the mobilization of a tribal nationalism that owed nothing to the past, but saw itself the herald of modernity. In place of the inherited and centuries-old codes of morality and legality, Nazi totalitarianism substituted only one source of authority and validity—the will of the führer. It was indeed, as Hermann Rauschning said long ago, the Revolution of Nihilism.

It was this characteristic of dynamic movement that distinguished Nazi totalitarianism from all previous sorts of Caesarean despotisms or Bonapartist tyrannies. Nazism demanded a total rupture with such static models of dictatorship, and instead sought the mobilization of the population through massive propaganda to obey Hitler's mercurial, constantly evolving, and in the end inscrutable will. One of the functions of this propaganda onslaught was to bring about the erosion of conscience in the hearts of his individual followers. In her book *Eichmann in Jerusalem,* Hannah Arendt enumerated a number of factors that contributed to this erosion of conscience. The first of these was linguistic. A conspicuous feature of the Nazi ideological worldview was a roster of slogans and catch-phrases, indulging in euphemisms such as "Final solution," "special treatment," "mercy killing," or "resettlement," whose purpose was to conceal the enormity of what was being done.

Second, and related, the Nazis created among their functionaries a pseudo-morality through warping a component that all ethical ideas contain: the notion of obligation and sacrifice. Such a grotesque twist was necessary precisely because the majority of murderers were not sadists or killers by nature. Himmler's stratagem for dealing with any feelings of pity such men may have harbored consisted in ramming home the message, not "What horrible things I did to people" but "What horrible things I had to watch in the pursuance of my duties, how heavily the task weighed down upon my shoulders!" Such a rationalization could assume the tincture of duty and thus anesthetize other moral qualms. Its success was indeed evident, as was noted in the recent debate about the conduct of so-called "ordinary Germans" engaged in mass murder of Jews in Poland, Russia, and the Ukraine. In the circumstances of war, the multiplication of death, the ever-present sense that one's own life hung in the balance, lessened the value of life generally. Notably on the eastern front, there was a deliberate brutalization of the troops, who were indoctrinated to regard their opponents as demonic *Untermenschen*. So too the civilian victims, especially the Jews, were to be regarded as parasites or vermin, whose elimination or destruction need cause no qualms of conscience at all. At home, the Nazi leadership was constantly disappointed by the failure of the population to welcome such radical plans to remodel society on racial lines. One factor in this failure was undoubtedly the refusal of the churches to participate. Rather, they defensively sought to create spheres of relative immunity, or as Eberhard Bethge (1985) has called them, "islands of nonconformity." Here the church sought to keep alive the traditional norms or moral behavior inherited from their forefathers and to draw the line at the regime's interference, penetration, and control. By such means the Nazi ambition to achieve total domination was never achieved.

With hindsight we could all wish that the churches had possessed the moral and theological strength to mobilize opposition to the increasingly radical acts of the Nazis, or had not been misled by a mistaken sense of national loyalty in collaborating to perpetuate the totalitarian system. But it is undeniable that the churches, especially the Protestant churches, were not equipped institutionally or theologically to face the pervasive political demands of those years. They found no adequate theology to develop criteria for the political behavior of their followers when faced with such radical challenges as National Socialism. Too often, as in case of the so-called "German Christians," theology was used as a means for providing ideological justification for political stances adopted for secular reasons.

Of course, the German churches were not alone in this predicament. All of Christian Europe was caught up in a series of major crises, both organizationally and spiritually, which profoundly affected the exercise of their authority and influence. In this century modern men and women have increasingly shaken off the moral tutelage of ecclesial institutions and rejected the authority of religious dogmas. Instead, with an alarming degree of wishful thinking, the belief has grown that the individual's ethical guidance can be found in purely secular immanentist terms, regardless of the claims of history or community. At the same time, the modern state, also without any willing reference to transcendental value, has advanced its own demands for supremacy. Richard Rubenstein pointed out that with the collapse of credible religious and moral restraints on the state, which has resulted in the inevitable depersonalization of the relations between the rulers and the ruled, the state's sovereignty in this age of triage can become supreme (Rubenstein 1983). The history of the twentieth century has seen an exponential growth of technology, an increasing bureaucratization of the state's machinery of control, and an unprecedented readiness to manipulate whole populations for the alleged benefit of the dominant political group. At the time, these forces have been accompanied by a corrosive decline in the acceptance of the moral codes and humanitarian ideals held by the churches.

Yet, it also has to be acknowledged that the churches themselves contributed to this situation. It was no accident that the confusion and disarray in the European churches after 1918 were the product of their stance in the immediately preceding years of the First World War, when Christian, especially Protestant, theology had been so widely used or misused to justify the war efforts in all the conflicting nations. The mutually exclusive claims by each nation to have God on its side only resulted in the discrediting of Christianity as a whole. Four years of war had shattered the presumption of divine benevolence and omnipotence. The church leaders' triumphalist proclamation of God's support, their enthusiastic promises of imminent and divinely-blest victory, and their subsequent legitimation of the ruthless slaughter of the trenches soon appeared to be nothing more than hollow hypocrisy. Above all, the contrast between the teachings of Christ and the actual conditions of the battlefields had produced widespread disillusionment and even contempt. It would not be too much to say that European Christianity has never recovered from these self-inflicted wounds.

In the 1920s and 1930s, therefore, the churches faced a major crisis of credibility (Buchheim 1953; Gotto and Repgen 1990). In Germany, the experiences of the war, and even more of the nation's defeat in 1918, were particularly crucial. Neither clergy nor laity were in any way prepared for the spiritual and organizational metanoia demanded by the hour. The dominant school of German Protestant liberal theologians collapsed in the shock of war and unparalleled destruction. In the aftermath, a host of rival, often mutually incompatible theologies were constructed. The results only publicly demonstrated their theological disarray and contributed still further to the undermining of the churches' position in society. With the rise of such dynamic and revolutionary forces as Nazism, Fascism, and Communism, the churches' message seemed too weak and ineffective to withstand the waves of hostility and hatred that engulfed the post-1918 societies. The absence of any adequate resistance to the Nazi onslaught should be regarded as part of the whole malaise of Christendom during this period. This is where, I suggest, the roots of the churches' failure are to be found. Even when it occurred, their opposition to Nazi totalitarianism was essentially a defensive backward-looking reaction, relying on inherited structures and values. The prophetic voice of Christianity was confused and timorous. As many church leaders were obliged to recognize, their view of the social order and moral standards, based on the conservative ideals of the past, seemed to have become almost irrevocably broken, or rendered irrelevant, by the rise of the Nazi alternative substitute religion or forces beyond control (Meier 1992).

These were conclusions that many church members were unwilling to face at the time and that church historians and commentators, for understandable reasons, have been unwilling to stress since. But it is clear that, with the renewal of aggressive war in 1939, their dilemma was only made worse. As the war progressed, those church leaders most ardently committed to the cause of peace and justice, such as Pope Pius XII, could not fail to recognize that their moral influence had markedly diminished. From 1941 onward, Hitler's decision to escalate his ideologically-prompted campaigns for mass slaughter in eastern Europe demonstrated that the moral and political barriers that had been built up over the centuries to define permissible limits of military and political action were now ruthlessly overthrown. Rubenstein has reminded us that the systematic bureaucratically administered extermination of millions of subject peoples has now become a temptation of government (Rubenstein 1983). Nothing in the history of the last fifty years (Conway 1982), since the fall of Nazism, can lead us to assume that this capacity or temptation for the misuse of political or ideological power has been repudiated. The grim prospect is that similar excesses may happen, and indeed have happened, again.

Since 1945, the European churches have struggled to come to terms with this disastrous legacy. Looking back we can see that the German Church Struggle clearly exemplified the dilemmas and deficiencies of the churches' political witness in the maelstrom of conflicting ideologies and power struggles. It also demonstrated the difficulties confronting political pronouncements by theologians and the dangers of being misled by false political theologies in revolutionary situations. Theologically speaking, the problem of how the church best can mobilize its followers to witness for peace and justice in a world beset by political violence and injustice remains to be solved. It is to the credit of some farsighted Christian leaders, such as the first postwar German chancellor, Konrad Adenauer, or more recently the Polish pope, John Paul II, that they have recognized the need to rebuild the shattered Christian community amongst the ravaged and divided European nations and, in particular, to restore and revitalize the sense of ethical obligation, both individually and internationally. As they have rightly pointed out, the perversions of recent European history, whether in a Nazi or Communist guise, warn us of the consequences for any political or social system that deliberately repudiates the ethics of the past. How to ensure that the churches' political witness will be appropriate for the kind of pluralistic, democratic, and individualistic society now emerging in the remodeled Europe is a task presented to today's generation of church leaders (Baum 1996).

# 2

# Roman Catholic Theologians and National Socialism

## Adaptation to Nazi Ideology

THOMAS RUSTER

1

BY THE SUMMER OF 1933, Catholics in Germany had begun explicitly to express their enthusiasm for the new Nazi regime. Many Catholics had earlier wanted to join this attractive national movement, but until 1933 the bishops in their dioceses had prohibited, at least selectively, membership in the NSDAP (*Nationalsozialistische Deutsche Arbeiterpartei*) and the presence of uniformed members of the NSDAP at Mass. But Hitler's declaration at the Reichstag on March 12, 1933, that he would protect the rights of the Christian churches, the subsequent pronouncement of the German Episcopal Conference on March 28, 1933, that "the prohibitions and warnings" against National Socialism were "no longer necessary," and, finally, the concordat between the Vatican and the German Reich cleared the way for a collaboration between Catholics and Nazis (Dietrich 1988).

Such prominent theologians as Karl Adam, Joseph Lortz, and Michael Schmaus took the opportunity to publish articles urging a positive relationship between Catholicism and National Socialism. They encouraged Catholics to accept elements of the new regime's ideology and tried to dissipate the mental reservations and scruples that might trouble the Catholic faithful. They also hoped to change the political radicalism of the government by adapting to some elements of the Nazi weltanschauung. Some theologians hoped that a display of support might be able to prove that Catholics, even in a Nazi state, could still be good Germans. These political hopes were rooted in the national pressures that motivated their theological reasoning. Since the French Revolution, religious faith has had to prove its relevance to its members, and several prominent German theologians hoped that the popular power of the Nazi movement with its "romantic" and organic worldview would allow Catholics to maintain their faith and still remain loyal German citizens. When they praised the *"völkische Bewegung"* connected to the Nazi state and to Germany's popular traditions, they maintained that political life and their faith could be joined. When they accepted the religious organic model of romantic racism, they intended that "blood," that is, nature, and spirit could be united in their faith. When they spoke about nationalism, they also opposed the Roman, that is, Vatican, domination of national churches (Bucher 1998, 143–79; Ruster 1997, 99–112; Hürten 1992).

Several theologians tried to adapt to the Nazi order in order to prove their nationalistic credentials. Which dogma or theological tradition offered sustenance for this adaptation? Could the Catholic theological tradition be consonant with the Nazi Weltanschauung? Finally, what does it mean for the validity of theology when a principle could be so misused that it facilitated the adaptation of Catholicism to the totalitarianism of the Nazi state? How can such a misuse of theology be avoided? These questions have been asked for decades and can only be probed by reflecting on the theological positions offered.

## 2

In 1933 Joseph Lortz (1887–1975) was already a professor of ecclesiastical history at Braunsberg and later (1935) would hold the same position in Münster. He was well known for his *Geschichte der Kirche in ideengeschichtlicher Betrachtung* (1927/29). In 1939/40, he published his famous work *Die Reformation in Deutschland,* one of the most noteworthy attempts in Catholic theology to investigate objectively the theology of Martin Luther (Lautenschläger 1987). In 1933, Lortz sought to establish a positive relationship between Catholicism and National Socialism at the University of Münster (Lortz 1933).

For Lortz as for so many Catholics, the success of National Socialism meant a great victory over Communism. From his point of view, Germans could now live in the beginning of a new era of national renewal under National Socialism, in which German Catholics would be explicitly integrated into the *Volk.* Lortz was enthusiastic over Hitler's book *Mein Kampf* and reproached Catholics for not having enthusiastically accepted this blueprint of the Nazi Weltanschauung.

Lortz himself was not a systematic theologian and so only superficially discussed the fundamental ideological correspondence between Catholicism and National Socialism. For him it was enough that both opposed Communism, liberalism, democracy, relativism, and public immorality. Both affirmed, he felt, the natural order of creation through blood and race. Both hoped to maintain the *"Ständische Gesellschaftsordnung"* (order of estates in the society), a traditional position for politically conservative Germans. As the principal unifying idea uniting Catholicism and Nazi ideology, Lortz asserted that the emphasis on community rights over individualism as well as common interest over private interest could serve to help bind the church to the new ideology.

Lortz's aim was to cement the allegiance of Catholics to the new state. He listed, therefore, an array of the advantages for the institutional church. The Catholic church, now a part of the political solution, could concentrate its activities on the spiritual aspect of the human condition. A proper relationship among the confessions could also now begin to emerge, because the denominational concerns would become sublimated into national goals. And, finally, the church in Germany could be strengthened against the unifying and controlling tendencies of the Vatican. Lortz did not mention any concrete support that the Catholics could give to the Nazi state, but the ideological consonance could not help but strengthen Hitler's regime.

**3**

Michael Schmaus (1897–1993) was Professor of Dogmatic Theology in Münster (1933–45) and afterward in Munich. His *Katholische Dogmatik* (four volumes) has until recently often been used as a foundational text in theology, and he is frequently viewed as a precursor to Vatican II. In Münster on July 7, 1933, his lecture, "Begegnungen zwischen katholischem Christentum und nationalsozialistischer Weltanschauung" (Confrontation between Catholic Christianity and the National Socialist Worldview) (Schmaus 1933), listed the tenets of the party platform of the NSDAP point by point and suggested that some of Hitler's assertions reflected the Catholic theological tradition (Breuning 1969, 192–94; Heinzmann 1987).

According to Schmaus's opinion, the last two centuries had been dominated by the ideas of the French Revolution, that is, by the principles of freedom and equality. The revolutionary realization of these ideas had effectively undermined the natural and hierarchical order underpinning European societies. During this period, traditional organic societies had become atomistic, characterized by no internal or cohesive unity. The political ideals of liberalism, democracy, individualism, and rationalism were, he felt, opposed by the Catholic church and by National Socialism, which had based its ideology on the principles of community, *Volk* (nation), *Bindung* (commitment), and authority. The new state hoped to realize the priority of community and society over individual rights, the replacement of the liberal financial-capitalistic order of economy by a more corporative and productive order, and the transformation of a society divided by class struggle into an organic community. Schmaus felt that he could agree to virtually every point of the Nazi program, because the church had continuously opposed the ideas of the French Revolution and modernity. Schmaus, therefore, hoped to illustrate the correspondence between the Catholic and the National Socialist principles along several lines.

• The church was to be seen essentially as an ideal entity that could affirm every type of political community and because the natural order was to be viewed, at least partially, as an image of the supernatural. There was to be no fundamental contradiction between the church as such and other "natural" communities along the lines of the scholastic schema that asserted that the supernatural was to be constructed on a natural foundation.

• Divine Providence has given to every nation a special position in God's plan and task. The difference between Germany and Nigeria, for example, was to be accepted as a distinction that corresponds to the will and intention of God. Accordingly, history as a whole could be viewed as being organized by the *providentia Dei*. The German nation was designed, he insisted, to have a special place in this cosmic order. Describing the relation between the church and the nations, Schmaus asserted that the church is not really *international*, but *supernational*, and did not neglect the national. *Supernational* would be analogous to *supernatural*, and here Schmaus stressed the scholastic axiom that the supernatural supposes and works through the natural. God's grace builds on the natural order. Grace as God's gift, therefore, can and should cooperate with the individuality of the German people.

• Hierarchical authority as reflecting the will of God was essential to the church and was the organizing principle of Nazism. The Christian faith had historically supported the political authority of the state, because such power was seen as ultimately grounded in God's plan. Human beings, it was felt, had to be guided by authority because of original sin, which made freedom without authority impossible. For Schmaus, however, there was also an irrational and dangerous energy powering the Nazi ideology and Party. Catholic faith and its spiritual tradition could help excise this danger by providing spiritual boundaries that would mitigate the irrationalism in Nazi ideology. Catholics, therefore, could agree with many of the Nazi aims directed against modernity and might even be able to help modify the Party program by nurturing the movement through the church's message. In essence, Schmaus felt that the Nazi regime could not really survive without Catholic support. He used a set of such traditional theological concepts and models as those centering around the nature-grace relationship, the providence of God, the order of creation, and original sin. His arguments helped to explicate the Catholic interest in accommodation in these early stages of the Reich.

## 4

Karl Adam (1876–1966) was Professor of Dogmatic Theology in Tübingen (Krieg 1992; Kreidler 1988; Ruster 1997, 197–207). His most successful and often reprinted book was *Das Wesen des Katholizismus* (1924). Because of his vivacious and expressive language as well as an outlook that tapped German romanticism, he has been seen by some as a modern theologian. His opposition to modernity, democracy, and liberalism, however, was simultaneously unambiguous. In 1933 he felt that the time was ripe to relate his theology more toward the Nazi worldview. His article "Deutsches Volkstum und katholisches Christentum" (Adam 1933) was an intended glorification of the new state and its führer, Adolf Hitler. Adam used the word *blood* throughout his work. After he had some conflicts with the Sturm Abteilung (SA) men during a lecture in Tübingen, he apparently did not complete the article, whose second part had been announced at the end of the first.

Adam himself praised Hitler as a prophet coming from the "Catholic south." The divinely ordained mission of the German people, he felt, could best be explained by noting the connection between blood and spirit, especially between German blood and the Christian religion. Adam felt that Hitler himself had fulfilled this much-awaited German and Catholic goal (Scherzberg 2001). Hitler was felt to be the man who connected Christianity and the German *Volk* in his own person. For Adam, the essential and earlier unification of the Catholic church and the German Reich seemed to be occurring again during his lifetime and could be seen as the fulfillment of an historical development beginning even before the First Reich. Since the baptism of Pippin, the German nation (*deutsches Volkstum*) and German Christianity, he insisted, had coexisted and had nourished one another, even though at times the relationship had been uneasy.

Referring also to the so-called scholastic axiom *gratia non destruit naturam sed supponit et perficiat eam,* Adam identified nature with blood, race, *Volkstum,* and nation. The church represented the supernatural segment and rested on nature like the second floor sits atop the first. Adam argued that the Catholic religion in Germany was dependent on and nourished by German blood. Catholicism, therefore, was to affirm the contributions of the German race, the importance of the purity of blood, and the nation. Nationalism and Catholicism, therefore, were not at odds with one another. The kingdom of God was to be perceived as both the national and religious goal of the German people; otherwise a fundamental and essential part of Catholic doctrine would be abrogated (Adam 1933, 59). Supernature then was not merely spiritual, but rather could only be made existent through the relation of spirit and blood. Supernature was not to be separate from nature. As a consequence, the natural order itself was assumed to participate in the redemption of humanity.

As a minority in the population, German Catholics could welcome Adam's inclusivistic theology. Concerning Jews, Adam actually declared that purity of blood was itself a Jewish commandment (Adam 1933, 61), which, of course, tended in his mind and that of others to mitigate Nazi anti-Semitism. Because the Jewish *Volk* is and would always be different from the German *Volk,* even nationally minded and assimilated German Jews, Adam insisted, would logically at least have to accept the anti-Semitic measures being implemented by the Nazi government. Germans, he asserted in a not surprising twist of Christian precepts, actually had a religious duty to be anti-Semitic so that Germany remained a Christian society.

Adam's theological argument based on nature and grace would logically lead to a full acceptance of Nazi ideology and the elimination of Jewish influence from German society. He viewed the acceptance of racism, nationalism, and hostility toward the Jews as acceptable attitudes that Catholics should maintain in Germany. His immediate aim was to prove that Nazism and the Catholic faith were not in conflict with one another. The new state was to be given a heightened status due to its support of the church and its members. Adam also insisted grace and the kingdom of God would be furthered in this new political configuration. It seemed useful that the Nazi state should be allowed legitimately to exist and that Catholics should not resist their civil authorities. Such a collaboration of Nazis and Catholics, representing nature and grace, would of itself allow God's kingdom to move toward fulfillment. The establishment of Hitler's regime seemed to be the partial fulfillment of Karl Adam's eschatological vision. 'Blood', 'race', and 'nation' did not, as other Catholics later suggested, really belong to God's eschatological process. In hindsight, Adam's enthusiasm for the regime had twisted his theological sensitivity.

## 5

In 1933, Karl Eschweiler (1886–1936) was Professor of Dogmatic Theology in the eastern Prussian town of Braunsberg. His book *Die zwei Wege der neueren Theologie* (1926) was probably one of the best works of Catholic theology to emerge in the Weimar period. He joined the NSDAP in 1933. When he died in 1936, his funeral took place in the presence of SA-men and standard-bearers of the party (Ruster 1997, 293–304; Berger 1998, 156–62).

The cutting issue related to church/state issues that Eschweiler discerned in 1933 was political. He insisted that the churches should surrender their influence in the political parties that were closely connected to their confessions. The depoliticization of the Christian churches required by the NSDAP and realized by the concordat at least for Catholics was in Eschweiler's opinion the finale in the process overcoming the Westphalian Peace of 1648, which had begun the process of marginalizing the Christian churches. As a result of Hitler's ascent to power, Eschweiler felt that he could rejoice in the new Nazi order in Germany. The theological point at issue, which centered his theological reflections, was contained in article 24 of the Party program that demanded that the freedom of all religious confessions in the state was to be affirmed as long as the churches did not offend against the moral sense of the German *Volk* (Eschweiler 1933). Could Catholics consent to this viewpoint? That became the principal question posed in Eschweiler's commentary on the times.

Eschweiler related article 24 of the NSDAP program to the philosophical theology of Thomas Aquinas, which stated that the soul was to be seen as the formative principle of the body ("anima intellectiva est una et unica forma corporis"). He identified *anima* with the religious confession and *corpus* with the moral sense of the German race. According to Eschweiler, for pupils of Thomas Aquinas, it would be self-evident that the grace of faith for its own existence required that humans be born into a *Volk,* that is, into the German community (Eschweiler 1933, 456). The soul could only act through a specific body, which is what article 24 was trying to say, at least according to Eschweiler. For such Catholics as Eschweiler, it was absolutely normative to think in these terms to ensure that Christianity could reassert its relevance.

The church was to become for Eschweiler the soul of the new state. The church was not to have any material power in temporal matters, but only to exert its influence through the spirit. The demands of the NSDAP and the concordat concerning the depoliticization of the church could, theologically at least, be accepted in this context. But the Nazi state also needed the church to legitimate its own authority, at least Hitler seemed to think. Without the support of the church the Nazi state would lose the unifying cement that religion could help provide, and Eschweiler felt that this sociopolitical fact was designed to draw the two together.

## 6

Robert Grosche (1888–1967) and also Damasus Winzen outlined their views of what a Catholic–National Socialist accommodation would be like. They organized their reflections theologically around the concept of a *Reichstheologie,* which was historically designed to fuse Christianity and the secular order (Breuning 1969, 238–52). To delineate the theological and secular concepts of *Reich,* that is, empire, with all the ideological connotations that this term had for Christians concerned with the spiritual and secular orders through the centuries, would mean, they felt, that the relational model of nature and supernature, order of creation, and *anima forma corporis* would not be conceptually powerful enough.

In 1933 Robert Grosche was a chaplain for students in Cologne. He had been an active member of the Catholic *Jugendbewegung* (youth movement) in the second decade of the twentieth century. During World War I, he became dean of the cathedral in Cologne. In 1933 and 1934, he published several articles centering around the theme of establishing a foundation for Christian politics that would be useful for German Catholics in the Third Reich (Grosche 1933a; Grosche 1933b; Grosche 1934).

Grosche recognized the anti-liberal tradition thriving in conservative Europe, which had failed in organizing European states (Goritzka 1999). Catholicism had historically and, it seemed in 1933, correctly been a principal supporter of this antimodernist tradition, which derived its nourishment from the traditional concept of God's kingdom explicated in the Middle Ages but destroyed ideologically after the French Revolution. The Reich, he asserted, was originally and theologically a Christian eschatological term; Grosche saw it as one of the central dogmas organizing Christianity. Essentially the Reich was a goal that, when reached, would be the realization of peace for the world, a *pax Christi.* In secular mythology, the Reich was to connect Charlemagne, the Holy Roman Empire, Bismarck, and now Hitler. Grosche questioned, of course, whether the Nazi state was really qualified as the next step toward the realization of the theological concept of *Reich,* but he cautiously offered an affirmative answer to this question.

He formulated his argument around the notion of a theology of history, which was grounded in the results of the Council of Chalcedon. Here Jesus Christ had been proclaimed as one person with a divine and a human nature, which are neither separated nor mixed. Grosche's theological reflection combined the doctrine of the two natures of Christ with a theology of history. For him, only Christians could have a real history in the true meaning of the word. For pagans time was an eternal cycle repeating the same events. History for Christians moved from a beginning to the promise of fulfillment that was to be found in Jesus Christ. The unification of the two natures in Jesus was viewed as the proleptic anticipation of the end of history. Since Jesus lived, all time was now to be viewed as an historical transformation of the world that had already been spiritually completed in Jesus Christ. Grosche concluded that spiritual impulses always would precede and anticipate secular events. He felt, therefore, that this proper order of Christian history was in his day becoming a reality with the establishment of the Third Reich. The definition of the infallibility of the pope in 1870 on a spiritual level, for example, was to be seen as merely the prelude to the 1933 political decisions made by Germans. The principle of authority in both the church and the state, he asserted, was to take precedence over the freedom of speech and voting, that is, democracy, which divided humans in society (Grosche 1933a, 48).

Grosche, however, did not favor a theocracy. The dogma of Chalcedon itself prohibited the theocratic model. Grosche reminded his readers that the rejection of theocracy had already been taken in Chalcedon in the year 451. Historically, the two powers, church and state, were ideally conceived as existing in one and the same Reich, although unmixed. It would be *monophysistic* (that is, the heresy that affirmed the concept of only one nature in Christ) to establish the Reich under the sole rule of the church or of the state. Church and state should be joined in the Reich and simultaneously should maintain their own independent realities. It was now time for advancing toward the already destined Christian Reich, he maintained, although the final end would not soon be reached. Grosche saw evidence that the Reich was emerging in Germany through the Nazi movement. The foundations for this Reich seemed to be embodied in the *Führer Prinzip,* the organic German community, and the emergence of a realized corporate political theory reflecting the medieval ideal. Grosche was convinced that if ever there were to be an authentic Christian Reich, it could only exist under the dominion of Germany, which had already demonstrated its essential identity with the conceptual *Reich* that had helped power European political theory and history since medieval times. Both the Third Reich and the historical tradition that had shaped the concept of the Reich in the development of German political thought shared an acceptable hegemonical perspective. He felt that the state, however, could not become the embodied Reich by itself, since it had to be blessed by the church. The task for German Catholics, therefore, was to advance the realization of the spiritual Reich through the assistance of the state. Only in its relation to the Christian concept of *Reich* could the Nazi state become Christian (Grosche 1933b, 99). In essence, both the church and state had to cooperate for the legitimate Reich to emerge. Similarly Winzen viewed current events through the lenses of *Reichstheologie.*

Damasus Winzen OSB (Order of St. Benedict) was a monk in the abbey of Maria Laach. At the famous *Führertagung* at Maria Laach in 1933, a meeting of the leading conservative Catholics sympathizing with the Nazi movement, he presented a lecture, "Gedanken zu einer 'Theologie des Reiches' " (Winzen 1933a; Winzen 1933b).

Winzen's perspective is close to that of Grosche. The Reich was for Winzen the end of the political willing and longing of Germans. According to Winzen, a purely political state could never become the authentic Reich, since such a polity was merely a temporal entity, an artificial construction designed to serve the interests of the economy. All states, of course, have been based on power, but in its authentic meaning the Reich was to be based on God's plan that was rooted in the close relationship between the temporal Reich and church. The earthly Reich, he insisted, was to exist in relation to the church and was nothing

other than the realization of the kingdom of Christ in the contemporary physical and political community. God's Reich ultimately had to be based on the
priest and king, Jesus Christ, the real ruler and redemptor of the world.

  Winzen's thought was patterned after the model of Augustinian sacramental theology. From this perspective the church would provide God's blessing,
while the state would be the recipient. When the church engaged the state in establishing the common good, a type of transubstantiation actually would take
place and the true Reich would emerge, since the sacramental authority of the
church was in actuality consecrating the state and its government. The church
was seen to have a vocation and a duty to lead all peoples along with their limi-
tations to the universality of the Reich. Because of its sacramental power, the
church was actually, according to Winzen, the only institution with an ability to
incorporate states into the Reich. The authentic Reich, Winzen insisted, had
not yet been realized. But the foundation and the possibilities for God's Reich
were in the hands of Catholics in Nazi Germany. The concept of *Führer*, the notion of the organic community, and the idea of a national task or goal suggested
to him that Hitler's state was a significant step toward the Reich that God intended (Winzen 1933a). He insisted, however, that the deepest longing of the
German people could not be fulfilled before the anointed ruler of this earthly
Reich (Hitler) would place his own crown on the altar of the king of kings
(Jesus Christ) (Winzen 1933a, 16). Winzen's dream was certainly unrealistic,
but his theological reflections do suggest the enthusiasm with which Hitler was
being greeted in this early period of adaptation.

7

When theologians want to express their political opinions, not surprisingly
they use theological terms and models, which normatively help to determine
the flow of their arguments. From a perceived correspondence of common interests (Lortz) to a deeply perceived unity between church and state in the
Reich, based on the mystery of the hypostatic union (Grosche) or the unification of word and element in the sacrament (Winzen), almost every union of
state and church could become possible and would seem like the unfolding of
God's plan. In the case of each of these theologians, it would be difficult to decide which came first, theology or historical reality. Did the choice of the theological schema that was responsible for the final result or did the intention to
achieve an acceptable political and theological union ultimately influence the

choice of the schema? The theological speculations considered above do suggest the need that each man had to prove that his nationalist credentials were compatible with his religious ideals. Here was finally, they thought, a regime that epitomized the anti-liberal and anti-democratic perspectives supported by the church since the French Revolution. In the cases presented here, the theologians used the principles peculiar to their own professional specializations.

These men were theologically creative. In their political reflections, they tried to maintain the original meaning of their theological or philosophical perspectives. The Catholic tradition relies on theologians' continuously reappropriating the thoughts of their predecessors and then urges them to amplify how the past can fit the contemporary culture of the current era. Theology is supposed to engage culture. The insights of 1933, however, were theologically framed to accommodate Nazism for the sake of political expediency. Catholics were determined to continue making the case that they were as nationalist as their Protestant contemporaries. They accommodated the Christian faith to the realities of politics and have illustrated for us how ahistorical theological concepts were doomed to failure when confronting modern political ideologies. They failed to engage in any substantive political critique (Berger 1998, 191–252; 323–423).

Because theology deals with ontological values, it is a dangerous affair. Error comes easily when theologians lose sight of what reappropriation means. Nature, at least in its original tradition, should not be identified with 'blood' and 'race' as some German theologians tried to do in 1933. It is interesting to see that Karl Barth, who stressed the otherness of the revealing God very clearly and who urged theologians to resist hyphenated Christianity, was more prepared to resist the National Socialist ideology than were his Catholic theological contemporaries. The attempt to adapt Christian faith to the Nazi Weltanschauung can be seen in hindsight as a dangerous move, since it favors the solutions that can introduce an insidious corruption that can subsequently reduce the Christian faith to a supportive role in relation to political ideology. These Catholic theologians tried to reconcile Nazi ideology, seen by some as a pseudoreligion (Lease 1995), with their Christian faith. By naturalizing theological doctrines, they hoped to achieve a political accommodation with the new regime (Ruster 2000; Bärsch 1998), but they actually jeopardized the transcendent foundation of their faith.

# 3

# The Conflict Between Engelbert Krebs and the Third Reich

ROBERT A. KRIEG

## 1

THE THIRD REICH deliberately set out in 1933 to decrease the number of professors in the seventeen departments of Catholic theology then existing at German universities and *Hochschulen.* Beginning in 1933, National Socialist leaders put pressure on politically questionable professors in these departments to resign, and they usually managed to get their way, even if it took a few years. After a professor vacated a position, the Reich frequently neglected to replace the professor, or on occasion moved the academic chair to another department. The Ministry of Education went a step further in 1939: it closed the University of Munich's department of Catholic theology and four of Bavaria's philosophical-theological *Hochschulen:* Bamberg, Freising, Passau, and Regensburg. During 1944 and 1945 the advance of the Russian troops forced the evacuation of the schools at Braunsberg and Breslau. As a result, only ten departments of Catholic theology remained at the end of the war, and each of them was smaller than it had been in 1933 (Mussinghoff 1979; Stasiewski 1971; Stasiewski 1984).

Books and articles have already provided detailed accounts of the histories of these theology faculties, of some of their members, and of the interaction between these departments and Hitler's government (Bäumer 1983; Bäumer 1984; Heim 1997). One aspect that warrants study is the correlation between the theology and the politics of German Catholic theologians during the Third Reich. It is one thing to know how a specific theologian acted in response to

Nazism; it is another to understand how the scholar's theological ideas shaped his political actions (Dietrich 1987; Dietrich 1988; Krieg 1999).

Engelbert Krebs (1881–1950) was a widely respected theologian at the University of Freiburg when Adolf Hitler became Germany's new chancellor on January 31, 1933. Krebs stood, however, as a threat to the Nazi state because of his participation in the Catholic Center Party and his positive view of Jews and Judaism. In 1934 and 1935, Krebs wrote critiques of the Reich as it increasingly violated its concordat with the Vatican (Junghanns 1980; O'Meara 1998). The Reich dismissed Krebs from his professorship in 1937 and eventually tried to imprison him. Krebs's opposition to National Socialism sprang from his theology of the church. According to Krebs, the church should work for the coming of God's reign. It must be an advocate for justice and a voice for truth as well as a religious institution, a community of believers, and a bearer of the sacraments (Dulles 1987). This inclusive view of the church inspired and guided Krebs's political stance.

## 2

Born into a banking family on September 4, 1881, in Freiburg im Breisgau, Engelbert Krebs matriculated at the University of Freiburg in the autumn of 1900. At the same time, he entered the seminary for the Diocese of Freiburg. During his first year of studies, Krebs heard the lectures of Heinrich Finke, a medieval historian active in the Görres Gesellschaft, and of Adolf Dyroff, an idealist philosopher specializing in Christian spirituality. Krebs moved to the University of Munich for the autumn and winter of his second year of studies, attending the lectures of the patristic scholar Odilo Rottmanner, OSB, and the neoscholastic philosopher Georg Freiherr von Hertling. Krebs was deeply impressed by both scholars, especially Hertling (O'Meara 1998, 129), who shared with Krebs the vision of German Catholicism that Hertling himself had received from Joseph Görres (O'Meara 1982, 126–33; O'Meara 1991, 155–60; Schwaiger 1984; Schatz 1986, 67–69). Krebs returned to Freiburg in the spring of 1902 and, under the direction of Dyroff, completed his doctorate in philosophy during 1903, writing a dissertation on the medieval mystic Dietrich von Freiburg in Saxony (Junghanns 1980, 3–19).

Krebs began his theological studies in the autumn of 1903 at Rome's Camposanto Teutonico. Among his teachers were Heinrich Seuse Denifle, O.P.

(Order of Preachers), and Franz Ehrle, S.J. (Society of Jesus), the prefect of the Vatican Library. Krebs was ordained a priest in 1906 and served in parishes in the Diocese of Freiburg for the next two years. He returned to Rome from 1908 through 1910 and studied with Franz Josef Dölger. Finishing a dissertation on the notion of the Logos as savior in first-century Christian literature, he received his doctorate in theology from the University of Freiburg in 1909. Next, he demonstrated his scholarly competence in both philosophy and theology by completing a second dissertation on Meister Eckhart's Dominican student Hervaeus Natalis. Krebs was "habilitated" in "scholastic studies" at the University of Freiburg in 1911 (Junghanns 1980, 20–38).

Krebs was immediately offered Freiburg's chair in pastoral theology, which had been held by his mentor, Cornelius Krieg (d. 1911). Choosing instead to wait for an opening in dogmatic theology, he worked as an adjunct professor at Freiburg for the next eight years, teaching courses in philosophy as well as in theology. He addressed issues posed by the Baden School of neo-Kantianism and published scholarly texts on the writings of Johann Baptist Hirscher, the history-of-religions approach to the early church, and the notion of salvation. Eventually receiving a professorship in dogmatic theology at the University of Freiburg, Krebs gave his inaugural lecture, titled "The Problems of Moral Values and Their Presentation in Catholic Dogmatic Theology," on June 8, 1917 (Krebs 1917). He was formally appointed a regular professor of theology at the University of Freiburg on October 1, 1919, succeeding Carl Braig (Junghanns 1980, 40–101).

Krebs backed the German government's policies during the First World War. He wrote articles on the war's progress, highlighting what he perceived to be the moral and religious basis of Germany's cause (Krebs 1915). Belonging to the Committee for the Defense of German and Catholic Interests, he visited the front lines, drove the wounded to hospitals, and called for improvements in the prisoner-of-war camps. He also explained to his readers the criticisms of Germany's war efforts by the Belgian cardinal Désiré Joseph Mercier, Archbishop of Mechelin (Krebs 1917–18). Krebs's initial support for his nation's military action was typical of German Catholics who were intent on demonstrating their patriotism (Hürten 1992, 35–48).

Krebs emerged as a dogmatic and historical theologian during the 1920s. He published scholarly texts in Christology and ecclesiology, including studies on the beliefs of the Syrian and Russian Orthodox churches. He wrote the first volume of *Dogma und Leben* in 1921, revising it in 1923. He completed the second volume in 1925. He published the widely read *Das Kennzeichen seiner Jünger* (1921), which also appeared as *A Little Book on Christian Charity* (1927). His research on medieval thought bore fruit in texts on mysticism such as *Grundfragen der kirchlichen Mystik* (1921). Further, he wrote on the relationship between Catholicism and Protestantism, on Joseph Wittig's progressive theological views, and on Jews and Judaism (Junghanns 1980, 73–77, 94–137). As an adjunct professor, Krebs had advised the promising student Martin Heidegger in academic matters and had also witnessed his wedding. But he watched their collegial relationship cool during the 1920s as the philosopher no longer practiced his faith (Ott 1993; O'Meara 1998, 135–40). Drawing on his experience as a chaplain at Freiburg's Hochschule for women, Krebs published articles on Germany's social and educational biases against women (Krebs 1922a). Perhaps because of his feminist views, Krebs was visited by the philosopher Edith Stein in April 1930 (Junghanns 1980, 54–58). Krebs's interest in the universal church prompted him to travel around the world from March 1, 1926, to February 16, 1927, visiting the United States, Japan, China, Korea, Indonesia, Ceylon, Egypt, and the Holy Land. Upon his return to Freiburg, he wrote *Um die Erde* (1928), in which he recounted his travels and reflected on Catholicism in non-European societies.

Krebs celebrated his twenty-fifth anniversary of priestly ordination on July 1, 1931. During the prior months, he had published two books on the history of dogma, *St. Augustinus als Mensch und Kirchenlehrer* (1930) and *Gottesgebärerin* (1931).

## 3

After the Reichstag passed the Enabling Act on March 23, 1933, Krebs found himself in the Third Reich, and, although he had lived in constructive ways in a monarchy and a democracy, he found himself excluded from the Nazi state (Bäumer 1983). Krebs immediately perceived the dangers of the political situation in 1933. On March 22, 1933, he noted in his private journal that Nazi leaders were intimidating many of the representatives in the Reichstag into voting for the Enabling Act. He initially looked for positive aspects in the Reich. For example, after officials of the Catholic Church and the Nazi government signed their concordat on July 22, 1933, he wrote an article tactfully praising the new agreement between Rome and Berlin, but also warning Catholics to stay alert to the new situation's "dangers" (Krebs 1933a). Further, searching for an alternative to the *"Führerprinzip"* in higher education, he proposed ways of strengthening German universities in "Die Aufgabe der Universität im neuen Reich" (Krebs 1933b). In this vein, he also gave a lecture at the University of Freiburg on June 1, 1933, explaining that a strong, centralized government in Berlin would be valid only if it respected the authority of God and the church (Krebs 1933c).

For his part, Krebs refused to smooth over his differences with National Socialism. The Reich required all professors to fill out questionnaires in 1933 and 1934 so that the regime could pinpoint its "enemies." In response, Krebs made it clear that he had always voted for the Center Party (Heiber 1991, 280–81; Ruster 1994, 312–13).

Moreover, Krebs did not hide or renounce his convictions regarding Jews and Judaism. He spoke out against the dismissal of Jewish professors from the University of Freiburg in April 1933 (Ott 1993, 147). In doing so, he upheld the position that he had publicly expressed for more than ten years. In 1922 Krebs had published an article urging Catholic students to respect their Jewish peers (Krebs 1922b). In 1926 he wrote a pamphlet, *Urkirche und Judentum,* which appeared as an article in Fordham University's journal, *Thought* (Krebs 1927a). He held that Christians must regard Judaism as the home in which they were born and that they must respect Jews as bearers of God's teachings (Krebs 1927a). In 1933, Krebs reiterated his views in the *Lexikon für Theologie und Kirche.* In the entry "Judentum und Christentum," he asserted: "Jewish belief constitutes the preparation, womb, and continuing witness for Christian faith." After explaining this assertion, he discussed the kinship between the Jewish and Christian faiths. He ended the article by observing that "[t]he differentiation between Christian faith as fulfillment and Jewish faith, which remains steadfastly committed to being an unfulfilled preparation, is irreconcilable as a differentiation of convictions, but it should not become a differentiation lacking in love" (Krebs 1933d). Krebs's outspoken, positive view of Judaism has stood out in relation to the covert, religious anti-Semitism among most German Catholics (Scholder 1986, 322–54; Dietrich 1988, 50–94).

As Hitler's government entered into its second year, Krebs gave a public lecture—entitled "Jesuitischer und deutscher Geist"—in Freiburg on February 15, 1934, in which he argued that a state's authority is derived from God's authority. Hitler's government had exercised good judgment by declaring that it opposed atheism, for example, in Bolshevism, and wanted to work with the Catholic and Protestant churches in overcoming atheism in German society.

An instance of the proper integration of the German *"Geist"* and the Christian *"Geist"* occurred, Krebs said, in the Jesuits, for they brought together both "spirits" in their lives and mission (Krebs 1934). Outraged by this idea, Freiburg's Nazi Youth Association and Nazi Student Association destroyed the lecture's reprints.

An unfortunate incident took place in August 1934. Among many friends and associates at his brother's house in the Black Forest village of St. Märgen, Krebs stated: "We are being governed by robbers, murders, and criminals." Afterward, he learned that his remark had somehow made its way to the Gestapo (Bäumer 1983, 279).

Krebs came into overt conflict with the Reich by publishing two scholarly articles in 1935. In opposition to Alfred Rosenberg's *Der Mythus des 20. Jahrhunderts* (1930), he wrote "Arteigenes Christentum," arguing that Catholicism cannot be turned into a national church without betraying its very essence (Krebs 1935). Further, he published an essay on Johann Adam Möhler's *Athanasius* (1827)—a book that Joseph Görres had praised in 1837. While much of Krebs's text is comprised of selections from Möhler's book, an introduction by Krebs explained that Athanasius had opposed the Roman emperor Constantine's interference in the church during the struggle with Arianism. Athanasius's opposition to the state had significant implications for German Catholics, Krebs noted (Krebs 1934–35). Without being specific, Krebs's message was clear: Catholics should resist the Reich's efforts to control the church.

Krebs's conflict with the Nazi regime moved into the juridical sphere in the mid-1930s. From 1935 through 1938 the regime closed Catholic newspapers, seized church-owned properties, and conducted show trials against priests, sisters, and brothers who were accused of sexual misconduct or the misuse of funds (Hürten 1992, 362–79). In response, Pope Pius XI issued his encyclical *Mit brennender Sorge* in 1937. Krebs's formal struggle with the Reich began in November 1935 when he asked the university's administration to obtain a visa for him to travel to Austria so that he could lecture on mysticism. When he received no response to his request, he made it again in December and was eventually told by the rector's office that he should not accept the invitation to Vienna because the Reich would not likely grant him permission to leave the country. On April 1, 1936, Krebs's request was returned to him without a decision (Bäumer 1983, 278–79).

Krebs's situation became more precarious when the Minister of Justice alerted the Minister of Cult and Instruction on April 2, 1936, that it was investigating Krebs because of his alleged statement of August 1934 against the Reich. In turn, the Minister of Cult and Instruction informed the university's rector on April 18 that he should suspend Krebs from his teaching until the investigation was completed. Although Freiburg's Archbishop Conrad Gröber sought to stop this suspension, the rector announced that Krebs's courses were canceled until further notice. On May 23, 1936, the Reich charged that Krebs was an enemy of the state because of his reported criticism of Nazi leaders in 1934 at St. Märgen. Moreover, it claimed that Krebs was a Communist, for he had attended meetings of labor groups, had participated in the left wing of the Catholic Center Party, and had recommended that Baden's Grand Duke abdicate in favor of democracy. The formal proceedings dragged on for many months, during which, in July 1936, the Reich revoked Krebs's passport (Bäumer 1983, 172–78).

On February 22, 1937, the University of Freiburg received word from the Minister of Cult and Instruction in Karlsruhe that, in making his alleged comment in August 1934, Krebs had violated article 6 of the law concerning the reordering of the civil service. Permitted to submit a written self-defense within three days, Krebs argued that article 6 did not pertain to him because according to the Vatican's concordat with the State of Baden ecclesiastical authorities as well as civil authorities must review charges against a priest-professor. Krebs learned on July 19 that the Ministry of Justice had withdrawn its charges against him because of a lack of witnesses. Nevertheless, the Minister of Education informed Krebs on August 31, 1937, that he was henceforth retired from the University of Freiburg. Soon afterward, the University moved Krebs's academic chair from the theology department to the departments of law and politics (Bäumer 1983, 280).

Krebs was not at a complete loss without his professorship. He devoted himself to writing entries for forthcoming Catholic encyclopedias that were being edited in China and Japan. Moreover, Archbishop Gröber appointed Krebs to lecture at St. Peter's Seminary in Freiburg, conferring on him the church's honorary title of monsignor (Junghanns 1980, 179–210). The relationship between Gröber and Krebs, however, was strained because of the archbishop's efforts to accommodate the Nazi regime and also because of his criticism of theologians interested in Germany's renewal in theology and liturgy (Ott 1984; Vorgrimler 1966, 32–40; Rahner 1994).

Krebs again became a target of Nazi ire after he gave a sermon on the Feast of St. James the Greater (July 25) in 1943 at a mass in the Black Forest village of

Oedsdach im Renchtal. Developing the theme of love from the biblical readings for the day, he observed: "To be sure, one may fight against one's enemies, but one may not hate them." This statement offended a Luftwaffe lieutenant at the mass, who then reported Krebs to the Nazi authorities. The Gestapo interrogated Krebs on October 20, 1943, and, on November 29, they searched through his house. Afterward they incarcerated Krebs in Karlsruhe, tentatively sentencing him to a prison camp. This action was blocked, however, when a physician submitted an official report on Krebs's poor health, including his anemia. Releasing Krebs from jail, the Reich informed him on December 28, 1943, that he was not allowed to say Mass, preach, or hear confessions. Archbishop Gröber intervened and secured permission for Krebs to celebrate Mass in private (Junghanns 1980, 211–14; Bäumer 1983, 280–81).

After several illnesses, Krebs died in Freiburg of a kidney infection on November 29, 1950, at the age of sixty-nine (Junghanns 1980, 215–44). During the Third Reich, Krebs kept the vision of Catholicism in Germany that he had acquired from Joseph Görres and Georg Freiherr von Hertling and that he had pursued under Wilhelm II and in the Weimar Republic. According to this vision, the church should not withdraw from modernity into a "ghetto" but should interact with contemporary society, contributing to Germany's common good and culture. This general view expressed itself in Krebs's specific understanding of the church.

## 4

In his theology, Krebs deliberately drew on scholars from the twelfth to the twentieth centuries and enriched their ideas with his own insights and his intellectual synthesis of the Christian faith. He mined both the neo-Platonic and Aristotelian traditions, studying the Franciscan St. Bonaventure and the Dominicans St. Thomas Aquinas, Hervaeus Natalis (d. 1323), and Vincent de Contenson (d. 1674). Yet, in an age of neoscholasticism, he moved beyond medieval thought by viewing modern scholarship favorably. Attracted to theologies that see the church in relation to the coming of God's kingdom, he turned to Bernhard Galura (d. 1856), Franz Anton Staudenmaier (d. 1856), and Johannes Baptist Hirscher (d. 1865). Further, he took seriously texts that recast the past's wisdom in contemporary categories, especially the writings of Matthias Joseph Scheeben (d. 1888), Hermann Schell (d. 1906), and Wilhelm Koch (d. 1955). By the end of his life, Krebs had published approximately

twenty-six books and 340 articles. He laid out his major theological ideas in
*Dogma und Leben.*

The two-volume *Dogma und Leben* in 1,209 pages is Krebs's "summa"
(Junghanns 1980, 235–95). The first volume (457 pages) treats seven major
topics of Catholic belief: faith, God, the Trinity, creation, original sin, salvation
in Jesus Christ, and Mary (Krebs 1923). The second volume (752 pages) dis-
cusses six themes related to Christ's saving work through the church: the
church's teaching office (for example, papal infallibility), its priestly office and
sacraments, its pastoral office (for example, the role of the bishops), the church
as the mystical body of Christ, grace beyond this life (for example, purgatory),
and the advent of God's new creation (Krebs 1925). Needless to say, Krebs intended this work to be a presentation of the most important tenets of Catholicism, summarizing significant conciliar and papal teachings on the selected
topics. He expressed his originality by relying on personal language instead of
neoscholastic terminology, discussing modern issues (for example, suffering),
and developing the theme that love of God entails love of neighbor. It is this
theme that undergirded the scholar's opposition to the Third Reich.

Weaving the topic of love through both volumes, Krebs articulated the belief that love is the primary reality of the Christian faith. In his view, one of the
church's distinguishing marks is its compassion for all people, communicated
through its charitable works around the world (Krebs 1923, 30). The source of
this charity is the triune God. "God the Father and the Son love the world in the
Holy Spirit. Thus the love inflamed in the soul by the Spirit—if one truly loves
the Father and the Son—must love all of creation in the Father and the Son, for
the Father has always conceived of creation in the Son and has brought it into
existence in the Spirit" (Krebs 1923, 224). Out of devotion to the triune God,
the church commits itself to the well-being of all people (Krebs 1923, 226).
Jesus Christ displayed God's compassion for all men and women and conveyed
it symbolically by washing his disciples' feet before going to his death. It is
Christ himself, therefore, who strengthens the church's generosity (Krebs 1923,
385). In particular, Christ empowers believers through the church's sacraments
to the love of God and neighbor (Krebs 1925, 65). This sacramental action anticipates God's new creation when the faithful will fully share in God's life and
the communion of the saints (Krebs 1925, 609–11). Finally, God will judge
human beings according to their degree of generosity to those in need (Matt.
25:31–46). "Love of God and Christian love of neighbor are in essence identi-
cal. Whoever loves God loves therefore everything that bears God's influence,

indeed loves God's resemblance in all people. Deficient love of neighbor is a sign of deficient love of God" (Krebs 1925, 701).

What is the church's role in the human effort to love God and neighbor? The church, which is "the mystical body of Christ," witnesses to the coming of God's new creation (Krebs 1925, 11). "The kingdom of God grows not only out of the invisible seeds of grace, but also out of the externally perceivable seeds, namely, out of God's hearable word, which Christ has strewn by means of his visible sowers in the fields of the world" (Krebs 1925, 12). To a degree, the church already participates in God's new reign. However, it is not itself the fullness of this reality. The church is united with the coming of God's new creation, but it does not encompass it. "The church is the union of the intentional building up of and the vibrant growing into the kingdom of God" (Krebs 1925, 12). For this reason, the church plays a sacramental role in history; it is a "visible vessel" of God's love for all human beings (Krebs 1925, 720). While the Holy Spirit works invisibly throughout the world transforming people's hearts and minds, it desires that the church make God's love concretely evident in every land and culture. "Thus the vessel of [divine] love is the church, the mustard seed or the wheat seed, the grape vine or the mystical body, made knowable in a visible reality, in which [people] should grow together" (Krebs 1925, 720). In sum, the church's vocation is to attest to the advent of God's new creation.

In *Dogma und Leben* Krebs developed a theology that sees the entire human family in relation to the mystery of Jesus Christ, and yet he simultaneously recognizes that God's love in Christ extends to all human beings regardless of their religious affiliation. In other words, Krebs held a "Christocentrism" that affirmed the universality of God's grace. He expressed this orientation at the start of volume 1 by referring to Andrew's testimony to Peter about his encounter with Jesus Christ: " 'We have found the Messiah' (John 1:41). How much delight concerning life's deepest yearning . . . lies in these words. . . . Through the fortunate possession of our dogmatic faith, we Catholic Christians hold in common with those ordinary people at the Sea of Gennesaret [in A.D. 28] this delight, this inner security and joy" (Krebs 1923, v). Complementing this thought, Krebs concluded his first volume by discussing Christ as the new Adam, the initiator of the new creation (Krebs 1923, 443). In the opening pages of volume 2, Krebs again noted his Christocentric orientation: "In all parts [of this volume] the theme is always the same; we are always speaking only of Christ, living and working in his mystical body, the church" (Krebs 1925, 25). Following through on this orientation, he ended the second volume with the image of the second coming of Christ and the new Jerusalem (Rev. 21:1–5).

This emphasis on Christ as the center and future of human life anchored belief in the universal character of God's grace. For Krebs, love of Christ includes respect and care for all people. Hence, Krebs recognized the validity of Judaism (Krebs 1923, 80–84). Moreover, he steered clear of a triumphal view of Catholicism. In particular, he did not promote the idea that the church is the full embodiment of Christ and hence of God's kingdom—an idea that some theologians have derived from the incarnational ecclesiology of Johann Adam Möhler (Brosseder 1988–89; Himes 1997; Pottmeyer 1997, 151–53). The church witnesses to a transcendent reality that has not yet come fully into history.

The theme of love of neighbor, which stands out in Krebs's *Dogma und Leben,* also emerges in Krebs's other writings. For example, in *A Little Book on Christian Charity* Krebs wrote: "True charity looks around with a kindly eye to find a fellow man groaning under a heavy burden. Kindly and patiently, with due consideration for human frailty and weakness, the charitable man stoops and helps him bear his burden" (Krebs 1927b, 75). In other writings, Krebs reinforced the theme of love with related ideas: theology as reflection on actual Christian life, divine revelation as a personal encounter with God, history as a journey to God's kingdom, and the graced character of creation.

In sum, Krebs reasoned that because the divine love that characterizes God's triune life also fashioned and sustains creation, God desires that the Holy Spirit draw all of creation and history toward union with the Father in Jesus Christ. The church witnesses to this reality in its communal life and human services; these activities attest to the second coming of Christ, whose Holy Spirit reaches out to all people. What did this theological view mean for Christian life in Germany under Hitler? According to Krebs, a commitment to the coming of God's reign meant that one could not support a government whose leaders showed no respect for the inherent dignity of all human beings, even if these officials had reached a concordat with the Vatican. His opposition to the Nazi regime rested, therefore, not upon his political convictions, which in fact remained ambiguous about democracy, but upon his religious convictions. From the outset, Krebs perceived that Hitler's Third Reich contradicted God's kingdom, the "*Reich Gottes.*"

**5**

The majority of the German Catholic theologians did not support National Socialism, but neither did they oppose it (Bäumer 1983, 273; Scholder 1986; Scholder 1988; Hürten 1992). As priests, they followed the lead of Pope Pius XI, the German bishops, and eventually Pope Pius XII by complying with the concordat's clause that clergy would not engage in "politics." Many German Catholic theologians did not object to the concordat's clause because, as neoscholastics, they held that Catholic philosophy and theology had very few points of contact with contemporary issues and modern thought. However, a few theologians initially supported Hitler's regime; among them were Karl Adam (Tübingen), Karl Eschweiler (Braunsberg), Joseph Lortz (Braunsberg and Münster), and Michael Schmaus (Münster) (Bäumer 1984). By contrast, some of their colleagues spoke out against the Nazi state; these included Romano Guardini (Berlin), Engelbert Krebs (Freiburg), Wilhelm Neuss (Bonn), Joseph Schmidlin (Münster), and Georg Schreiber (Münster) (Damberg 1993; Krieg 1997, 115–36).

Krebs developed a theology of love of neighbor that sees the church witnessing to the coming of God's kingdom. In other words, the church is an advocate for the well-being of all people and is also a spokesperson for the truth. Although Krebs did not explicitly speak in these terms, he conveyed these aspects of the church's mission as he promoted concrete social causes. He emphasized the model of church as servant during the Weimar Republic by aiding the efforts of workers, women, Catholics, and Jews to gain respect in the public realm and to establish organizations through which they could work to achieve their aspirations in German society (Krebs 1924, 29–68). He emphasized the model of church as prophet during Hitler's twelve years by speaking on behalf of his Jewish colleagues, criticizing the regime's interference in the church, and preaching on love of one's enemies. In other words, Krebs's political actions during the Weimar Republic and the Third Reich sprang from the conviction—learned specifically from Johann Baptist Hirscher (Krebs 1913; Pottmeyer 1997)—that the church's task is to promote God's reign in the world.

It would be wrong to suggest, however, that Krebs crafted a post-Vatican II liberation theology. Because he worked within the theological horizon of the First Vatican Council, he implicitly assumed that the ideal political arrangement would be for church and state to have a close formal relationship. Hence, remaining faithful to Pope Pius IX's *Syllabus of Errors* (1864), Krebs rejected in theory the separation between church and state. At the same time, Krebs observed the ways that the church was in fact thriving in democracies. For example, while maintaining in *Die Kirche und das neue Europa* that Catholicism should serve as the formal cornerstone of the European nations, he also noted that the church had secured legal rights within the Weimar Republic, and that it was operating well in this complex situation (Krebs 1924, 15–28). Further, he marveled in *Um die Erde* that the Catholic church in the New World was flourishing amid the secularism of the United States (Krebs 1928, 166–93). After Pope Pius XII's Christmas sermon of 1944, in which the pontiff endorsed democracy as the preferred form of government (Sigmund 1994, 274), Krebs may have wanted publicly to agree with this view. However, his health after 1944 prohibited him from undertaking scholarship and resuming his public role in the church and Germany.

Unfortunately, Krebs never wrote a retrospect on his life and thought. For this reason, we cannot say with certainty how his ideas evolved. For example, it would have clarified his theology as well as his political thought if he had said after 1945 how he perceived the Second World War and also how his view of the First World War had changed since 1918. By the fact that he challenged the Nazi regime, he had seemingly distanced himself by the mid-1930s from his nationalism of the early 1900s. Krebs's writings and actions after 1932 suggest that he respected the values of modernity and envisioned the church as taking a more positive stance to the contemporary world. In short, Krebs stood within the trajectory of Catholicism that eventually generated the Second Vatican Council's Pastoral Constitution on the Church in the Modern World, *Gaudium et spes* (1965).

This study of Krebs's theology and politics may have uncovered a clue for understanding the political ideas of Catholic theologians under Hitler. German theologians' views of the Third Reich may have been a function of their notions of the church's relationship to God's kingdom. The more a theologian identified the church with God's reign, the more he tended to stress that the church must safeguard its own existence at all costs, that it has the primary responsibility of protecting its members, its sacramental life and institutions. Hence, the theologians who saw the church as the embodiment of God's kingdom likely judged that the Vatican's signing of the concordat in July 1933 was a responsible act of self-preservation. By contrast, the more a theologian distinguished between the church and God's reign, the more he tended to emphasize that the church's first duty is to a transcendent reality of truth, justice, and love. For this reason, these theologians likely viewed the Vatican's signing of the concordat as a compromise of the church's mission. Opponents, including Krebs, held a vision of God's new creation in relation to which they condemned the Nazi leaders' motives and actions. This concluding thought stands as a hypothesis that needs to be tested in further studies of German Catholic theologians.

# 4

# Between Nationalism and Resistance

## The Path of Father Albert Coppenrath in the Third Reich

KEVIN P. SPICER

THE POSITION of the Catholic church during the Third Reich is recognizable through certain representative figures. These figures serve as religious indicators or barometers making it possible for historians to ask to what degree were the church's theological assumptions and pastoral methods suited to confront Nazism. Many historians today conclude that as a collective social unit the Catholic church failed for the most part to stem the tide of terror perpetrated by the Third Reich. This failure is borne out in Detlef Schmiechen-Ackermann's recent study on the diaspora Catholics in Hannover, in which he concluded that, according to his consulted sources, a "thesis of a consistent and enduring resistant Catholic milieu" in the face of National Socialism could not be supported. In this account, however, Schmiechen-Ackermann does note that there were many individual practicing Catholics who exhibited "significant forms of refusal and political opposition" (Schmiechen-Ackermann 1988, 462–76). Schmiechen-Ackermann's conclusion is significant because it offers a middle ground between those who offer an overly apologetic defense of the institutional church (Volk 1980) and those who condemn her for not doing enough (Hamerow 1997; Lewy 1964). The majority of individual Catholics, including the lower clergy, fell somewhere in the middle. That is, they regularly had to negotiate their allegiance to the state and fulfill their duties as Roman Catholics without a great deal of clear guidance from their local ordinary.

The choices that Father Albert Coppenrath (1883–1960) made during the Third Reich provide a case study that reveals how individual Catholic clerics maneuvered both to balance their own citizenship and perceived obligation to the Fatherland and to broker their church's position amidst a continued encroachment of the state into church life. As Nazism attempted to displace the moral dimension of Christianity, priests such as Coppenrath attempted to engage themselves in a kind of subversive discourse with the Nazi regime in order to insert the church's ethical position into every issue. And although priests such as Coppenrath were up against a regime that had a disproportionate amount of political and social power, they still sustained some sense of their own moral meaning against overwhelming odds.

1

Angered over the amount of espionage generated by the actions and statements of Fr. Albert Coppenrath, pastor of St. Matthias Church on the Winterfeldtplatz in Berlin, an official of the Gestapo shrieked: "This damned Westphalian *Dickkopf* on Winterfeldtplatz keeps us busy!" (Coppenrath 1948, 13). Coppenrath, however, exploited this offensive remark and used it in the title of his memoirs. In this manner, both local Nazi authorities and government officials saw Coppenrath as a thorn in the state's side, a stubborn scourge whose persistent use of "pulpit announcements" to inform his congregation of Nazi inconsistencies with Catholic principles and practice brought him into further conflict with the Nazi state (Roth 1937). From Coppenrath's perspective, these "announcements" merely attempted to impose an exercise of nuancing discrimination on Catholics as they did their best to wrestle with two mutually exclusive ideologies: National Socialism and Christianity. Coppenrath never saw himself, however, as one who worked against the Fatherland. Coppenrath always considered himself to be of strong "patriotic" character, which, he explained, meant "oriented to the Fatherland." This love of the Fatherland came from the influence of Coppenrath's father, Hermann, who was a treasurer to the Kaiser and a Prussian army officer. The senior Coppenrath had instilled in his son the importance of the qualities of order, duty, and loyalty to the nation. At the same time, Albert was also taught the traditions of his family's faith, Roman Catholicism.

Ordained in 1908 for the Diocese of Münster, Albert was soon able to show the fruit of his upbringing. During the First World War, for example, he sponsored mailings to German soldiers in the battlefield from his parish, St. Ludger, in Duisburg, and, as a result, received the Civil Service Cross for his efforts (Jauch 1997, 97). Later, in 1929, upon the suggestion of his local ordinary, Johannes Poggenburg, Bishop of Münster (1913–33), Coppenrath accepted the pastorship of St. Matthias in Berlin (Coppenrath 1948, 24). These dual loyalties, however, soon came into conflict as the Nazi state developed and brought Coppenrath, an outspoken man and church leader, into the forefront of church-state tensions in Nazi Germany.

At first, Coppenrath, like many of his fellow Germans, trusted Hitler and his government to solve the ills that plagued Germany. On May 29, 1933, for example, in a letter to a friend, Coppenrath wrote that he had no difficulty with the new situation in Germany, adding "even the grimmest party fanatic, if he is honest, cannot deny that National Socialism has already brought a good many things to our Volk and Fatherland" (Coppenrath 1948, 25). In early 1934, in a parish report, Coppenrath also reiterated his belief in the deeds of the new government when he wrote:

> If we allow our gazes now to go beyond the boundaries of our parish toward our Volk and Fatherland, there are also, thanks to God, many pleasing things to mention: the day of Potsdam with the statement that both Christian confessions are to constitute the foundation of the state; the revival of national consciousness that has in many circles of the Volk since 1919 been miserably extinct; the cleaning of our public life from the disgusting publication of trash and dirt in literature; the active and effective measures to defeat unemployment; the solemn proclamation of sanctity and esteem for marriage; the conclusion of the Concordat between the government and the Holy See. (Coppenrath 1948, 25)

Coppenrath then concluded his parish report with a benediction that so moved the congregation that the editors of the newspaper *Germania* requested a copy to use in the issue of April 20, 1934, for Hitler's birthday. In this prayer, Coppenrath adopted Nazi rhetoric using terms such as "blood and soil" and re-iterating the "Yes" of the people; but instead of directing this rhetoric toward Hitler, the Party, or government, Coppenrath adapted the language for religious aims as intercessions to God (Coppenrath 1948, 25–26).

Coppenrath did not always transfer his "Yes" to God to a "Yes" for the state. Rather, he preferred to stay out of politics altogether, a practice he had begun to exercise long before the Nazis came to power. He believed that for the ordained minister the practice of engaging in party politics from the pulpit could only harm his ministry and alienate his parishioners (Coppenrath 1948, 24–25). However, he made one exception to this rule, and that was in a pulpit announcement on December 9, 1934, before the plebiscite on the return of the Saar to Germany. On this occasion, like many patriotic Germans, he argued for the return of the Saar that had been "forcefully and against the will of the inhabitants separated from the German motherland" (Coppenrath 1948, 62). Before he supported this motion, however, he explained to his congregation at all the Sunday masses that this issue of the plebiscite did not deal in "affairs of the party." Instead, he stated, it was a "national question of great significance" (Coppenrath 1948, 62).

In this manner, Coppenrath's primary concern was his ministry as pastor of the huge St. Matthias community. Through the help of three chaplains, Coppenrath and his assistants served the more than 15,000 parishioners of the Schöneberg parish (Coppenrath 1938, 77). Pastoral ministry and coordinating the various parish associations filled his hours and, according to him, left him exhausted without any energy to pursue politics either outside or inside the church (Coppenrath 1948, 24). This did not mean, however, that he did not question the intentions of the state. On June 28, 1933, Coppenrath had already disagreed with a friend concerning the nature of National Socialism. Coppenrath wrote: "As you put it, the NSDAP program undoubtedly has many good aspects, if only the practice were not sometimes quite different" (Coppenrath 1948, 26).

The "practice" that he referred to was the apparent attack on church principles and organizations by both leading and local Nazi officials and groups. Although Coppenrath's early pulpit announcements revealed his disbelief that Nazis would act in such a way, especially after the promises made by Hitler in March 1933 in Potsdam, his attitude soon changed. As a result, he continually had to remind his listeners that in the face of the contrary, the führer had earlier declared that Christianity would form the "foundation of the moral life of our Volk" (Coppenrath 1948, 29). However, the barrage of actions by the Hitler Youth against his own parish and statements by Goebbels and Rosenberg soon made Coppenrath question the intentions of the state. While Coppenrath was normally an affable man who had a close relationship with the people he served, he could quickly "become gruff" if expected to do something outside "the moral or traditional rules" (Jauch 1997, 99). He also had a way of confronting a situation by getting his point across, but always in a way that ensured his own safety. In August 1937, for example, immediately following a complete exoneration on charges that he had caused unrest among the Volk, Coppenrath began to receive mailings from the German Freedom Party, whose literature

pointed out the hostility of National Socialism toward religion. Fearing entrap-
ment by the Gestapo, Coppenrath immediately sent the literature to the local
police office. At the same time, Coppenrath used the opportunity to get his
views across. In a cover letter, Coppenrath wrote: "Although I not only as a
Catholic priest, but also as an upright German, unfortunately cannot deny that
the factual statements of this letter are in most part justified, I refuse fundamentally the obvious hostility toward the state and consider it my duty to hand
over this letter." By this time, Coppenrath's manner of outspokenness was recognized by the Gestapo, which verbally responded to his letter: "Your cover letter was certainly a real Coppenrath!" (Coppenrath 1948, 148).

## 2

The event that most jolted Coppenrath's faith in the new government was the
SS murder of Erich Klausener (1885–1934), leader of Berlin's Catholic Action,
during the Röhm Purge. Immediately after the murder, State Secretary Koenig
of the Department of Transportation contacted Coppenrath, Klausener's
parish priest, and asked him to bring the horrible news to Klausener's wife. In
their conversation, Koenig also pointed out that the government had ruled
Klausener's death a suicide. Infuriated over the news, Coppenrath delivered it
to Frau Klausener and accompanied her to her husband's office. SS guards refused them entry because the government planned to cremate Klausener's
body (Coppenrath 1948, 42–46).

Even before Coppenrath had publicly commented on the murder of
Klausener, the Nazi propaganda machine had already created the story that the
former Catholic Action leader had joined the group around General Kurt von
Schleicher (1882–1934) and other "so-called traitors" of the Fatherland. Know-
ing Klausener's esteemed character quite well, Coppenrath refused to accept
such a dubious story and soon began a campaign through pulpit announcements to rectify Klausener's tarnished name. On July 1, 1934, Coppenrath announced the news of Klausener's death to his parish community and stressed
how deeply Klausener loved his *Volk* and his Fatherland (Coppenrath 1948,
44–45). This statement had serious ramifications because Goebbels had already labeled the "conspirators" as traitors to Germany. In addition, on July 3,
Hitler's cabinet legalized the murders through a law promulgated for the self-
defense of the state (Noakes and Pridham 1984, 182). Coppenrath ignored

concerns for his own well-being even though he realized he might be arrested by the Gestapo. He publicly stated, "No one who knew Klausener will believe this fraud!" (Coppenrath 1948, 43). The state, in Coppenrath's eyes, had obviously made a grave error in their judgment of the Catholic Action leader. On July 7, 1934, Coppenrath continued to follow his conviction of Klausener's innocence and presided over a requiem mass for the deceased, joined by his curates, by Nicolaus Bares (1871–1935), Bishop of Berlin (1933–35), by chancery officials, and by members of Klausener's family. Afterward they interred Klausener's ashes in the parish cemetery (Adolph 1972, 176). The Sunday following the internment, Coppenrath, ignoring the advice of the Berlin Chancery to act with "restraint" and "refrain from adding to the obituary" of the deceased provided by the diocese, described the burial of Klausener's ashes to the congregation at all masses. Then he drew their attention to a report from the Vatican newspaper, *L'Osservatore Romano,* that encouraged rejection of the state's claim of suicide. Finally, he told his congregation that the deceased's body had been burned without the permission of the family and against the teachings of the church (Coppenrath 1948, 47–49).

The week following his bold pulpit announcement, Coppenrath took his previously scheduled yearly vacation. Upon his return, a "gentleman," presumably a member of the Gestapo, visited him and advised him to "disappear" for his own safety (Coppenrath 1948, 49). Coppenrath ignored the advice and refused to hide, because, in his own mind, he had done nothing wrong. Coppenrath firmly held that he only spoke out in accordance with his duty as a priest and pastor and in so doing told the truth. The Gestapo, however, saw the situation through a different lens. In their eyes, Coppenrath's statements created unrest in the population and his announcements focused unwanted attention on the incidents of June 30. Therefore, on September 5, 1934, the Gestapo invited the pastor to appear at their local office for questioning concerning his recent public statements. Interestingly enough, during this interview the Gestapo agents were less concerned with direct comments concerning Klausener's death and more concerned with other more editorial comments made by Coppenrath. Evidently, a Catholic Gestapo informant had reported that in reference to the death of Klausener, Coppenrath had chosen a particular passage from an "epistle," extraneous to the assigned biblical texts for the day, to warn his congregation to guard themselves "against false prophets who come to you in sheep's clothing, but inwardly are ravenous wolves. You will know them by their fruits." Coppenrath reveled in the agents' confusion and explained that he did not "choose" this text, but that it was the text from the Gospel of Matthew 7:15–16 that was read every seventh Sunday after Pentecost (Coppenrath 1948, 59). Consequently, the Gestapo agents released Coppenrath, who, subsequently, on September 9 in a pulpit announcement described to his congregation at all the Sunday masses the events of the interrogation.

Coppenrath, however, did not relent in his desire to see Klausener's name rectified. Instead, one week later, on September 16, 1934, at an opening of a new meeting and recreation site for the youth of St. Matthias near Lichtenrade, Coppenrath consecrated the site "Erich-Klausener-Place." Then Coppenrath declared to the thousands present there that day: "[W]e name this site not for an enemy of the state, but for a man who loved his Volk and Fatherland with a burning love . . . We name this site not for a man who committed suicide, but for a man who lived as a faithful Catholic and died as a true Catholic. We name this site after a man whose slogan continually and always was: 'Everything for Germany—Germany for Christ!' " (Coppenrath 1948, 60).

In December 1934, Coppenrath's campaign for Klausener intensified when he suggested to Bishop Bares that he take up a collection to construct a memorial in honor of Dr. Klausener. The memorial would take the form of the first station of the cross at St. Matthias cemetery. Bishop Bares sympathized with Coppenrath and granted this request because he had already written Hitler in July and November 1934 to declare Klausener's innocence and his own disbelief of the director's suicide (Coppenrath 1948, 52–53). Bares also asked Coppenrath to prepare a statement to be read on February 10, 1935, in all diocesan parishes before the collection. Although the collection announcement circumvented the question of suicide, it did call attention to Klausener's service to the church and his faith in God (Lagebericht 1935). In light of the church's stringent teaching on suicide that normally precluded any chance of a soul's attaining salvation in the next life, not to mention the sanctioning of a memorial for a person who had committed suicide in this life, the collection for a memorial alone, endorsed by the bishop, made it clear to all the faithful that the Berlin diocese refused to accept the official government report on Klausener's death (Eichmann 1934, 21, 49, 428). The collection was taken up at the doors of the church and netted 4,836 Reichsmarks (RM), of which 622 RM came from Coppenrath's parish (Coppenrath 1948, 63).

On February 16, 1935, Lammers, on behalf of Hitler, wrote Bares and asked him to reconsider building the memorial in order to avoid provoking "immense agitation among the public" (Lammers 1935). For the moment, Bares heeded Lammers' "polite" warning; however, he refused to allow the issue to die. Instead, Bares argued that no further action could be taken until a "complete explanation of the situation" could be obtained (Coppenrath 1948, 64). Bares planned to continue seeking the truth into Klausener's death; yet Bares' own untimely death on March 1, 1935, prevented further investigation.

On February 27, 1935, however, the Gestapo did take further action in the Klausener affair and confiscated the monies collected for the memorial along with an additional 5,000 RM from the designated diocesan bank account. In addition, they interrogated Coppenrath three times, on April 12, 1935, February 3, 1936, and April 7, 1936, concerning the collection for the Klausener memorial. Each time Coppenrath fully admitted that he had written the announcement for the collection and had also informed his congregation on numerous occasions that the Gestapo had confiscated the money. He also made the Gestapo aware that they had confiscated 5,000 RM of the diocese's money that had nothing to do with the collection. Upon investigation, the Gestapo returned the surplus. Coppenrath remained resolute in his determination to honor Klausener's name, however. When allegedly asked whether he would pursue the erection of the memorial, he answered: "Obviously, at least as far as it depends on me! I do not possess 5,000 RM; however, since the confiscation of the collection, I have played the lottery and on the day I win 5,000 RM, I will give that for the building of the memorial" (Coppenrath 1948, 72). The Gestapo accepted his challenge and requested a proceeding against both Coppenrath and Vicar General Paul Steinmann (1871–1937) before the *Sondergericht* (Special Court). The court refused to hear the case, citing a lack of evidence to support infringement of the Law Against Malicious Intent of December 20, 1934, and sent the case back to the District Court of Berlin (Coppenrath 1937). But on September 30, 1937, the State attorney general proceeded with a case against both men and charged Coppenrath with "encouraging the collection" and "writing the relevant appeal" and Steinmann with "sending the appeal to the parish offices" (Coppenrath 1948, 73). Consequently, on July 4, 1938, the court announced its decision and found Coppenrath guilty of instigating the collection on political grounds. However, the court suspended the case against Coppenrath because the act was committed before April 30, 1938, and, therefore, the perpetrators had fallen under the

Amnesty Law, which nullified penalties of six months or less in honor of the *Anschluß* with Austria (Coppenrath 1948, 73–74).

3

Coppenrath's persistence with the Klausener affair and his other pulpit announcements on a variety of topics brought him under the close scrutiny of the Gestapo. This scrutiny in turn led to numerous invitations to appear before local Gestapo authorities for questioning. On one particular Wednesday, October 30, 1935, during an interrogation session, Gestapo officials asked Coppenrath why he did not fly the swastika flag from the church on the day of the funeral of Gauleiter Wilhelm Loeper (1883–1935). Coppenrath admitted that he had forgotten to fly the flag on that particular day, but said he had regularly flown it from the rectory and the parish youth house (Germania 1935). Later in November, in a meeting that he requested with an agent of the local Gestapo, he would learn that he was one of thirteen Berlin pastors who did not fly the flag; however, because of his pulpit announcements and statements regarding the Klausener affair, the Gestapo had chosen to intimidate him (Coppenrath 1948, 103–4). On November 1, 1935, for example, the Gestapo agents followed the interrogation with a one-hour-long house search and then invited Coppenrath to accompany them to their headquarters on Alexanderplatz. There Coppenrath spent the evening in a jail cell and the next morning had to appear before a summary court. At court Coppenrath held his composure in face of the charge against him and used the courtroom to lodge complaints against the Hitler Youth who had vandalized church property and demonstrated near the church during Sunday Eucharist. He also argued that he had not purchased an additional swastika flag large enough for the church because of the expense (*Germania* 1935). At this point, however, Coppenrath realized that he was probably being arrested not only because of an offense against the flag ordinance, but also because of his pulpit announcements. Therefore, in his defense, he voluntarily added that his pulpit announcements were being made in response to the "scandalous attacks on Christianity and the Catholic church." In addition, he noted that he had no "political intentions," but sought only to "safeguard legitimate interests and fulfill [his] pastoral duty" (Coppenrath 1948, 101). This time the court sided with Coppenrath, who received only a nominal 50 RM fine for his offense against the flag order. The court also did not declare him hostile to the state, a fact that overjoyed the pastor.

**4**

Possibly because of his love for country or because of respecting his own contemporaries, Coppenrath continued to trust the authority and the structure of Nazi power in his land. Unlike many of his confreres, he survived many interrogations and two arrests unscathed. This survival did not mean that Coppenrath did not fear reprisal by the Gestapo. In March 1938, Coppenrath confided to several priest friends that the idea that he might have to go to prison for a prolonged period of time terrified him. His 1935 experience in a Gestapo holding cell on Alexanderplatz awakened him to the horrors the state could inflict upon its "enemies." In the same 1938 conversation, Coppenrath also revealed that he questioned the German bishops' response to the state following the death of Klausener. For him and many others, this was a moment of lost opportunity (Adolph 1987, 235–36). However, Coppenrath only shared these opinions with his closest of friends. In public, Coppenrath limited his criticism to pulpit announcements. Nevertheless, the Gestapo viewed these announcements as a means to disturb the peace within the state and so Coppenrath's safety was constantly in danger. Possibly to justify delivering future announcements, he used the announcements to describe his encounters with the Gestapo to his congregation. Yet he did not push his parishioners to resistance and normally reported that the Gestapo had treated him in a just manner or had not harmed him in any way (Coppenrath 1948, 102). In one case, after several members of his parish blocked an attempt by an unidentified Gestapo agent to confiscate an edition of the weekly church newspaper, Coppenrath even warned his congregation never to "reproach a police officer or even to take steps against him" because he carried this out on "instruction of a higher authority" (Coppenrath 1948, 88). After the war, Coppenrath argued that he had made such statements to protect those around him. If resistance to the encroachment of the state in the life of the church had to be made, Coppenrath wanted to take the sole responsibility. In another sense he did not wish to be responsible for another person's arrest and imprisonment (Coppenrath 1948, 40, 79–80).

As Coppenrath himself admitted, he was and remained throughout his life a committed nationalist (Coppenrath 1948, 5). He, too, refused to accept anything that he did as a pastor as "politically motivated." Instead, Coppenrath always argued that he limited himself to the pastoral sphere, questioning those things and events that brought offense to Roman Catholicism. In the eyes of senior Nazi officials, however, Coppenrath was a troublemaker and clearly unreliable. Others also viewed Coppenrath's comments as "politically motivated." As early as April 1934, a Berlin cabaret performer asked his audience: "What is new in politics?" He continued, "Unfortunately, I do not know what is going on since I was not in St. Matthias church last Sunday!" The audience understood and appreciated the joking remark (Coppenrath 1948, 28). However, this was not a laughing matter for Coppenrath.

Coppenrath was a strong personality who could stand on his own in the face of injustice. Coppenrath was not always alone, however; he received the constant support of his parishioners. Upon return from his first overnight in jail owing to the court's decision concerning his offense to the national flag, for example, his parishioners greeted him with well-wishes in person, in written letters, and through telephone calls. In addition, flowers and financial gifts to help pay the 50 RM fine followed in the days thereafter (Coppenrath 1948, 102).

Coppenrath's luck ended, however, as the war began. At first, he refrained from any pulpit announcements or comments on the "religious situation" because of the war. However, because of recent attacks on the church by Rosenberg's pen, Coppenrath felt compelled to speak out against these attacks. In his homily on October 18, 1940, Coppenrath discussed the sins of the church in relation to the claims of some scholars. While Coppenrath admitted that there were definite "weaknesscs and shortcomings" evidenced within the two-thousand-year history of the church, he noted that in relation to "numerous families and groups, governments and rulers . . . [who] have shown such a wealth of scandals, such a full barrel of sins, of corruptibility and lies and deception and robberies and murder and immorality, the scandals and sins in the 2000 year history of the church, no matter how sad and disgraceful, almost disappear in comparison" (Coppenrath 1948, 168). On October 20, 1940, Coppenrath mentioned who these detractors were, namely Rosenberg and Corvin, whose *Mythus* and *Pfaffenspiegel*, respectively, continued to be used against the church. He then quoted Johann Gottfried Herder, who had said that "without the Catholic church Europe would have become a desert and the loot of the Mongols." "We should add," Coppenrath stated, "without the Catholic church, Europe would in the future be a desert and a loot for the—barbarians" (Coppenrath 1948, 169). On November 3, 1940, he then followed his two homilies with a pulpit announcement that criticized the intelligence of those who denounced him to the Gestapo for their lack of understanding of his comments

(Coppenrath 1948, 170–71). On November 9, 1940, in relation to his last three comments, especially his disparaging remarks about Rosenberg, Coppenrath was visited by the Gestapo. The two Gestapo officers invited the pastor to accompany them to their headquarters on Alexanderplatz. At this point, he realized something was wrong because, first, he did not receive the written summons to appear for questioning that had always been the normal protocol prior to this event and, second, on November 7, an official of the Gestapo had secretly informed him that someone would soon be coming for him (Coppenrath 1948, 171–73). The Gestapo detained Coppenrath in the holding cells of the headquarters until his unexpected release on December 5, 1940. Before his release, however, the police official on duty warned Coppenrath not to bring politics to the pulpit. Coppenrath argued that he had never done that. Later, as he left his cell, he gave the Hitler salute to the master of the watch almost in mockery, because he was not allowed to use the salute as a prisoner (Coppenrath 1948, 192–93). Upon his return to St. Matthias, on Sunday, December 8, Coppenrath thanked his parishioners who had prayed for him during his absence. After a brief vacation in Münster, Coppenrath returned to find shortly thereafter an official letter prohibiting him from residing in or visiting any part of the diocese of Berlin (Coppenrath 1948, 200). Coppenrath accepted this letter on the threat of further arrest and returned to his native Münster. After this move, he did not engage in any more "subversive" actions against the state.

5

Coppenrath was a proud nationalistic German who loved his country. Like thousands of other German Catholics, he wanted to be included in the revival of the German Reich. Because Coppenrath did not wish to be labeled an "enemy of the Reich"—a title that Bismarck gave Catholics during the *Kulturkampf*—he and thousands like him found themselves reaffirming their traditional support of any government, including that of the Nazis, that staunchly supported family life and attacked liberalism and Communism. The perceived success of Hitler's government in combating unemployment and attacking lax morality in German society also encouraged Coppenrath and others to welcome the Nazi government. As a result, Hitler's March 1933 promises made to the churches and the July 1933 concordat received, even if only quietly, Coppenrath's stamp of approval.

The murder of Erich Klausener, its subsequent cover-up, and the false accusations made against him that followed his murder, however, awakened Coppenrath to the harsh realities of National Socialism. In addition, the ever-increasing encroachment of the state into organizations (youth groups, Caritas) that the church previously supervised provoked the outspoken Coppenrath to express his objections. Coppenrath was particularly careful, however, to protest against those events that only directly affected his church and ministry. For this reason, he refused to call himself an opponent of the government and always denied engaging in political resistance. The Gestapo, of course, viewed Coppenrath from a different angle. According to police announcements, he was a disturber of the peace who aroused resentment against the Nazi regime. Consequently, they labeled Coppenrath politically untrustworthy and ordered him to be watched continuously. They also interrogated him regularly.

On this latter point, Coppenrath may currently be judged as one who resisted the regime. And although, as he continually stressed even after the war, his pulpit protests were religiously motivated to safeguard pastoral care and to create a religious counter-space to protect the church's realm of influence, state officials perceived Coppenrath as one who intentionally delved into political matters and who resisted the measures of the state (Kershaw 1993, 161; Schmädeke and Steinbach 1985, 1122). In the opinion of state officials, Coppenrath was a political opponent of the regime who refused to limit his comments to pastoral affairs.

Nevertheless, Coppenrath's love for his people, his commitment to German nationalism, and his attempts to fulfill his pastoral duties would today probably seem too limited and almost like an evasion of responsibility from within the narrow walls of the German Catholicism of his time. In this context, the central question is whether some priests like Coppenrath at all times could work within an anti-Christian state like Nazi Germany without compromising their beliefs. As suggested earlier, Coppenrath attempted to channel the church's teaching while at the same time to press his parishioners to look anew at the policies of their state. Certainly in delivering his pulpit announcements before the war, Coppenrath stubbornly stood out in aspiring to expose any wrongdoing against the institutional church and German people. This form of bearing witness was eventually diminished by the outbreak of World War II. His personal faith during the war then became an oddity against the ultimate inadequacy of any institution in Germany to confront head-on the evils of Nazism. And though the power of his faith was unmistakable, he does not always convince people today of the potency of that faith to oppose an institution as evil as Nazism.

Coppenrath's witness, however, demands our respect. He offered a limited though worthy counter-possibility to his fellow churchmen at the time. His disappointment with the bishop's limited response to the government following the death of Klausener, for example, was convincing because it also seemed a reminder to himself not to blindly trust Nazism. In this way, Coppenrath's experiences can allow us to see what it was like to be a priest, struggling with Nazism from within the limited confines of his own religious tradition. His witnessing, however, will always be overshadowed by his church's inability to peer out of her own institutional needs into an evil present and denounce it unequivocally.

# 5

# National Socialism as a Force for German Protestant Renewal?

Pastors and Parishioners Respond
to Adolf Hitler's "National Renewal"

KYLE T. JANTZEN

## 1

IN RECENT YEARS, the focus of German Church Struggle history has shifted somewhat from the theological strife to the social and political context in which the German churches functioned. Even so, historians have remained constant in their basic assessment of the German Protestant response to the transition from the Weimar Republic to the National Socialist Third Reich (Scholder 1988, 1:3–216; Scholder 1989, 35–60; Wright 1974; Wright 1977, 398–418; Dahm 1968, 29–49; Jacobs 1983, 108–35; Klan 1987, 432–43; King 1982, 52–71; Borg 1966, 186–206; Borg 1984). Briefly put, German Protestantism suffered a profound shock from the defeat in World War I, not least on account of the spiritual significance attributed to the conflict by pastors and theologians. Moreover, the collapse of the Kaiser's Reich abruptly shattered the sacred "union of throne and altar" that had defined the relationship of Protestants to their princely rulers since the Reformation. With the exception of minority groups like the Religious Socialists and the *Christliche Welt* liberals, German Protestants did not adjust well to the new political realities of the Weimar Republic.

Culturally and sociologically, active Protestants were largely drawn to the German National People's Party (DNVP), the leading conservative party in Weimar politics. Attracted by its monarchist and patriotic platform, up to 80 percent of Protestant pastors allied themselves with the DNVP, giving rise to the contemporary witticism "The church is politically neutral, but it votes German National" (Dahm 1965, 145 and 104; Klan 1987, 440). Historian Martin Greschat recently analyzed this political orientation and advanced the argument that German Protestant pastors typically held a "national-conservative basic attitude." Greschat contends that most pastors were captivated by the importance of the German *Volk* and hostile toward the Western powers. They regarded the domestic political division of the Weimar Republic as either a political syndrome or the destructive work of foreign powers, and yearned for a warmhearted national unity where commitment, order, and authority would constitute the core values (Greschat 1993, 67–103, especially 83). In the context of the German Church Struggle, I define *religious nationalism* as an ideological orientation in which (1) Protestant Christianity was understood as a faith that had been revealed uniquely in and that was to be lived primarily within the German national community, and in which (2) German nationalism was understood as incomplete without a Protestant Christian ethical foundation and symbolic presence (Smith 1995, 50–60, 141–50, 201–10; Scholder 1988, 1:74–87; Zabel 1976, 1–20).

In the realm of theology, the 1920s have now become known as the formative years for Karl Barth's dialectic theology, but far more dominant in Germany at the time was the trend toward nationalistic political theology. Steeped in natural theology, political theologians like Emmanuel Hirsch, Werner Elert, Paul Althaus, Wilhelm Stapel, and Gerhard Kittel exalted race—in this case, the German *Volk*—as the preeminent divinely created order (Ericksen 1985, 42–62, 84–109, 130–66; Tiefel 1972, 326–36). They accentuated the dichotomy between Luther's two kingdoms, between the realms of the law and the gospel, so that "state and church simply had nothing more to say to each other: whatever the state had to do for the sake of God's will it knew better than the church" and the church could only confirm the will of the state (Scholder 1988, 1:421). Enmeshed in this theology, Wilhelm Stapel argued in 1933: "The totalitarian state controls all law, all morality. The church has all that concerns the kingdom of heaven. . . . The morality which the church teaches must be that which grows in the hearts of the *Volk* to which the church brings the gospel, for morality belongs to the 'nomos' of the *Volk*" (that is, the "law of life that determines its internal and external form, its cultus, its ethics, its constitution and its law in accordance with its nature") (Stapel 1933, 65–70, in Scholder 1988, 1:422, 421).

With a social, political, and theological background so conservatively ori-

ented toward nation and authority, it is no wonder that many German Protestants were predisposed to welcome Hitler's rise to power in 1933—even if they
had misgivings about the National Socialist Party's obsession with race, its violent tendencies, or its unclear position on the independence of the land
churches (Wright 1977, 393–418; Scholder 1988, 1:99–119; Conway 1968,
6–15, 328–38; Barnett 1992, 9–29; Nowak 1987, 352–64; Baranowski 1987,
53–78; Pierard 1978, 8–29). One of the chief expressions of this national-
conservative attitude was the rapid growth of the pro-National Socialist Faith
Movement of the German Christians, which sought to unite Protestant Christianity with National Socialist ideology and values (Bergen 1996; Lächele
1994).

    While these issues have been repeatedly explored in the history of the national church scene, less understood is the extent to which the adulation of
Hitler's "national renewal" voiced by Protestant theologians and land church
leaders was echoed locally by Protestant parish clergy and laypeople. While a
complete explanation of clerical nationalism and the reception of National Socialism in German Protestant parishes would necessitate a compilation of findings from throughout Germany, some provisional observations can be gleaned
from research in three regions, drawing on source material from the church
district of Nauen, located immediately northwest of Berlin.

2

Nauen's twenty-eight parish churches and their filial congregations offer a
meaningful view into local religious life for three reasons. First, the district was
situated in the Berlin-Brandenburg church province of the Old Prussian Union
Church, the largest and most conflict-ridden Protestant church in the Third
Reich. Second, it was near enough to Berlin that individual pastors (and parishioners) were well informed about Hitler, National Socialist rule, and the critical
developments in the church struggle. Third, it was primarily rural and agricultural; its village churches were central institutions and its pastors were principal figures in local life.

    The history of the church struggle in the parishes may well demonstrate
more vividly than national church histories both the profound influence of the
National Socialist-sponsored national renewal over German Protestants during the early years of the Third Reich and the limited power of the total claims
of the National Socialist state within the Protestant community. In 1933 and

1934, the religious nationalism spawned by Hitler's movement appeared to over half of the parishes in the Nauen district not as a looming ideological or church-political threat (nor even as a benign political shift to the right), but as a welcome catalyst for Protestant revival. However, as the church policy of the Third Reich and the hostility of the National Socialist German Workers' Party (NSDAP) toward the Protestant churches grew clearer during 1935, parish clergy and laypeople began to express antipathy for the kind of National Socialist-Protestant synthesis advocated by members of the German Christian Movement. In Nauen, the staunchest opposition to the "nazification" of the churches appeared in the organization of campaigns to block the appointment of German Christian clergymen to vacant pastorates.

The infrequence of legal or political consequences for these campaigns suggests that—whether or not direct opposition to the National Socialist regime was possible—Protestants in the Nauen district were relatively free to determine the course of their own religious lives during the National Socialist era. Capable of blocking out most interference from German Christian land church authorities, the local church opposition frequently employed Scripture and Reformation Confessions against German Christian higher church authorities. At times, these ethical and theological critiques spilled over into political criticism of National Socialist ideology and national leaders, which National Socialist functionaries considered to be resistance against the total claims of the party-state. From the parish perspective, however, Protestant religious opposition to National Socialist church policy and the German Christian Movement's activities was far from decisive and frequently obscured by Protestant political ambivalence toward (or worse yet, support for) the National Socialist movement and Hitler government. Early histories of the German Church Struggle conflated opposition to National Socialist religious policy and the campaigns of the pro-NSDAP German Christian Movement with resistance to Adolf Hitler and his government. In 1959, Friedrich Baumgärtel seriously undermined that interpretation with an analysis of church leaders' positive reception of National Socialism. More recently, religious historians have described the behavior of the churches in more nuanced terms, such as "partial co-operation," "functional resistance," "non-conformity," and "dissent" (Norden 1985, 227–39; Nowak 1987, 352–64).

In the Nauen church district, Protestant Christians were deeply attracted by the National Socialist "national renewal" first and foremost because they believed that along with the political transformation of 1933, there would be an associated moral renewal of the German *Volk*. This belief is clearly seen in the various speeches delivered at that year's annual district church assembly. Nauen Superintendent Graßhoff announced the church's task as "the inner restoration of the German soul and of our beloved Protestant church." In language rich with biblical allusion, he declared, "God has spoken to our German *Volk* through a great transformation. An epoch in German history has come to an end, a new period has begun" ("Kreiskirchentag in Nauen" 1933). Graßhoff hailed the end of party grumbling, class conflict, moral laxity, and godlessness in Germany, and anticipated a new era of sobriety, discipline, strong leadership, and the will of the nation to follow. Noting the astonishing speed of this transition, Graßhoff wondered, "What a miracle has come over us" ("Kreiskirchentag in Nauen" 1933).

The Nauen superintendent believed that the transformation he envisioned would be the beginning of a revolutionary spiritual resurrection of the German racial community. Thus enlivened, Germans would possess a profound new national character: dependable, loyal, and infused with a strong sense of the German racial community. Ultimately, this metamorphosis would accomplish the salvation of Germany from the specter of degeneration depicted by Oswald Spengler in *The Decline of the West*. At the climax of his speech, Graßhoff issued a challenge to the lay and clerical leaders in his church district: "The decision about whether or not the new structure of our state will be blessed by God lies in our hands. God has given our *Volk* a great opportunity. If we Christians fail now, then the final end of the entire external political structure is in vain. Then the West will indeed finally crumble, just as the Roman Empire crumbled" ("Kreiskirchentag in Nauen" 1933). With that ominous warning, Graßhoff completed his speech—a powerful, mutually reinforcing amalgam of National Socialism, spiritual renewal, and volkish rebirth.

Other meetings during the 1933 district church assembly echoed the tone set by Superintendent Graßhoff's speech. The women's assembly gathered under the theme "Ready for Service," an attitude Pastor Cramer of the Kremmen parish extolled during "this great, fateful time for our *Volk*." In glowing terms, Nauen women were told of Hitler's deep piety and the manner in which "the young chancellor of the *Volk* openly professed his faith in God and promoted the work of the Christian churches" ("Kreiskirchentag in Nauen" 1933). Even more impressive was the men's assembly, where the speaker was none other than General Superintendent Otto Dibelius, defender of the National Socialist "national renewal" and exponent of the church as an independent force for moral renewal within German society. Since the National Socialist seizure of power, Dibelius had justified German political developments in a radio address to America, preached the inaugural sermon for the new Reichstag on March 21 in Potsdam, and participated in the laudatory Easter Proclamation of the Old Prussian Union Church. Based on that, Superintendent Graßhoff of Nauen presented him as an important churchman who stood firmly behind the new political awakening of Germany and advocated a strong, independent Protestant church(Graßhoff 1933a; Scholder 1988, 1:232).

## 3

There is no disputing the fact that the revolutionary atmosphere of 1933 animated Nauen parishes. Reports from pastors about conditions in their parishes paint a vivid picture of the mood of ecclesiastical life in the early phase of the National Socialist regime. Along with the belief in the power of the national renewal promoted by the National Socialist government to produce moral renewal, these pastors praised National Socialism for its aggressive anti-Communism.

In Bötzow, Pastor Georg Gartenschläger explained: "Parish life stands strongly under the mark of the battle against Bolshevism. An assault on the pastor would be countered in the red press with an article: 'With Bible and Revolver against Workers.' " Though perhaps exaggerated, Gartenschläger's remarks were not isolated, given that his parish Bible studies revolved around the odd triad of "marriage, family, and the battle against Bolshevism" (Gartenschläger 1933). Gartenschläger and his parishioners also articulated their patriotic and anti-Bolshevik convictions by erecting a "practical memorial" to their fallen veterans, a twenty-eight-candle chandelier. Because the burning candles commemorated the deaths of local soldiers, the chandelier reinforced the priority of the Fatherland and created "an especially warm bond between family and church" (Gartenschläger 1933).

Pastor Ziegel of Bredow was another cleric on the watch for leftist attacks against Christianity. However, by May 1933 he could only report: "Recently here, as almost everywhere, communism and social democracy have grown completely silent." Still cautious, Ziegel voiced the concern of Bredow Protestants: "We know well that the threatening danger to our church is not yet definitively eliminated, and we will therefore remain alert, though above all in the effort to win back the parishioners gone astray and distanced from the church" (Ziegel 1933).

Clergy generally reported sharp increases in the level of interest among their parishioners in spring 1933. In Fehrbellin, an astounding 540 (or more than 28 percent) of Pastor Günther Harder's parishioners attended an evening service on April 30. That constituted a presence unequalled in his "unfortunately unchurchish parish" since the outbreak of war in 1914 (Harder 1933). In nearby Kremmen, Pastor Cramer noticed the attention of his parishioners grow during the church elections of autumn 1932. Two German Christian parish councilors elected at that time had transformed his parish council through their "lively interest" in the inner affairs of the church (Cramer 1933).

No pastor in the Nauen district described that political effect during the first months of National Socialist rule as vividly as Pastor Lux of Groß Behnitz. Attendance at his church had surged, and Lux attributed it to National Socialism:

> The political movements of the last year and first months of this year have had a strong effect throughout our parishes. With them, everything has advanced in the greatest peace and order. On National Remembrance Day, for the first time, the swastika flag of the SA stood beside the flag of the military association in the church, and the members of the SA in Groß Behnitz, Klein Behnitz and from the neighboring towns took part in the Remembrance service *en masse*, in their brown uniforms. (Lux 1933)

Ten days later, on March 21, there was an illuminated parade through the town, followed by a giant bonfire and speeches by local political leaders, who echoed the speech of the Reich president at the Potsdam Garrison Church earlier in the day.

Similarly, on National Labor Day (May 1) Lux held special services in both Groß and Klein Behnitz. Attendance at those services was higher than even Lux had experienced during his fifteen years there. As he reported, "Every strata and every house was represented" (Lux 1933). Lux's sermons that day invoked the image of awakening north and south winds, a natural reference to the political awakening of Germany by Hitler and his movement. The balance of the May Day celebrations in Groß and Klein Behnitz reinforced the centrality of the National Socialist political revolution. After Lux's morning service in Groß Behnitz, his congregation listened to a speech by the Reich president. Later, he proceeded to Klein Behnitz for an afternoon service. In both parishes, "Hitler linden" trees were planted, and the towns were illuminated yet again (Lux 1933).

In his report about these momentous events, Lux reiterated his belief in the potential of the new political climate present in the early days of National Socialism to foster a revival in the fortunes of German Protestantism. "God grant," he wrote, "that the strong national movement may also be accompanied by an upturn of church life" (Lux 1933). Actually, that potential was already being realized in the enthusiastic inquiries of Groß and Klein Behnitz citizens about the Word of God, the request of the Groß Behnitz volunteer fire department to attend church en masse, and the appeal of the local military association for Lux to conduct a special camp service for a jubilee they were celebrating.

Evidence from parish statistics sustains the testimony of local pastors that Protestant renewal in their parishes was linked to the broader phenomenon of the National Socialist "national renewal." Participation in church, defined here as the ratio of communicants to baptized parishioners, rose almost 5 percent in the Nauen district from 1932 to 1933 ("Statistische Übersichten" undated). However, the situation varied greatly from parish to parish. Participation shot up 83 percent in Beetz, 57 percent in Bredow, 54 percent in Paaren, and 41 percent in Bötzow. Five other parishes saw their participation levels rise between 17 and 25 percent, and five more rose between 1 and 10 percent. In the ten parishes in which participation declined, five pastors were within two years of the end of their ministry careers and appear to have been less energetic, while another two young pastors were publicly opposed to the mixture of nationalist politics and Protestant Christianity. Thus, the general surge in lay participation across the Nauen district appears to reflect the political influence of National Socialism.

The initial wave of interest in Protestant Christianity at the beginning of the National Socialist era was not sustained throughout the prewar years. That conclusion is supported by the changing rates of official withdrawal from the Old Prussian Union Land Church in the Nauen district. Simply put, fewer Protestants left their church between 1933 and 1935 than in any other time between 1932 and 1939. However, after the initial decline, the rate of withdrawal increased markedly from 1935 to 1939.

In sum, the pastoral reports of a surge of religious nationalism (Grasshoff 1933b) and of the participation of community and National Socialist organizations in church services in early 1933, coupled with the dramatic emergence of the German Christian Movement in the district synodal election of 1933 (and membership of local pastors in the Movement), suggest that a good deal of the temporary revitalization of public religious observance among Protestants in the Nauen district was a response to the national renewal promoted by the new National Socialist government. Statistics on baptisms, church weddings, membership growth, and participation in communion services reflect this same trend. They all peaked in the first years of the Third Reich, then declined in the years immediately before the Second World War.

The fact that many pastors experienced a significant, tangible revitalization of church life in their parishes is vital for understanding the clerical response to Adolf Hitler and his National Socialist government during its early years. In the Nauen church district, many pastors promoted the well-being of the German racial community as a spiritual value and strongly advocated the creation of a unitary Protestant Reich church. National Socialists espoused traditional values in family, religious, and national life, which pastors found conducive for their ministries. That clergy missed or ignored the brutal, illegal, and arbitrary nature of National Socialism is not quite as difficult to understand in light of its positive impact on parish life.

For some pastors, the revitalizing aspect of the national renewal that accompanied the National Socialist political takeover created confusion between their temporal and divine loyalties. Already in 1933, one pastor (probably Superintendent Graßhoff himself) expressed the fear that if he preached the concept *"Volk* is of God," then his parishioners would fail to see the need for their own conversion to the message of Christ. He admitted that he was leery of preaching the unpopular formula *"Volk* is of God, but *Volk* is fallen," since that challenged the prevailing National Socialist belief in the superiority of the German racial community. His solution—after much soul searching—was a compromise. He decided to preach that anyone who took up the National Socialist struggle with his own strength, boasting about his own exploits, would be lost before God. That said, anyone who came to the crucified Christ, abandoned his sinful nature, and entered the National Socialist struggle as a faithful Christian would be considered to be participating in a holy act (Unidentified Nauener 1933). This rather crude formulation is typical of German Protestant attempts to inject spiritual vitality into the National Socialist movement, and reveals the slippery slope of adapting to the popularity of National Socialism and thereby departing from Christian truth.

This tension between the claims of the *Volk* and the claims of the Christian faith reappears often, as in a 1936 confirmation program. One session was entitled "Religion from the Blood? Religion as Revelation," a question and answer that implied a critique of the *völkish* notion of a blood-bound faith community. In contrast to that, a second session revolved around the "Christianization of the Germans" and the overarching theme reflected the preoccupation of local leaders with the fusion of Christianity and national identity: "All for Germany, Germany for Christ" (Nauen District Church Office 1936a).

As late as 1939, confusion reigned in the mind of Pastor Konrad Isleib of Hakenberg, near Nauen. In a letter to his friend, Interim Superintendent Ulrich Bettac, Isleib argued the case for creating a unitary Reich church, asserting that it was both vital for the well-being of the *Volk* and the expectation of the führer. A member of the moderate wing of the German Christians, Isleib betrayed his movement's utter inability to bridge the gap between the ultimate claims of both Christianity and National Socialism when he wrote, "The Fatherland stands above everything, just as it always has been for us, even when . . . naturally, our conscience—bound to God and his Word—speaks the final word" (Isleib 1939). The Fatherland stands above all, but the conscience speaks the final word. If this was an unusually confused attempt to decide whether national or Christian identity was preeminent, others refused to worry about such inconsistencies. Pastor Gartenschläger of Bötzow summed it up when he proclaimed the "great fighting goal" of "unity between *Volk* and church" (Gartenschläger 1933).

## 4

As state-church policy grew more authoritarian and National Socialist Party animosity toward the churches increased, the trials of church politics and administrative deadlock provoked several fundamental criticisms of the National Socialist state among clergy in Nauen. By 1938, Interim Superintendent Bettac was despondent about the church-political divisions in the Nauen district, and linked them to the broader political atmosphere of National Socialist Germany. Frustrated with radical German Christians, he wrote, "I cannot say it any other way—consciously or unconsciously, [the German Christians], on behalf of the state, are destroying the bothersome church" (Bettac 1938).

The following year, Bettac was openly skeptical about the possibility of any unity between church and state in the Third Reich. Disagreeing with the prognosis of his overheated colleague, Pastor Isleib of Hakenberg, Bettac argued that the National Socialist state "declares that it is not and does not want to be Christian." How could a union of state and church possibly be achieved, he continued, as long as the state kept advancing its totalitarian claims over everything, including the church? For Bettac, the danger of state interference in and control over the churches constituted a greater threat than the ongoing conflict over matters of faith within the churches (Bettac 1939a).

In the Nauen district, the most energetic individual resistance against the union of national and Protestant ideology came from Pastor Herbert Posth of the Berge parish. A staunch member of the Confessing Church, Posth rejected the prevailing nationalist theology. In an article he wrote for a 1935 edition of the Nauen district newsletter, Posth stated, "One is *born* into the *Volk,* one belongs to it through blood and race, one is *called* into the church by the Holy Spirit in the Word of God . . . independent of blood and race" (Posth 1935). Three years later, in the course of a dispute with the Brandenburg church authorities, Posth reiterated his view: "The opinion [that] the church should 'promote the life of faith of the members of the *Volk*' contradicts the clear Word of God. . . . It amounts to disobedience against the Word of Christ to preach the gospel to *all* nations—the word *Volk*-member [*Volksgenosse*] is not a church word at all, but rather a political word" (Posth 1938).

One of Posth's young charges in the Confessing Church, Vicar Priester, was also accused of agitating against the National Socialist state—not least because he rejected the authority of the Old Prussian Land church. Priester denied he was an enemy of the state, but raised concerns about National Socialist religious policy. He criticized ideologues like Rosenberg who proclaimed the pagan Germanic worldview as the only source of happiness for Germans and who denounced the Christian religion as bad for the national community. Priester concluded, "If the warning and guiding word of the church is interpreted as agitation against the state, if the church is suspected and defamed as an enemy of the state in its care for the souls of the *Volk,* then it must suffer this reproach, but out of truthfulness towards its Lord must not be silent" (Priester 1936). While shunning direct political opposition to National Socialism, Priester understood that his ultimate loyalty belonged to the God of the Bible and not to the führer of politics.

In addition to the individual clergy who rejected the German Christian movement or objected to state policies that undermined the spiritual life of German Protestantism, pastors and parishioners in the Nauen district frequently combined forces in struggles over the most contentious of parish events during the Third Reich: the appointment of new pastors. In Nauen, pastoral appointments were a constant concern. As a result of the many retirements, deaths, and transfers of clergy in the district, only six of the 28 pastorates (21 percent) were cared for by the same pastor from before the National Socialist seizure of power in 1933 to the outbreak of World War II in 1939 (*Evang. Sonntagsblatt für den Kirchenkreis Nauen* 1935–40; Nauen District Church Office 1931–35; 1935–38; 1936b; 1937; 1938; 1939a; 1939b; 1939–44; 1940; 1941; 1942; 1943; 1944; *Pfarralmanach für die Kirchenprovinz Berlin-Brandenburg* 1937/1939; *Evang. Sonntagsblatt für den Kirchenkreis Nauen* 1935–40). During that period, fourteen pastors were appointed to permanent positions, only three of whom were German Christians with allegiances to racial determinism and authoritarian church leadership that contradicted orthodox Protestant doctrine and practice: Werner Andrich in Vehlefanz, Friedrich Siems in Nauen and Kurt Herzog in Wansdorf (Bettac 1937b).

**5**

Confessing church clergy and laity proved able, time and again, to block the appointment of German Christian candidates. Just how capable the Confessing church was to control pastoral appointments is clear from a letter from Interim Superintendent Bettac to Mrs. Eichler, a leading parishioner in Leegebruch, near Vehlefanz, in October 1939. With every intention of blocking any unwanted German Christians, Bettac explained that a permanent pastoral appointment in Vehlefanz had to be delayed and informed her that a new curate would be arriving soon. Admitting that he did not know the new curate's church-political alignment, Bettac wrote: "If I may give you advice *confidentially,* it is this: As soon as [the curate] Herr Pastor Klähn is there, establish his church-political position through an open inquiry. If he is not a 'German Christian,' I would ask you to work with him, but if he is a 'German Christian,' reject him and turn to me again, so that we may obtain another temporary pastor there" (Bettac 1939c; Bettac 1939d). As Bettac understood, land church authorities were simply unwilling to place temporary or permanent clergy into positions in which they were manifestly unwelcome. Bettac and the Confessing church pastors of the district exploited that fact for the purposes of keeping new German Christians out of the Nauen district, and accomplished their goal wherever they could count on the support of a sufficient number of determined parishioners.

If German Christians were largely unsuccessful in their attempts to influence pastoral appointments in the Nauen district, the Confessing church proved surprisingly adept at the task. Examples from Groß Behnitz and Nauen illustrate the means by which they accomplished their purposes. In Groß Behnitz, the appointment of Confessing church pastor Kurt Fritzsche was contested in March 1938, six months after it was announced and after the allotted period for parishioners to object to the appointment had elapsed. Fritzsche's critics (105 parishioners signed the complaint, including the mayors and schoolteachers in Groß and Klein Behnitz) interpreted his membership in the Confessing church as antagonistic toward both the German *Volk* and the National Socialist movement. They argued that Fritzsche's teaching "rends the racial community" and rejected the idea that "there could be some other law for a German church as there is for the German *Volk*." Several times they repeated the assertion that Fritzsche's church politics were un-German and illegal, and claimed that Fritzsche's Confessing church believed itself able to set aside not only the authority of the Land church government, but also "the sovereignty of the state" (Günther et al. 1938). Perhaps more clearly than many of their clergy, these parishioners recognized the total claims of the National Socialist regime and understood the implications of their pastor's refusal to submit his confessionally informed theology to those claims.

This grievance was answered by two petitions in support of Fritzsche's appointment, signed by 392 parishioners from Groß and Klein Behnitz, including the patron and five other parish councilors. Demanding the speedy investiture of Fritzsche, they reminded the Consistory that no protests against his appointment had been submitted within the allotted time span (Parish Council of Groß and Klein Behnitz 1938). Then the patron of the Groß Behnitz parish, Dr. von Borsig, wrote an angry letter to the Consistory. He complained that he had not received any news about the promised confirmation of Fritzsche's appointment. Surmising that it had been delayed "by the petitions of irresponsible parishioners," von Borsig reminded the Consistory that there was no legal basis for procrastination and described the situation as a "serious attack on my rights as patron" (von Borsig 1938). Von Borsig condemned "the most awful demagogic manner" in which signatures were gathered by Fritzsche's opponents and asserted that roughly 75 percent of adult parishioners from Klein Behnitz and 80 percent from Groß Behnitz had signed petitions on behalf of Fritzsche. "There could hardly be a more impressive number," claimed the patron, who added that between forty and fifty signatures on the petition for Fritzsche were parishioners who were renouncing their signatures on the protest against his appointment. Summing up his expansive attack on the dilatory Consistory, von Borsig depicted the vast majority of the complainants against Fritzsche as participants in "efforts hostile to Christianity" and as people "who have never had any time for Christianity and the church" (von Borsig 1938).

This letter placed the Brandenburg Consistory in a difficult position, for while they agreed with the substance of the grievance against Fritzsche, they had no legal basis on which to overturn the appointment and were forced to justify their lack of action to Fritzsche's opponents by expressing faith in Fritzsche's willingness to work with the Consistory and hope that he would drift away from his Confessing church colleagues (Brandenburg Consistory 1938).

While the church-political clashes in Groß Behnitz demonstrated that the Confessing church could place its own candidates into pastoral positions and defend them with a mixture of popular support and patron power, events in Nauen showed that the determination of Confessing church forces could successfully block a German Christian candidate in the most important parish of the district.

## 6

The problems in Nauen began in 1935, when the former German Christian pastor Gerhard Schumann was joined by a more radically nationalist German Christian, Friedrich Siems ("Einspruch gegen die Wahl des Herrn Pfarrer Andrich . . ." undated). By 1937, the moderate Schumann had retired and Siems was the head pastor in Nauen. Siems was politically active, and not only within the church. He was an old National Socialist party member, served as a local party official, and had married the daughter of the deputy mayor. One of his colleagues was convinced this activity explained Siems's appointment to the coveted pastorate in Nauen (Bettac 1937a).

The first wave of open conflict swept through the parish in the spring of 1939. The candidate nominated for the vacant associate pastorate was Pastor Werner Andrich from neighboring Vehlefanz. Like Pastor Siems, Andrich belonged to the radical Thuringian German Christian movement. In a revival of previous church-political battles, Confessing church parishioners in Nauen launched a grievance against the election of Andrich, based largely on the argument that the German Christian minority in the Nauen parish was already served by Pastor Siems, and that a second German Christian pastor would be unfair ("Einspruch gegen die Wahl des Herrn Pfarrer Andrich . . ." undated). The protesters argued that they represented the majority in the parish who stood by the "old faith," and they appealed to a Prussian church precedent: in a divided parish, multiple appointments should be divided between rival church-political groups ("Einspruch gegen die Wahl des Herrn Pfarrer Andrich . . ." undated).

On top of this basic charge, they piled on other grievances: that Andrich had managed his parish finances irregularly in Vehlefanz and was under investigation there; that his clothes were unclean; that he baptized children born to parents who had formally withdrawn from the church; that he conducted funerals for others who had abandoned church membership; that he had played with his confirmation students while dressed in his bathing suit; that he called the parish women's association a coffee club; and finally, that his own parish found him unbearable and that the elders there said he was not always truthful ("Einspruch gegen die Wahl des Herrn Pfarrer Andrich . . ." undated). If some of these complaints seem trivial, together they demonstrated a concerted effort by the majority of active parishioners in Nauen to thwart the appointment of Pastor Andrich.

Other grievances were more substantial, taking issue with Andrich's teaching and ministry. Complainants cited seven errors, including the failure to employ the trinitarian invocation, the elevation of the führer as a model of Christian piety, and the exaltation of the religious unity of the German *Volk* under National Socialism above the Word of God. According to the grievance, Andrich had claimed that Jesus Christ gave Christians the power to fulfill the divinely created order of National Socialism, and had stated that it was his highest aim as a preacher to spur his hearers on to an ever more devoted service to the movement. The protesting parishioners replied that there was no single form of government approved by God and that seeking God's kingdom and righteousness was the Christian's highest duty. They charged Andrich with blurring the Christian distinction between Christians and non-Christians in his quest for the religious unity of the German Volk ("Einspruch gegen die Wahl des Herrn Pfarrer Andrich . . ." undated; Ossenkop 1939).

Despite this list of grievances, Interim Superintendent Bettac remained pessimistic about the chances of overturning the appointment of the German Christian Andrich. Bettac suspected that the Brandenburg Consistory in Berlin would use the appointment in Nauen for two purposes: first, to rescue Andrich from the uncomfortable circumstances of his current parish, since it appeared that the child Andrich and his new wife were then expecting was going to be a "seven month child," conceived out of wedlock; and second, to appoint a German Christian superintendent based in Andrich's old parish, in place of Bettac, who was staunchly opposed to appointing German Christians (Bettac 1939b).

Bettac tried to avert land church interference by appealing to the head of the local Women's Aid, Mrs. Krüger, to convince the seemingly ill-informed patron of the parish, Mayor Urban of Nauen, to withdraw his nomination of Andrich. Bettac bemoaned the fact that Mayor Urban had not consulted with his counterpart in Vehlefanz about Andrich, nor with the neighboring pastor in Velten, nor with Bettac himself. Bettac, as interim superintendent, had initiated a pair of grievances against Andrich and was well placed to give advice. Concerning the opinion of complainants in Nauen that Andrich lacked any semblance of pastoral dignity, Bettac knew prominent parishioners in Vehlefanz who described Andrich as a "harlequin." Frustrated with the lack of disciplinary action against Andrich, Bettac vented his anger over the "scandal" of the Brandenburg Consistory's continual protection of the German Christian clergy (Bettac 1939b).

Krüger did as Bettac had requested, and tried to explain to the mayor the long history of conflict between her 170-member organization and the Nauen German Christian Pastor Siems. Krüger made it clear that the Women's Aid steered clear of church politics and expected at least a neutral pastor, if not a member of the Confessing church—in short, one who would hold theologically orthodox services and cooperate with the women of the parish (Krüger 1939).

Thanks to these and other efforts, the appointment of the German Christian Werner Andrich in Nauen was scuttled (Nauen District Church Office 1939b). However, the saga of the associate pastorate continued into 1940. When the position came open, local members of the Confessing church again demanded a candidate who would conform to their neglected church-political orientation.

And so there came to Nauen the candidate of choice, one preacher by the name of Gustav Gille. He preached a candidation sermon from Luke 16:10 ("Whoever can be trusted with very little can also be trusted with much, and whoever is dishonest with very little will also be dishonest with much") (Gille 1940a), charging the Nauen congregation to maintain a high level of political loyalty but otherwise simply urging them to imitate God's faithfulness. He used the customary formula of service, including the trinitarian version of the invocation and the Apostles' Creed ("Predigt gehalten bei der Probeaufstellung am 21. Jan. 1940 in Nauen durch P. Gille" 1940; "Wir Endesunterzeichneten erheben hiermit Einspruch gegen Lehre, Gaben und Wandel des Herrn Hilfspredigers Gille" 1940; Nauen District Synod Executive 1940a). In short, he appeared to be a theologically orthodox young pastor. As such, the parish council in Nauen supported his appointment.

Then came the explosion. It soon became apparent that Pastor Gille was in fact from the extreme racial-nationalist wing of the German Christians. He had in the past regularly deviated from the Apostles' Creed because he did not fully subscribe to it, and generally held German Christian religious celebrations instead of the prescribed land church services (Nauen parishioners 1940a).

Immediately, Nauen parishioners began to circulate petitions. Some accused Gille of neglecting to preach about Jesus Christ, of belittling God by conflating divine and human faithfulness, and of emphasizing human obedience as the way to God rather than Jesus' atoning death and resurrection. Others stated simply that they wanted an associate pastor who would preach on the basis of the Bible and the traditional confessions. Both of these important grievance petitions were spearheaded by women in the Nauen Women's Aid (Troost et al. undated).

When this first round of petitions was rebuffed (Brandenburg Consistory 1940a; Brandenburg Consistory 1940b), the protestors from Nauen wrote angry letters to the land church authorities, reiterating their grievances and adding a few others: that Gille had portrayed Jesus only as a model teacher, and not as the Savior too; and that Gille had led the children into a renewal of Old Testament legalism and works rather than pointing his listeners toward Christ (Nauen parishioners 1940b).

Gille, Siems, and the mayor of Nauen did their best to rebut these accusations. Patron Mayor Urban of Nauen had informed the Brandenburg Consistory that no matter what happened in the case of Gustav Gille, he would continue to nominate German Christian candidates for the position in Nauen (Brandenburg Consistory 1940c). In spite of these threats, the Nauen District Synod Executive accepted the parishioners' grievances against Gille and urged the Brandenburg Consistory to overturn his appointment. The synod executive argued that Gille had dishonestly used the full trinitarian invocation and the Apostles' Creed in his candidation sermon in order to deceive the parishioners about his true theological position (Nauen District Synod Executive 1940a).

Further, they understood that Gille had tricked the parish with the full connivance of head pastor Siems. On top of that, they introduced the complaint that Gille had preached his candidation sermon without looking at the congregation in Nauen as well as their recent discovery that Gille had a record of divisive German Christian agitation in his old parish (Nauen District Synod Executive 1940a ). Indeed, Gille's history proved reliable. As an indication of his style during the conflict in Nauen, he insulted Mrs. Krüger of the Women's Aid on her barrenness and argued that those opposed to him were merely a clique of academics, officials, and small business owners (Nauen District Synod Executive 1940a).

This last item points to a similar feature of disputes between the Confessing church and the German Christian movement in other parishes. Throughout the conflict, both sides claimed to speak as the voice of the parish. For his part, Curate Gille claimed the existence of a three-hundred-member German Christian group in Nauen, and argued that the parish groups behind the grievances comprised only a vocal minority who did not have the greater interests of the parish at heart. In complete contrast, the speakers bringing the charges against Gille claimed to speak for a group of almost three hundred themselves, including 170 in the Women's Association, 69 in the Evangelical Union, and 51 in the Christian Fellowship. Moreover, according to the report of the synod executive, the German Christian group consisted of a few regular attendees and many guests, while the protesting groups were comprised of the leading participants in parish life (Nauen District Synod Executive 1940a.).

By the time the Nauen District Synod Executive had rendered its judgment, however, Gille had returned to his former parish in Sachsen-Anhalt and to his position as an officer in the German army (Nauen District Synod Executive 1940b; Gille 1940b). Nonetheless, his supporters continued to agitate on his behalf. Pastor Siems was incensed at the Nauen District Synod Executive rejection of Gille, and wrote a letter from the Eastern Front criticizing the Women's Aid for its misuse of many old women and its adoption of "parliamentary methods of a democratic past." Rather than listen to the "small circle" of complainants, the Consistory ought to turn to "people capable of judgment, who really stand in the contemporary, pulsating life of the Third Reich." Siems argued that the Women's Aid had separated itself from parish life by refusing to work with him when he was present in Nauen, and suggested that Patron

Mayor Urban was looking to the interests of the majority of the twelve thousand souls in the Nauen parish when he nominated Gille, whom Siems praised for his " 'manly' attitude" in the face of the hatred of his opponents (Siems 1940). Mayor Urban also defended Gille and castigated the Consistory's treatment of the Nauen parishioners engaged with National Socialism as "a snubbing and a clear violation." He was incensed that they had abandoned his candidate Gille, "a front soldier since the beginning of the war!!!" and he reminded the Consistory about a 1940 regulation recommending the appointment of veterans. Attacking the Confessing church opponents of his nominee, Mayor Urban pointed out that they could only gather about 120 signatures, which he described as "a storm in a water glass!" and "a marxist maneuver" (Urban 1941a).

Although Mayor Urban continued to support the nomination of Gille for the vacant Nauen parish until June 1941 (Urban 1941b), he finally gave up trying and nominated another war veteran, a disabled military chaplain and vicar named Erich Schröder, in April 1942 (Urban 1942). Schröder, a vicar in Nauen for eight months in 1939 and 1940, found himself in Russia with the army and could not get away for a candidation service in Nauen until well into 1943. Faced with the prospect of yet another round of protests from the Confessing church in Nauen, Schröder explained to Interim Superintendent Simon of Oranienburg that he had no interest in any church-political group whatsoever. Describing his many experiences as a soldier and then military chaplain, Schröder made it clear that his constant exposure to mortal danger drove him to the simple message of salvation in Christ, which he preached and ministered from the Word of God and the Reformation Confessions (Schröder 1942). This explanation must have been enough to satisfy both the Nauen parish and the Brandenburg Consistory, since Schröder was called to Nauen in May 1943 (Schröder 1943). With that, the four-year struggle to appoint an associate pastor in Nauen ended.

## 7

What can be concluded, then, from the dramatic effect of National Socialism and the political transformation of 1933 upon the parishes of the Nauen district, from the occasional criticism of National Socialist ideology and leaders by local Protestant clergy in the middle and later 1930s, and from the staunch defense of ecclesiastical independence and fidelity to Scripture and the Reformation Confessions made by pastors and parishioners alike? These church-political events and their outcomes form an enlightening window through which to see the church struggle as it filtered down from Berlin (and other land church capitals) into the parishes across the country. Such a view confirms that the church struggle was not just a phenomenon of high-church politics, but a reality of ordinary Protestant life. It also reveals ways in which the basic contest of the church struggle was played out through the unique forms of parish life—not least in the important local matter of the appointment of clergy.

Moreover, local church conditions portray more vividly the divided, even confused, nature of the German Protestant response to National Socialism. Far from providing a warning about the dangers of authoritarian leadership, racial ideology, or political violence, parish clergy from Nauen and the surrounding area mistakenly welcomed the National Socialist movement as a return to a lost national and religious tradition and a stimulus to ecclesiastical revival. There was neither direct confrontation in the face of National Socialist misrule nor significant public criticism of its most obvious evils.

To stop at that point, however, is to diminish the importance of the fact that the clergy and laity affiliated and allied with the Confessing church evaded and even defied the authority of the Brandenburg Consistory. As they publicly fought for the independence of their churches from German Christian heresy, these German Protestants asserted the existence of a sphere of public life beyond the control of the National Socialist regime. In so doing, they opposed the total claims so often and clearly advanced by National Socialist leaders from Hitler down to the host of local party officials.

Often this opposition was denied by Protestants, including most prominent figures in the Confessing church, who accepted the political claims of National Socialism and believed that Hitler himself wished no evil upon the churches. That confusion and political failure does not change the fact that unlike millions of their fellow Germans, those Protestants in the Confessing church who defended ecclesiastical independence maintained a worldview in which National Socialism was not a god and did not claim their ultimate allegiance.

That so many in the Nauen district could affirm this position publicly through participation in the Confessing church points out the limits of National Socialist rule at the local level and raises anew the difficult question of the unachieved potential of political resistance in the churches. Ultimately, it was the long-term growth of cultural Protestantism in Germany and the ubiquitous national-conservative mind-set of the pastors, and not the totalitarian power of National Socialism, that hindered the proclamation of the gospel as the "living and active" Word of God that "penetrates even to dividing soul and spirit . . . [and] judges the thoughts and attitudes of the heart" (Hebrews 4:12, New International Version). That same gospel might have provided a firm basis for widespread political resistance against National Socialism in Germany, had it not been so enmeshed in an authoritarian political environment cultivated under centuries of deference to German princes and emperors. The radicalism of the National Socialist regime exposed the dangers of that passivity toward political authority. It was only after the defeat of Adolf Hitler's regime that Protestant church leaders began to understand the extent to which they were bound in "solidarity of guilt" with their fellow German citizens (Beckmann 1950, 26–27).

# 6

# Sowing *Volksgemeinschaft* in Bavaria's Stony Village Soil

## Catholic Peasant Rejection of Anti-Polish Racial Policy, 1939–1945

JOHN J. DELANEY

1

NAZI PROPAGANDA aimed to promote *Volksgemeinschaft*, or a People's Racial Community, which often lacked appeal in rural Bavaria and was unsuccessful in controlling either attitudes or behavior. This assertion is sustained by examining the behavior of Bavaria's Catholic peasants toward Polish POWs, civilians, and forced laborers during World War II. Driven by their racial definition of community, the Nazis did their best to make Bavarian peasants treat Poles as subhumans. Yet the peasants, influenced by religious and communal factors, generally refused to treat them as such. Why?

The Nazi images of a united *Volk*, although powerful, were hardly accurate or representative. To understand why, we must consider crucial cultural and regional differences at work in the reception and hence the effectiveness of the propaganda that promoted racial and exclusionist definitions of community. Bavaria's Catholic subculture possessed a preexisting and competing ideology, which left its staunch believers prepared to fend off *some* theses of such propaganda. Beyond these ideological factors were the economic pressures at work in Bavaria's labor-starved rural economy, the peasantry's resentment of policies perceived to be contrary to their own self-interest, and the control peasants continued to exercise in their personal lives.

Religious and communal factors influenced peasant attitudes and behavior toward the Polish laborers, who lived in their homes and worked beside them on their farms. These peasants could not adhere to the racial policy of the Nazi regime. Their resistance is significant, but limited in nature and very pointed in its application. That resistance did not seek to topple the regime. To be sure, the larger picture of this period shows that Bavarian peasants were citizens of the Third Reich. They willingly fed it, answered its military draft, and fought its wars. A small percentage of peasants even joined the Nazi Party or served the regime as local peasant leaders. Thus both directly and indirectly Bavaria's Catholic peasants were crucial and essential participants who shored up, indeed empowered, the Third Reich.

At the same time, however, rural Catholic Bavaria offered very low levels of formal support tied to Nazi convictions. As citizens of the Reich, there was much they would go along with and even accept. That acceptance, however, knew definite limits. Nazi assaults on their church and intrusions into their farmyards were stubbornly resisted in a wide range of overt and covert acts. Even local Nazis could differ with policies from Berlin if those policies were viewed as burdensome, unnecessary, or contrary to local interests (Peterson 1969, xi–xxiii, 404–27; Boberach 1971). In short, even Nazi state power knew limits. It depended on enforcement by local functionaries and compliance by individual peasants. Wherever they could safely manage it, the predominately non-Nazi Catholic peasantry sought to preserve their relative autonomy, preexisting values, and preferred patterns of everyday life. This self-defense was especially the case in their parishes and on their farms. For Nazi anti-Polish racial policy to gain acceptance in rural Bavaria, it had to succeed in those two peasant strongholds.

2

It would be a mistake to attempt to gauge the effectiveness of Nazi racist propaganda as though it operated in a vacuum. In reality it was forced to compete with preexisting values. Because Nazi racism advocated hatred of non-Germans—whether Catholic or not—the party found itself in fundamental conflict with the Catholic church, which had long preached the opposite. The Nazi position contradicted Catholic teachings that religious faith was primary, regardless of "race" or ethnicity. Such teachings were the basis, in regions like Catholic Bavaria, of moral and ethical norms that provided community standards and personal guidance in the conduct of everyday life. Unlike the Nazis' racially defined *Volksgemeinschaft,* Catholic teaching explicitly included all who accepted its doctrines and were baptized, regardless of race and nationality. Nazi racism also ran up against inculcated humanistic values that postulated concepts such as the brotherhood of mankind. By dint of repetition, Catholic ideas had become firmly rooted among Bavarian peasants. These ideas enjoyed a much longer history than the racism of Nazism, itself an upstart movement occasionally scorned during its years of struggle in rural Catholic Bavaria for its atheism, hostility to religion, and political arrogance (Pridham 1973, 146–83, 266–67).

Other significant factors strongly reinforced religious values. Apart from church teachings, there was the church itself as a societal institution. Its traditions, holy days, and festivals provided the spiritual and social celebrations observed by peasants not only year round, but also year in and year out. The local network of the church permeated every aspect of the villagers' lives (Blessing 1988, 3–111). Sunday Mass was well attended; priests possessed great standing and power in the community even beyond the Nazi seizure of power. Well into World War II, some local clergy even countermanded Nazi prohibitions placed on weekday celebrations of holy days (Witetschek 1971, 3:199). Edward N. Peterson has observed that there was "a remarkable feature of [Bavaria's] Catholic villages: the priest often made the decision about who would join the party and therewith remain in control of the village (Peterson 1969, 412)." Sundays offered priests the opportunity to instruct parishioners on church teachings and to remind them of their Christian obligations. Moreover, the pulpit was not just for religious messages. It also fulfilled an informational and instructional function of a political nature (Peterson 1969, 314; Kershaw 1983, 198–201). The parish priest was often a community's crucial link to the outside world, a fact not lost on disgruntled Nazi functionaries. Rounding out the factors that account for the priests' secure presence in the village were personal relationships. In administering the sacraments that accompanied birth and death, the priest established intimate contact with his parishioners at the points of joy and crisis in their lives. The youth of the community were raised with religious instruction, joined Catholic youth organizations, and participated, along with their parents, in parish events (Horn 1979, 561–82). Even village charitable systems fell within the domain of the church. If Socialists elsewhere could claim to have lived with Social Democracy from cradle to grave, it seems fair to say that the church, where it was still a dominant force, had done the same for its followers. Thus in their attempt to penetrate Bavaria's many hamlets and thereby win over the hearts and minds of villagers, the Nazis and their weltanschauung faced a formidable competitor.

Within the community humanitarianism was reflected in the day-to-day relationships of peasants who had known each other since childhood. Even the lowest occupational groups—land laborers and milkers—were integrated into peasant family living and belonged to the community. They lived in peasant homes of medium- and small-size holdings, ate their meals in common, and socialized with the farmer's family in their free time. There were of course rotten and abusive as well as decent employers, and agricultural conditions were especially hard, but on the whole local laborers were not treated inhumanely (Delaney 1995, 267–73). Integration, not racial thinking, thus marked provincial social and economic life before the war years. Such was the case up through the late 1930s when foreigners, including Poles, first arrived to replace Germans who had migrated to the cities in search of easier and better paying work, or who had been drafted into the German army (Wunderlich 1961, 238–40; Delaney 1995, 105–10).

Within such tightly knit rural communities daily contact between villagers reinforced their common identity. Studies of rural villages elsewhere stress a basic cause for this identity: the need for mutual aid in farm communities plus the power of social pressures in a small community (Lee 1981, 90; Mooser 1979, 260).

3

How did Nazi propaganda impact peasant values and village life? As a weapon of Nazi racial thinking, it was employed in an attempt to mobilize, direct, and manipulate the minds of German citizens. The larger goal was to (re)educate the German people to Nazi thinking and to promote a People's Racial Community. This goal applied to a wide variety of topics of which Poland, Poles, and German-Polish relations were a special target. Poland was portrayed as a terror state whose deeds included international violence, murder, and robbery. The Polish nation fared no better on a cultural level. Goebbels smeared it as incapable of developing culture, citing "inferiority" of its "racial" stock. In short, Slavs were considered subhuman.

The Nazis produced reels and reams of vicious anti-Polish propaganda just before their invasion of Poland and continued to do so during the brief campaign (Welch 1993, 90–98; Zeman 1973, 104, 107; Steinert 1977, 51). Here is an example originally highlighted by Ulrich Herbert: "Every day, the German Press publishes photos of atrocities from the former Poland, along with reports that Poles are being exemplarily punished for those deeds, i.e. they are being shot" (Herbert 1997, 67). Once Polish POWs and civilian laborers were introduced into and exploited for the benefit of the labor-starved German war economy, the Nazis began to issue restrictive edicts. This step beyond propaganda was a further attempt to influence German minds. Once again, the aim was to encourage racial thinking, alter behavior, and promote the concept of a People's Racial Community.

Laws and edicts were released via official channels throughout Bavaria and were accompanied by a renewed propaganda campaign by 1940. Already by the fall of 1939, Germans and Poles had been thrown together but instructed to avoid one another. As observed by Robert Gellately, the Poles, like their employers in Lower Franconia, were rural folk and overwhelmingly Catholic. Such circumstances, he noted, were hardly conducive to the enforcement of stringent non-fraternization policies (Gellately 1990, 222). In addition, Germans were instructed to recognize the racial distinctions that allegedly rendered one group superior to another. Michael Burleigh recently remarked that "elementary human contact [of German peasants and Polish workers] was [not] permissible from a Nazi biological perspective, but matters looked otherwise to devout Bavarians and Silesians" (Burleigh 2000, 779). In fact, reports filed by security agents and Party officials in late 1939 show that a spirit of domination and subordination did not reign in the countryside (August 1984, 305–10).

Peasants, especially Catholic ones, were both open and inviting, as suggested in the following extended passage from an intelligence report of the Sicherheitsdienst (SD) (Steinert 1977, 56; Kitchen 1995, 155; Boberach 1984, 3:476; and August 1984, 347, n. 164).

Although various offices within the party and government have already issued guidelines for the treatment of Polish prisoners of war, we still receive numerous reports on a daily basis regarding overly friendly behavior on the part of a portion of the population toward such Polish prisoners. It is evident from a number of reports that, especially in rural areas, the social distance between the farming population and the Polish POWs is not being sufficiently preserved. Thus it has been frequently noted that Polish workers have been taken into the family on the farms where they are employed.

> Farmers have permitted their female help and in some instances even their daughters to go out dancing with Polish prisoners. We have had reports from Catholic areas that Polish prisoners are often brought in closed groups to church or that they have participated, together with the farmers to whom they have been allocated, in church services. (Herbert 1990, 136–37)

The SD continued to report on peasant behavior deemed objectionable right up to war's end.

Prior to the war, the peasants' desperate need for farm help also undermined attempts to infuse racial thinking. Reports from all over Bavaria show they welcomed the Poles. Some farmers competed with each other by paying those Poles who arrived early almost twice the wage later allowed by the state. The reception of the Poles in the countryside was generally positive. Some farmers even petitioned local authorities to release POWs from camps and assign them to live at the family farms where they already worked by day. The time lost marching to and from camps was objectionable; housing individuals designated as "racially inferior" with one's family was not. Racial policy was thus also rejected on a practical level (Delaney 1995, 152; Großmann 1984a, 593; Janta 1944, 126–38). In short, many Polish land laborers were taken on by the peasantry in the regional traditions accorded Bavarian *Knechte* or farmhands who preceded them. POWs were soon seen in civilian clothing. By early 1940, Nazi authorities were frankly admitting the failure of propaganda to promote the *Volksgemeinschaft* and the voluntary non-fraternization of races upon which it ultimately depended.

**4**

The Party addressed the situation with more edicts: the upshot of the directives called for the strict separation of Germans and Poles at places of worship and for non-fraternization at places of work; insisted that Poles wear identifiable insignia, be barred from cultural events, be restricted in their movement, be denied access to pubs and inns frequented by Germans; and in general insisted that Poles suffer humiliation and deprivation as was their biological due. Included among these was a deadly prohibition outlawing sexual relations between Germans and Poles (Reichsministerium des Innern 1940, 555–56; Bayerisches Gesetz und Verordnungs Blatt 1940, 7:37, sections 1.4, 1.6).

In areas throughout Germany where the Nazis were firmly in control, this stringent collection of repressive and inhumane laws was difficult to ignore and thus was usually enforced (Herbert 1997, 116–36). In the Bavarian countryside, however, such was often not the case. Despite claiming Munich as its birthplace, Nazism was in fact particularly weak in rural stretches of the predominately Catholic state. Before 1933 National Socialism did not capture much of rural Catholicism's block vote (Hagmann 1946, 21–22). In the July 1932 election, seventeen Catholic rural voting districts returned less than 15 percent for the NSDAP, while seventeen of the state's Protestant districts awarded the Nazis anywhere from a "low" of 55.8 percent to a staggering 83 percent of the vote. The Catholic rural environs of the state formed the core constituency of the Bavarian People's Party or BVP. In some places the BVP commanded an absolute majority. It even managed to retain 48 percent of the state vote in the unfree election of March 1933 (Kershaw 1983, 23). Clearly the Nazi Party was at a distinct political disadvantage before 1933. The disadvantage endured and became more pronounced within the context of the Church Struggle of the 1930s, which Peterson has described as a "cold civil war between a radical party and a conservative church" (Peterson 1969, 295; Höpfl 1997, 41–49, 70–83). Intrusive Nazi economic policy added to Catholic peasant discontent (Jucovy 1985, 244–55). The regime also showed favor to industry over agriculture (Corni 1990, 220–68). Industry's expansion resulted in a rural labor shortage that culminated in crisis and left farmers angry and bitter (Kershaw 1983 33–65). By 1939 the bulk of the Catholic peasantry had been effectively alienated from the coercive and largely discredited National Socialist state (Kershaw 1983, 185–223). The regime's racialist propaganda in rural Bavaria thus competed not only with preexisting values, it targeted a largely dissatisfied and often resentful population composed of tightly-knit communities and was thus forced to operate in a relatively unfavorable environment.

For all these reasons the Nazis' struggle against fraternization and decency between Bavaria's non-Nazi peasantry and the Poles assigned to them was an uphill battle in which the limits of the party's power were clear to all. Foremost among the immediate factors hindering the NSDAP was its organizational weakness. In some cases, Nazi administrators wrote off entire anti-Nazi villages that the party never succeeded in effectively penetrating (Peterson 1969, 404 ff.). More fundamental in importance is that hamlets, alpine villages, and individual family farms were often remote; many peasants could not be easily reached, much less observed and controlled. Once peasants were outside the village and in the fields, regulation was often next to impossible. The same held true within the four walls of non--and anti-Nazi households (Boberach 1984, 12:4518).

Thus farm life proceeded apace, and daily contact between many peasant families and *Zwangsarbeiter* (forced laborers) enabled relationships to develop along mundane instead of ideological lines. Daily contact resulted in familiarity that enabled human emotions, not racialist notions, to come to the fore. People largely living in their own world, who recognized their appreciation of others, were unlikely to sacrifice their feelings and identities to the fanatic claims of racist propaganda and racial definitions of community. One pro-Nazi flyer of the day urged the following: "Germans! The Pole can never be a comrade! . . . never forget that you belong to a master race" (Herbert 1997, 77–78; Großmann 1984b, 373, n. 124). There, in no uncertain terms, was the revolutionary outlook and value system that the regime urged the religiously grounded and conservatively minded peasantry to embrace. Separately and collectively these factors placed serious obstacles in the way of Nazi attempts to convince peasants to hate and discriminate against those young Poles whom the peasants regarded as fellow Catholics or simply unfortunate human beings whom they needed and were inclined to like (Boberach 1984, 3:528, 11:4262–63).

In light of the above, how then did the generally disaffected populace react to the Party's racist ideas and the foreign laborers in their midst? The obvious answer is with a variety of responses. Most striking were fraternization, charitable treatment, and the anti-racist opinions of clergymen. Nazi bureaucrats and security agents regarded such fraternization in the countryside as a serious problem (Boberach 1984, 11:4316). References to it appear throughout the war and fall into a number of revealing categories.

Common religious worship was an early concern of Nazis, who commented that it undermined the regime's efforts to segregate the two groups, to prejudice Germans, and to subjugate the newly arrived Poles. Thus, from the very inception of the wartime Reich, Germans and Poles attended Mass as fellow Catholics (Gestapo files 1939–1945, file 1058; Boberach 1984, 2:422, 3:709; Ziegler 1973, 272). Outside village chapels, the state attempted to convince German peasants that the Poles were biological enemies who belonged to separate racial communities. The contradiction was glaringly apparent and basic allegiances were rarely in doubt. Göring's guidelines of March 8, 1940, stipulated an end to common worship precisely because the practice exposed the contradictions of religious and political values (Ziegler 1973, 248; Boberach 1984, 12:4498).

Furthermore, some priests took up special collections on behalf of penniless forced laborers, and small gifts were solicited at mass and within the community (Boberach 1984, 3:528, 766; Witetschek 1971, 195; Witetschek 1967, 345–46). Civil greetings and kind words also played an important role. Openness brought people together—resulting in something as simple as a church tour where priests and Poles could share an appreciation of baroque design (Ziegler 1973, 260; Hehl 1985, column 1117). This simple example is but a small indication that Catholic Germans and Poles apparently could easily engage in a dialogue of sorts based on common traditions despite language barriers. Other results of openness included invitations to the rectory, sharing of a cigarette, conversation over a precious cup of coffee or a prohibited glass of Schnapps (Boberach 1984, 4:968). Deeds of this nature also encouraged the community to reach out to the Poles. Sacristans and later parishioners followed in their clergy's footsteps (Ziegler 1973, 266).

One surveillance analyst emphasized that the well-chosen words of priests urged parishioners to be charitable toward forced laborers: "Again and again Catholic priests hold up the following Church teaching before the rural population: What you do to the poorest of my brothers, you do unto me" (Boberach 1984, 11:4112). As a result, nonconformist behavior was reported throughout the countryside. Peasants indifferent or opposed to the regime's racial politics invited the Poles assigned to them into the local pub (Gestapo files 1939–1945, files 14819 and 7596; Witetschek 1967, 348; Boberach 1984, 4:1081). That act and others like it were considered betrayals of the racial community and were taken seriously enough to trigger Gestapo action. Even Fürst Karl August von Thurn und Taxis and his *Hauskaplan* were arrested for, among other things, refusing to accept the "German" greeting, and for speaking with Russian and Polish POWs (Ziegler 1973, 334, n. 1). Under the Nazis, all such behavior vis-à-vis Poles was condemned, with the tragic and ironic result that decency was illegal and good people became outlaws.

Good deeds and common decency were simply a beginning, not an end. In the countryside, daily contact between farming families and Polish laborers was a significant factor encouraging people to move beyond kind words and good deeds to forge working relationships, friendships, and even a family attachment to individual workers. Once Poles were on a family farm the treatment accorded them depended to a great extent upon the individual peasant to whom he or she had been assigned.

Catholic peasants of poor repute who had abused German farmhands prior to the war were often the same ones who abused foreign workers during the war. This was the situation for Anton Togarcek, assigned to a farmer near Karlstadt. Anton feared for his life after being grabbed by the throat and thrown to the ground over a trifling matter. He fled to the police with his story. The subsequent investigation yielded village witnesses who backed his story. They also identified the farmer as a hothead who was quick to shove and strike others (Gestapo files 1939–1945, file 6333). Every society has its mean and nasty types who prey on vulnerable or defenseless people. Bavaria was no different in that respect and thus some Poles were mistreated, indeed some terribly so. Their tragic fate ranged from lesser abuses such as being overworked or slapped around to terrifying and even deadly ones. The latter included prolonged Gestapo interrogation and even execution by the regime. Again, the fate of Polish farmhands largely hinged on the person or persons to whom they had been assigned. Some ideologically driven Nazi peasants did abuse their Polish workers. But by and large the weakness of people's personalities, not Nazi ideology, accounted for cruel behavior in the Catholic countryside (Delaney 1995, 265–73).

To a far greater extent, Poles in rural Catholic Bavaria were accepted in the spirit of Christian brotherhood or appreciated for their company, efforts, or agricultural skills (Kershaw 1983, 288). In such cases good relations became a springboard to friendships or at least cordial relationships. Although Poles were officially prohibited from eating at the family table, police sources report the readiness of peasants to share their meals with one who by official racial definition was inferior.

Instances of meals in common were accompanied and followed by reports of *Hausgemeinschaft*—situations in which individual German families and Polish laborers within one house lived as a community (Gestapo files 1939–1945, file 7251). To the pronounced frustration of Nazi bureaucrats and spies, the integration of Poles into the Catholic community proceeded apace with the peasantry's refusal to force most Catholic Poles to work on holy days that they themselves celebrated in violation of the law (Ziegler 1973, 280, 284). Much to the Nazis' chagrin, the Gestapo discovered that Poles even walked in pilgrimages, joined Corpus Christi processions, and enjoyed local festivals (Gestapo files 1939–1945, file 15748). Such developments point out that devout Catholics had more in common with forced laborers, who shared their faith and religious culture, than they did with intrusive Nazis who outlawed their traditional days of observance and celebration. The extent of this fissure between peasantry and Party was reflected in the fact that in time some Poles were included in private religious celebrations such as baptisms and weddings. During the war years some Poles obviously joined inner-family circles.

Nothing posed a greater threat to the Nazi ideal than *Rassenschände*—the "defilement" of the German race brought on by sexual intercourse between Germans and "sub-humans," in this case Poles. For this reason, Rassenschände, or "racial mixing, reports, which are widespread in the SD's *Meldungen aus dem Reich* documents by war's end, merited deadly terror and retribution. Poles accused of this racial crime were arrested and executed. German women suffered public humiliation by the authorities and frequently ended up in prison or a concentration camp (Gellately 1990, 234–36; Boberach 1984, 14:5337–41).

POWs and foreign laborers easily met local girls and women when assigned to work and live in villages. The story of twenty-year-old Pole Franz Zych and his Bavarian milkmaid is a typical one. When interrogated by the Gestapo he said: "With respect to the room, board, and treatment, I received from [farmer F.] . . . I had it really good. It was there I got to know [his daughter]. She and I worked together in the fields and in the barn. The first time I had sexual relations with her was four weeks ago in the barn." The rest, which the Gestapo was keenly intent on hearing, is not hard to imagine. The frequency and kind of sex couples engaged in impacted the sentences individuals received (Gestapo files 1939–1945, file 5352).

The story of a thirty-five-year-old farmer's daughter from Deggendorf County is another case in point. The loneliness of her life and close daily contact with the Polish POW assigned to her were not without their effect. By May 1940 their unions occurred wherever privacy permitted. Once discovered, a special court of the regime handed her a prison sentence of one year and five months (Staatsarchiv München, Sondergericht München 10441). Similar circumstances, patterns, consequences, and sentences appear elsewhere throughout Bavaria (Staatsarchiv München, Sondergericht München 11354, 11392).

In the first six months of 1942 alone, the area around Regensburg yielded 257 similar cases of outlawed sexual relations with foreigners including many Poles (Gellately, 1990, 240). In County Landshut, there were 122 discovered cases of prohibited sex with foreigners in the same year. County Landshut's population only stood at 30,357 in 1939 (Bayerisches Statistisches Landesamt

1953, 45–46). One is left to wonder as to the number of undiscovered cases there, elsewhere in Bavaria, and throughout Germany during the entire war.

The examples of many types of conduct presented here and the resultant frustration voiced by Nazis raise the issue of the regime's response to behavior it was unable to alter. Put quite simply, it resorted to terror. More than anything else, terror was an open admission of the failure of both the call for a *Volksgemeinschaft* and the racist propaganda directed against Poles in the Catholic community. Terror took many forms. Foremost among them were the arrests of priests who dared to speak out against racism, set examples for the community, or were otherwise hostile to the regime. Parishioners or villagers who refused to conform were, depending on the community and the Nazis in it, subject to severe threats and stern warnings from regional Gestapo authorities, local public humiliation, fines, jail sentences, or detention in concentration camps. Over time more pronounced propaganda campaigns were undertaken and stricter edicts were issued, but terror became the norm.

Actually, terror and propaganda in Nazi Germany were two sides of a single coin. If Goebbels and his machine were unsuccessful in beating certain ideas into the populace, Himmler's henchmen resorted to terror. Viewed from a distance, these events suggest an escalating development that the regime unsuccessfully sought to stem. This was clearly a reactive form of terror. It sought conformity from two populations with a future in the Third Reich. As such it was fundamentally different from the proactive, genocidal terror the Nazis inflicted on Europe's Jews. The function of the proactive terror was to eliminate the Jews, not to alter their behavior. In short, the Nazis' Janus-faced terror dictated that groups with a future were to conform; groups without a future were slated for destruction.

5

Much to the disappointment and anger of the regime and its surveillance operatives who secretly monitored public opinion, many Polish land laborers were well received on family farms in Bavaria's Catholic countryside when they arrived in 1939–40. By 1941 and 1942, *Tisch-* and *Hausgemeinschaft*—or increasingly closer communal living—became a real problem for Nazi authorities. According to surveillance operatives, persistent violation of edicts banning common religious worship was at the root of the problem. The sources indicate the problem's persistence into 1944 but references to fraternization and *Haus-*

*gemeinschaft* drop off in number. By 1945 SD agents, administrators, and the Gestapo were concerned with more pressing matters and rarely alluded to fraternization. The problem to which they referred and one with its own history is their well-grounded fear of retribution by the millions of mistreated foreign laborers found mostly in work camps and industry scattered throughout the Reich.

In essence, rural Bavaria's Catholic subculture was not defenseless before the dissemination of the Nazi racist propaganda that promoted the People's Racial Community. In the National Socialist struggle for the German heart and mind, the Nazi party pitted itself against rural Catholicism's political party and local traditions and never really triumphed. Thus, following the national seizure of power, it was largely regarded as an outside force. Secondly, the competing ideology possessed by practicing Catholics was entrenched, as opposed to the Nazi Weltanschauung, and thereby constituted an opposing worldview. Rural Bavarians were not saintly or model democrats. They neither rose up to protest persecution of the Communists, Socialists, and Jews, nor did they oppose the Second World War. But in an attempt to understand how the Nazi system worked, it is instructive to study areas in which the regime fell short of its goals. As individuals and members of tightly-knit communities, the peasantry, priests, and villagers were better able and more likely to fend off racist propaganda that targeted them and attempted to spread hate vis-à-vis the unfortunate Poles in their midst. Quite simply, the racist Nazi message in particular fell on stony ground.

Throughout the war years, rural Catholic Bavaria's deeply entrenched values maintained their predominance in social life. Instead of adopting Nazi values toward the Poles, many Bavarians engaged in popular opposition. Their rejection of Nazi propaganda and racial policy violated the law, was dangerous, and took real courage. The regime certainly viewed their behavior as oppositional. Lesser violations brought Germans and Poles before the Gestapo and yielded threats of concentration camp internment for any subsequent transgression. Serious violations, including prohibited sexual relations, were considered high political crimes against the People's Racial Community. The cruel and deadly sentences they produced did not stop the Bavarians. Granted, those so victimized by Nazi justice did not seek to topple the regime. For that reason historians holding fast to traditional definitions of resistance tend to minimize these peasants' historical significance and do not label them as resisters. But the sustained and myriad acts of Catholic villagers amounted to a staunch rejection of racial policy, and the rejection carried collective weight. The Nazis feared the strong personal relations of Germans and Poles, especially those marked by sexual relations. Their social and political consequences were viewed as threatening to a point of adversely affecting the People's Racial Community and, by extension, the future of the racial state. In the end, illicit relations of any type did manage to compromise Nazi racial policy. This popular opposition to racial policy produced a defeat for the Nazis and should be recorded as such.

The intangibles that initiated, conditioned, and determined German and Polish relationships stemmed from the peasants' provincial and religious traditions, not from the racial values of Hitler, Göring, Goebbels, and Himmler. Holding fast to their politically and religiously intertwined identities, both courageous and authoritative priests and the hard-headed conservative peasantry who constituted rural communities rejected radical calls for a People's Racial Community of masters and subhumans. Instead, they attempted to live in harmony with the Poles on their farms according to Bavaria's rural traditions, their consciences, and the teachings of their church. In short, racist propaganda and the *Volksgemeinschaft* were failures in much of rural Bavaria and can be demonstrated most clearly through the repressive edicts against fraternization that the Nazis issued and the terror that they used in an attempt to enforce them.

# 7

# The Priority of Diplomacy

Pius XII and the Holocaust During the Second World War

MICHAEL PHAYER

## 1

POPE PIUS XII believed his pontificate to be the most difficult of any in modern times. He was probably right, although Pius VII did not have an easy time of it with Napoleon Bonaparte. The Second World War certainly presented Pius XII with difficult practical situations, some of which could be dealt with diplomatically, an approach that suited Pope Pius.

The career and pontificate of Pius XII mirrored that of Benedict XV, whose papacy spanned the years of the Great War. Like Benedict, Pius hoped above all to play the role of a negotiator during World War II. President Franklin Roosevelt and Prime Minister Winston Churchill pulled the rug out from under Pope Pius when they called for an unconditional surrender at Casablanca in 1942. Bitterly disappointed at not being able to team up with Roosevelt, Pius spoke derisively thereafter about the "Big Three" to the German ambassador to the Vatican, Ernst von Weizsäcker.

Deprived of a positive role, Pius XII had to settle for alternative goals. These were defensive and threefold: safeguarding Europe from Communism, avoiding a showdown with Nazi Germany, and protecting the city of Rome from aerial and surface bombardment. At various times, one of these priorities would seem more important to Pius than the other two. During the first years of the war, Communism and Nazism preoccupied Pius, but by 1942 his highest priority became the preservation of Rome. When this danger passed in 1944 at the same time that Hitler's fall seemed a certainty, Pope Pius returned to his first concern, Communism.

Countering genocide was not among the priorities of Pius XII. Of course, before the war no one could have imagined the calamity that struck European Jewry, but it must be admitted that the murder of the Jews never came to rival in importance for Pope Pius the three concerns just mentioned. Once the Vatican recognized the fact of genocide, Pius intervened, to the extent that he did, only diplomatically. When it came to the Holocaust, Pius unfortunately intervened only timidly when compared to the daring risks he undertook regarding his three principal concerns.

Historians have long been occupied with the question of Pope Pius and the Holocaust. Recently, the English Catholic writer John Cornwell took on this task in *Hitler's Pope: The Secret History of Pius XII* (Cornwell 1999). Not unlike Rolf Hochhuth, the playwright whose characterization of Pius as a grasping and uncaring individual stained him indelibly, Cornwell has emphasized the pope's reserve and austerity in dealing with people and his portentous ways when it came to personal habits and public ceremonies whether liturgical or diplomatic. Unattractive as these characterizations are, they do not appear critical in connection with the Holocaust, as Cornwell was surely aware. So what made Pius "Hitler's Pope"? Cornwell claimed to have found two other flaws in Pius XII's personality: hunger for power and anti-Semitism. These were Cornwell's links to Hitler and the Holocaust. In short, it was not the exigencies of the war that dictated Pius XII's Holocaust-related decisions, but the inadequacies of his personality.

There is an alternative to Cornwell's thesis (Phayer 2000, chapter 6). The importance that Pius placed on Communism, Nazism, and Rome's destruction actually kept him from intervening strenuously on behalf of the victims of genocide and, at times, from intervening at all. Space not permitting any kind of thorough analysis of this thesis, I will attempt to illustrate it by carefully examining a few occurrences. Before proceeding to this view, let us scrutinize Cornwell's proposition more closely.

**2**

In *Hitler's Pope* there is considerable emphasis on the 1933 concordat between Germany and the Vatican. This emphasis is certainly justified. Pius XII cut his professional teeth working on concordatory agreements between the Vatican and several German states during the Weimar Republic. While acting as the Vatican secretary of state, Pius, then known as Eugenio Pacelli, negotiated the

1933 concordat. Ivo Zeiger, S.J., a Vatican collaborator in the concordatory ne-gotiations with the Third Reich, recalled Pacelli's determination and vigor while burning the midnight oil during Holy Week 1933, to redraft the as yet un-ratified concordat, characterizing him as "determined," "self-willed," "impervi-ous to criticism" (Muench 1946–47).

Nor can Cornwell be faulted for asserting that preserving the concordat was a major factor in Pius's failure to break with Hitler at the war's outset and throughout its duration. Pius, who ascended the throne of Peter the same year that World War II began, was well aware that Germany was the aggressor in the war and that Germans committed atrocities against Polish Catholics before the Holocaust during the early years of the war, but this awareness did not cause him to break off diplomatic relations with Hitler even when Konrad Preysing, the bishop of Berlin, advised him to do so.

After the war—even before it ended—Pope Pius sought assurances from Germany's conquerors and occupiers that they would acknowledge the validity of the concordat. John Cornwell does not explore the postwar era in *Hitler's Pope,* but there can be no doubt about Pius's continued preoccupation with the concordat. During the cold war the papal envoy to Germany, Bishop Aloysius Muench, slowly came to realize that Pius was continuing to interpret develop-ments in Germany "according to this or that phrase of the Concordat" (Muench 1946–47). In sum, the emphasis put on the concordat by the author of *Hitler's Pope* is certainly justified.

But how does this emphasis relate to the Holocaust? In Cornwell's think-ing, Pope Pius relentlessly followed a centrist papal policy that packed power in his hands. The concordat was the conduit that relayed church jurisdiction di-rectly to Rome, bypassing regional bishops. Rather than forfeit power by de-nouncing Hitler's Holocaust, Pius chose to preserve the concordat.

This line of thought contains several general weaknesses and one essential flaw that is particularly relevant to the Holocaust. Concordats have tradition-ally been part and parcel of Vatican diplomatic policy. That Pope Pius XII would follow in the footsteps of his predecessors cannot in any way come as a surprise. But was not the concordat with Germany singular, an exception to Vatican concordatory policy, in that it compromised principle to secure church power? This manner of thinking is teleological, not historical. In 1933 no one could guess the excesses that would result in Hitler's being named chancellor. The events of 1930–33 clearly indicated that Germany was moving away from democratic government. To seek to come to an understanding with the new, but not yet dictatorial, government of Hitler was certainly opportunistic, but not in any way unprincipled. Finally, Cornwell presses the concordat argument much too far when he argues that the Vatican worked a quid pro quo, trading Nazi recognition of the concordat for the German Catholic Center Party's vote in favor of the Enabling Act that transformed Hitler from a chancellor to a dictator. A number of motives can be attributed to Center Party politicians for voting for the act. There is no documentary evidence, however, that ties the concordat to the Enabling Act (Hürten 1992).

Anyone who is unfamiliar with German records would miss the essential flaw in Conwell's Concordat-Holocaust linkage. Pius was the perfect pope for Hitler, Cornwell would have us believe, because major decisions bearing on Germany would be reserved to the Vatican to satisfy Pius XII's hunger for autocratic power. To preserve that power Pius kept silent about the Holocaust. In point of fact Pius did not dictate what the German church should do about the Holocaust. Immediately after the war, the Bavarian Josef Müller, who had been active in the resistance against Hitler, told the American diplomat Harold Tittman that the German church preferred that the pope should stand aside, while the German hierarchy carried on the struggle against the Nazis inside Germany. The pope, Müller added, had followed this advice (Tittman 1945).

This arrangement left open, of course, the possibility that Pope Pius would urge the German bishops either toward confrontation with the Nazi government or toward accommodation. When Pius XII wrote to the German bishops at the time of their national meeting at Fulda in 1943, he advised them that what they had already said in 1942 about the Holocaust was sufficient. *But he clearly left the door to protest open for the bishops, giving them freedom to act autonomously.* Thus, the argument founders that centrist papal policy in general and Pius XII's craze for power in particular led to the accommodation of Hitler on the precise question of the Holocaust.

Besides Pius's excessive hunger for power and control, Cornwell sees anti-Semitism as the second reason why Pius XII was *Hitler's Pope.* Before examining whether Pius actually *was* anti-Semitic, let us assume for the sake of analysis that this was the case in order to test the point of view as it relates to the Holocaust. In Daniel Jonah Goldhagen's well-known book, *Hitler's Willing Executioners: Ordinary Germans and the Holocaust* (1996), the author assumed that anti-Semitism was the driving force behind the German murder of the Jews. A host of Holocaust scholars immediately objected, pointing out that individuals who were directly involved with the killing actually had various motives for their actions. The same point can be made, obviously, for Pius XII, who stands accused, after all, not of murdering Jews but of keeping silent about it.

We can pursue Cornwell's argument a step further by referring to Zofia Kossak-Sczcucka. Kossak was a self-acknowledged anti-Semite who felt that Poland would be much better off without its large Jewish minority population. So when the Germans began killing Jews en masse did she collaborate with them? No; she founded the *Zegota* resistance group that worked more hero- ically than any other group in Europe to save Jews. Kossak told the Polish Catholics that "Whoever remains silent in the face of murder becomes an ac- complice of the murder" (Tomaszewski and Werbowski 1994, 43). Clearly, anti- Semitism was not a certain predictor of Holocaust collaboration.

The phenomenon of Catholic Poland's producing both heroic rescuers and wicked collaborators puzzled the historian and sociologist Nechama Tec. Why, Tec asked, would some Poles act courageously, others savagely? Both were believing Catholics. Tec searched for a solution to the riddle. Catholics, Tec ul- timately decided, were morally ambiguous because on the one hand their church taught contempt for Jews as Christ killers, but, on the other hand, that murder was sinful. Moral ambiguity helped lead Catholics to respond to the Holocaust in extreme ways—some as rescuers but many others as Nazi collab- orators (Tec 1986, chap. 9).

Even if Pius XII were anti-Semitic, it does not follow that he would keep silent about the Holocaust on that account. Indeed, such a supposition stretches the imagination. The ten commandments of Hebrew scripture form the basis of Christian morality. Would Pope Pius be able to disregard the com- mandment, "You shall not kill"? In the face of scanty evidence such an assertion can only be viewed as highly conjectural and hypothetical.

What is the evidence behind the charge that Eugenio Pacelli was anti- Semitic? Cornwell relied heavily on a piece of correspondence dating back to 1919, the time of the Communist revolution in Munich following the Great War. In his report to the Vatican secretary of state, Pacelli provides second- hand details of a meeting between several diplomats and a Communist leader, a Jew. The letter indicates a strong political and social anti-Semitism on the part of either the narrator who attended the meeting or Pacelli, but probably both. Cornwell deserves credit for providing the public with this document.

But the significance of the letter as a link between Pius and the Holocaust is minor. The letter was not written at the time of prewar Nazi anti-Semitic poli- cies and actions, let alone during the wartime Holocaust years, but at the time of the Russian Revolution of November 1917 and subsequent postwar revolutions in Germany. Many Jews were involved in these Communist insurrections, and for a number of decades prior to them Communism had been outspokenly atheistic. Catholic animus in general and German Catholic hostility in particular against Communists was strong, and the combination of Jewishness and Communism augmented it. This anti-Semitic feeling is clearly present in Pacelli's letter. In short, the letter reflects opinions and outlooks that prevailed at the time of its writing. Can Cornwell legitimately conclude that Pope Pius harbored the same feelings when the Jews were murdered en masse from 1941 to 1945? To do so flies in the face of evidence to the contrary. Pius XII was deeply saddened by the Holocaust, even moved to tears because of it.

Beyond the 1919 letter, Cornwell found scant confirmation of his assertion that Pope Pius was an anti-Semite. Cornwell overlooked an address that Pacelli delivered in Hungary in 1938 on the occasion of the International Eucharistic Congress held in Budapest. The congress met in the spring at a time of increased anti-Semitism in Hungary, whose first anti-Semitic laws were at that moment being passed by the legislature. Secretary of State Pacelli, in addressing the congress, made reference to Jews "whose lips curse [Christ] and whose hearts reject Him even today" (Herczl 1993, 93). This statement indicates that Pacelli shared the predominant Catholic religious anti-Semitism of the day. But the address must be read in the context of the time, not in the context of the Holocaust.

There is, to conclude, little evidence suggesting that Pope Pius was anti-Semitic and no evidence suggesting that he was vociferously anti-Semite. Furthermore, if such evidence were at hand, one could not conclude from it that Pius acted on anti-Semitic sentiments during the Holocaust.

All this having been said, the major problem with Cornwell's anti-Semitic hypothesis lies elsewhere. The fact is that Pope Pius helped Jews on a number of occasions during the Holocaust, behavior that in Cornwell's mind is unbefitting an anti-Semite. After the war leading international authorities and Holocaust survivors themselves thanked Pius in person for his assistance, a fact that Cornwell barely acknowledged in *Hitler's Pope*.

The enigma of Pius XII is that he sometimes lent his support to Jews during the Holocaust and refrained from doing so at other times. The challenge to the historian is to try to explain this checkered conduct. To provide an account of Pius that ignores either his actions or inactions is to ignore part of the his-

torical record. Several individual cases can help show that concrete circumstances explain why Pope Pius did or did not intervene on behalf of the Jews.

## 3

When Germany invaded Poland, Hitler intended to decimate all Poles. Since
Catholics formed the great majority and led the country culturally and politically, they paid more dearly than Jews during the first years of the war. Poles in
Rome—the Jesuit General Wladimir Ledóchowski, the ambassador Kazimierz
Papée, and the primate August Hlond—urged Pope Pius to condemn the German invasion. He refused but did allow Vatican radio to be used to condemn
the atrocities being perpetrated against the Polish people. At no other time during World War II did the Holy See speak more bluntly: Germany uprooted the
Poles "in the depth of one of Europe's severest winters, on principles and by
methods that can be described only as brutal." Driven from their homes into
the General Gouvernement region, "Jews and Poles are being herded into separate ghettos, hermetically sealed" where they face starvation while Polish grain
is shipped to Germany (Hlond 1941). Thus, at the beginning of the war, Pius
evidently intended to guard the Vatican's neutrality when it came to the political sphere, but to speak out against moral outrages.

The latter policy ended very abruptly just a few months later. Hitler threatened the Vatican with retaliation if the Holy See interfered with Germany's
*Lebensraum* destiny. Hitler's threat implied physical retaliation against the Vatican (Scrivener 1945, 65–66). This threat was followed up by a German request
through diplomatic channels that Vatican radio desist from its criticism. With
that the Vatican suspended its broadcasts, Pius saying that he feared the Holy
See's criticisms would only make matters worse for the Poles. When Polish
church leaders rejected this excuse explicitly, Pius remained silent, but still engaged in resistance activities.

Hoping to rid Germany of the Nazis while keeping the country powerful,
Pius XII shattered the rules of neutrality by acting as an intermediary between
German resistance circles and England. David Alvarez and Robert Graham, S.J.
have brilliantly pointed out in *Nothing Sacred: Nazi Espionage Against the Vatican* how close Pius came to being caught red-handed in this affair (Alvarez and
Graham 1997, 24 ff). What I want to draw attention to here is the violation of
neutrality and the great risk involved.

In the summer of 1943 Pius twice more violated Vatican City's neutrality, first by once again collaborating with German resistance, and second by acting as an intermediary between England and Italy regarding the latter's withdrawal from the war. At the same time as these violations took place, Father Marie-Benoit Peteul of Marseilles pleaded with the pope for his help in rescuing Jews in the Italian-occupied region of France. The situation of the Jews in southeastern France became perilous when the Italian government fell and the Germans established a puppet government anew under Mussolini. No longer did the German foreign office have to negotiate with the Italians over their Jews. A desperate plan was hatched to have the Jews picked up by Italian boats and taken to safety in northern Africa, newly occupied by the Allies. To carry out this plan, the Americans and British would have to give consent, because they now controlled the Mediterranean Sea. Marie-Benoit hoped that the Vatican would allow him to speak to the American and English diplomats to the Holy See to win permission for the planned maritime escape, but the French mendicant was denied permission. Thus, Pope Pius was prepared to violate neutrality in diplomatic matters but not when it came to the Holocaust.

**4**

Pius XII's priorities suffered their severest test when the time came for Germany to seize Italian Jews. This effort began when over a thousand Roman Jews were taken into custody and a few days later shipped off to Auschwitz. Early in the war Pius's highest priority had been the defeat of the Soviet Union and thus the defeat of the threat of Communism. In the latter half of 1942 fear of an Allied aerial bombardment of Rome supplanted Communism as the pope's greatest anxiety. Then, in the summer of 1943 when the Germans occupied Rome, Communism fell back yet another rung, giving place to the Holy See's fears that the Germans would not honor the sovereignty of Vatican City or the person of the pope. At the same time, Pius kept a nervous eye on the activities of local Italian Communists.

Working easily with Ernst von Weizsäcker, Pius moved quickly to solidify the Holy See's relations with Germany. The Nazis, for once, were just as anxious to have cordial relations with the Holy See, and, shortly before the October 16 roundup of Jews, they requested that the Holy See announce publicly that the conduct of German occupation forces in Rome had been correct and civil as far as the Vatican was concerned. On October 19, without having said anything critical about the deportation of more than one thousand Roman Jews, Pope Pius issued the requested "good conduct" letter, and, at the same time, requested that Germany's occupational forces in Rome be enhanced so as to guard against Communist insurgents.

Pope Pius's actions on October 19, 1943, are open to interpretation. Pope Pius XII had three reasons for not protesting the October 1943 roundup of Roman Jews: danger to the remaining Jews in hiding, danger to himself, and danger to the city of Rome. For lack of documentary evidence we do not know which of these weighed most heavily on his mind. We know only that he remained voiceless. He may have refrained from speaking out for fear of jeopardizing the thousands of remaining Roman Jews. Historians speculate whether after the October 16 roundup of Jews Berlin gave a "stop order" regarding their seizure and, if so, whether the pope, using the "good conduct" letter as leverage, involved himself behind the scenes in bringing it about. It is quite clear, nevertheless, that by accommodating the Germans he disposed of two of his most pressing anxieties, Nazis and Roman Communists.

John Cornwell's account of the crisis of the Roman Jews and the pope is vivid but misleading. His narration does not make it clear that several simultaneous considerations and circumstances would have guided Pope Pius during the fall catastrophe. Above all, Cornwell gravely misrepresents the meeting between Secretary of State Cardinal Maglione and the German ambassador Weizsäcker. "Evidently," Cornwell contends, the German ambassador attempted "to persuade the Cardinal Secretary of State to ask Pacelli to protest vigorously against the deportations" (Cornwell 1999, 305). Nothing of the sort occurred, as Owen Chadwick pointed out two decades ago (Chadwick 1977). Rather, Weizsäcker hoped to dissuade the Holy See from making a straightforward protest. The German ambassador probably cautioned the Vatican that such a protest might endanger the remaining Roman Jews who could be subjected to a further more extensive roundup.

5

Did a time ever come when Pius XII seemed willing to intervene on behalf of the Jews? Yes, when, in his eyes, the circumstances were "right," or, in other words, when his other priorities were not in jeopardy or would not be endangered by his intervention. The first occasion came about late in 1943, only a few months after the October disaster. In December Italy's puppet Fascist regime issued a directive to provincial administrators ordering that all Jews be sent to concentration camps. *L'Osservatore Romano* protested and called the order un-Christian and inhuman both with regard to Mosaic and converted "Jews." To expose women, children, the lame, and the elderly to the harsh conditions of a concentration camp was a violation of the laws of God (*L'Osservatore Romano* 1943a). An American nun living in Rome and writing under the pen name of Jane Scrivener had taken no note at all of the Vatican's veiled demur of October 26 about the deportation of Jews, but characterized the December 3 article as a "strong protest" (Scrivener 1945, 65–66).

The following day the Fascist press responded by asserting that Jews were alien foreigners and as such subject to concentration camp detention. *L'Osservatore Romano* did not back off. On December 5 the Vatican paper objected that the Fascists had offered no satisfactory answers to the criticisms the Vatican had earlier made. Why, *L'Osservatore Romano* asked, did Fascists consider Jews born in Italy national enemies and aliens? What legal right did the state have to confiscate their property? Rather, *L'Osservatore Romano* insisted, the Fascists must obey public law, according to which the state lacked the jurisdiction to change the status of an Italian-born citizen. Again the Vatican asserted that in no event should the elderly, women, children, and the ill be subject to detention (*L'Osservatore Romano* 1943b).

Now why would the Vatican protest strongly in December 1943 against a detention order, but not a few months earlier in October when the Jews were not only rounded up and incarcerated, but straightaway shipped off to Auschwitz in boxcars? The explanation lies most likely in the fact that Germany was directly involved in the former incident, but not in the latter.

A subsequent development in the summer of 1944 throws further light on the matter of the Jews and the Vatican. When Jews in northern Italy faced possible "resettlement," the papacy was asked to intervene. Pius, now "eager to co-operate in the endeavor to save Jewish lives," told Myron Taylor, President Roosevelt's envoy to the pope, that he would urge Ambassador Weizsäcker to press his government to desist from further deportations. "The pope declared that neither history nor his conscience would forgive him if he made no effort to save at this psychological juncture further threatened lives" (Michaelis 1978, 395). Why would Pope Pius be "eager" to oppose Germany on behalf of Jews in August 1944, but not in 1943? Why would his conscience bother him in August 1944, but not in October 1943? The explanation lies again in the fact that in

June 1944 the Germans had evacuated Rome and no longer posed a physical threat to the city or to the Vatican itself.

While the pope's reassuring words to envoy Taylor may sound impressive, they should not be overestimated. He was not promising to speak out, after all, but only to speak to the German ambassador about the matter. There is no record in the *Weizsäcker Papiere* that he actually did so. But for the purposes of our analysis it is certain that the pope's conscience came into play only after his major fears were allayed. The Germans had evacuated Rome and the Americans had occupied it without any further significant damage to the city, and the Allied forces replaced the Germans in keeping an eye on local Communists.

## 6

Actually, I very much doubt that Pius XII underwent any basic change in mentality as the war drew to its end. The Second World War had begun with one great danger in Pius's eyes—Communism. As hostilities wound down, Pope Pius continued to view with great alarm the prospect of Soviet power in the middle of Germany, perched on the doorstep of western Europe. Two incidents support this assertion.

In April, 1945 the American and English diplomats Harold Tittman and d'Arcy Osborne, respectively, tried to disabuse Pius of his ideas on the general innocence of Germans for the country's atrocities by submitting photos of the Nazi death camps for him to review. The pictures indicated that not only the SS, but also German "civilians in general found nothing reprehensible about such crimes" (Osborne 1945). Immediately after the war, the Holy See did not oppose the punishment of individuals for war crimes, but Pius shunned the ministers' suggestion that the Holy See send representatives to the concentration camps so that they could judge the breadth of German guilt firsthand. Later, the Holy See would urge clemency for the convicted Holocaust perpetrators.

What bore heavily on the pope's mind became evident later that same year in September. To establish a bulkhead against Communism, Pius proposed to Generals Dwight Eisenhower and Mark Clark the outlandish idea of constructing a Catholic state in central western Europe, consisting of a number of nationalities, including the Germans and Austrians, under a resurrected Hapsburg monarchy. Ever the diplomat, Pope Pius did not have the time to moralize about the Holocaust (Foreign Service 1944–47).

7

A number of years ago Saul Friedlander pointed to some most troubling problems with Pope Pius's concentration on diplomacy. Hundreds of thousands of
Jews were murdered during the period between the battle of Stalingrad and the
end of the war. Regardless, Pius continued to work and to hope for a negotiated
peace that would keep the Soviet Union out of central Europe. How was it con-
ceivable, Friedlander asked, "that at the end of 1943 the pope and the highest
dignitaries of the church were still wishing for victorious resistance by the
Nazis in the east and therefore seemingly accepted by implication the maintenance, however temporary, of the entire nazi extermination machine?" (Friedlander 1964, 237).

Pope Pius's concentration on saving Christianity from Communism and
saving the city of Rome from destruction hindered him from addressing the
evil of genocide. This was a conscious choice on his part, as correspondence between Pius and the bishop of Berlin, Konrad von Preysing, demonstrates. In
1943 the Allies bombed Germany's cities, including the capital, relentlessly.
Writing to his friend of Weimar days, Preysing told Pius that, bad as the bombing was, worse was what was happening to Berlin's Jews. He referred to their deportation and extermination. In reply Pius sympathized with the plight of the
Jews and praised the Berlin canon, Bernhard Lichtenberg, for his prayer-
protests on their behalf. But Pius went on to say that his main duty was not to
do anything that might physically endanger the Eternal City because Christians
everywhere looked upon Rome as the center of Christendom (Pius XII 1944).

In the final analysis the reason that Pius XII did not speak out about the
Holocaust is that speaking out would have played havoc with all three of his
World War II goals. These aims were pursued diplomatically, a craft at which
Pius was adept. Additionally, nothing could be accomplished diplomatically
about the Holocaust, at least as far as the Nazis themselves were concerned.

This explanation of Pope Pius's actions leaves completely open the question of why he did not do more privately and clandestinely for the Jews during
the Holocaust. The answer to this question does not lie in Rolf Hochhuth's
characterization of a compassionless pope or in John Cornwell's accusation of
anti-Semitism, but simply in Pius XII's impaired judgment.

# 8

# Bystander, Resister, Victim

## Dietrich Bonhoeffer's Response to Nazism

STEPHEN R. HAYNES

## 1

IN THE UNITED STATES, interest in "Bonhoeffer and the Jews" has followed a pattern very similar to interest in the Holocaust itself. As Peter Novick argues in *The Holocaust in American Life* (1998), the Holocaust as we have come to know it is a post-1960s cultural phenomenon. Just so, attention to Bonhoeffer the anti-Nazi crusader (as opposed, for example, to Bonhoeffer the progenitor of radical theology) has been the result of steady evolution over the past thirty years. Novick maintains that the Holocaust as a distinct species of Nazi crime did not reach public consciousness until the mid-1960s. Similarly, "Bonhoeffer and the Jews" was barely discernible as a topic in Bonhoeffer studies before this time; conversely, most studies published since then have devoted at least superficial attention to the subject (Hughes 1966).

While it is possible that the cultural factors discussed by Novick are responsible for the relatively recent interest in Bonhoeffer's thinking about Jews and Nazi anti-Semitism, other forces have been at work as well. First, the 1960s saw the initiation of genuine church efforts to grapple with the Christian beliefs and attitudes that made the Holocaust possible. In Germany this process received momentum with the trial of Adolf Eichmann in Israel and the establishment of the "Jews and Christians" committee by the German Evangelical Church Convention. Second, during the 1960s historiography of the German Church Struggle underwent a "revisionist" shift, which subjected the less heroic aspects of the church's career under Nazism to acknowledgment and exploration (Conway 1964).

Third, the English publication of *No Rusty Swords* in 1965—with its inclusion of Bonhoeffer's essay "The Church and the Jewish Question" in a section dealing with "The Aryan Clauses"—made accessible for English-speaking readers Bonhoeffer's earliest reactions to Nazi anti-Semitism. Fourth, the publication of Eberhard Bethge's definitive biography of Bonhoeffer in 1967 provided added momentum for scholarly consideration of this topic. Another factor behind burgeoning interest in Bonhoeffer's stand against Nazi anti-Semitism may have been the Six-Day War and the Jewish struggle for survival that it highlighted. Finally, the emergence of the Jews in Bonhoeffer studies received impetus from published critiques by such Jewish scholars as Stephen S. Schwarzchild (1960). Since the late 1960s, such Jewish interpreters as Stanley Rosenbaum (1981) and Michael Goldberg (1986, 1995) have contributed to the scholarly discussion of Bonhoeffer and the Jews.

Within a few years these forces exercised a profound effect upon students of Bonhoeffer. By 1973, theologian William Jay Peck could make the claim that the Jews were a "decisive" part of Bonhoeffer's theological contribution (Peck 1973). Nonetheless, the abrupt emergence of the Jews in Bonhoeffer scholarship was followed by a painstaking process of analysis and assimilation. Only in 1995, for instance, did Eberhard Bethge acknowledge that the first edition of his biography suffered from "blindness . . . regarding the topic of the Jews" (Bethge 1995a, 30). This confession indicates that celebrating Bonhoeffer's brave stand against Nazi tyranny has not always meant close scrutiny of his record vis-à-vis Jews. In particular, reluctance to grapple with the less savory aspects of Bonhoeffer's theological understanding of the Jewish people has delayed a fully post-Holocaust assessment of Bonhoeffer's personal and theological legacy.

A post-Holocaust perspective on "Bonhoeffer and the Jews" can emerge by reassessing Dietrich's role as resister to Nazi totalitarianism. This reassessment will require not only reading Bonhoeffer's legacy through the lens of the Jews' fate under Hitler, but doing so in light of what the Holocaust teaches about the effects of Christian thinking and behavior on Jewish life. Among the insights at our disposal is a typology utilized by scholars of the Holocaust to classify the varieties of human behavior that made the Shoah possible. This typology will aid us in thinking beyond the dualism of murderous Nazis and innocent Jews by including the categories of bystander, resister, and rescuer.

To classify Bonhoeffer generically using these rubrics need not diminish his singularity (Godsey 1960). In fact, Bonhoeffer's uniqueness is accentuated when we recognize that between 1933 and 1945 he played several different roles, which can help us to understand the Holocaust. Furthermore, Bonhoeffer's story reveals something about the categories themselves. While movement between them could and did occur, it was neither uncomplicated nor decisive. Because the roles of bystander, resister, rescuer, and victim overlap in any faithful recounting of Bonhoeffer's career, his biography elucidates the human complexity of the Nazi era as well as the inadequacy of any behavioral typology that we apply to it.

## 2

When we examine Bonhoeffer's career under Nazi rule, "bystander" is not only the first designation that comes to mind, but the most controversial and the most difficult to document. Nonetheless, Bonhoeffer's role as temporary bystander in the face of Nazi anti-Semitism is one scholars have come increasingly to acknowledge. In a recent article, Kenneth C. Barnes describes Bonhoeffer's initial response to Jewish persecution as "hesitant and tentative, a far cry from the Bonhoeffer of later fame" (Barnes 1999, 112). Even as staunch a defender of Dietrich's reputation as Eberhard Bethge has intimated that during the early years of the Nazi regime he was a "silent bystander" (cf. Zerner 1994). In Bethge's view, Bonhoeffer occupied this role through 1938, because even in the aftermath of Kristallnacht he failed to join courageous Christians such as Julius van Jan, Helmut Gollwitzer, and Karl Immer in speaking out against anti-Jewish violence.

Of course, the designation "bystander" must be applied very carefully. Because he eventually took a decisive stand on behalf of the Nazis' Jewish victims, Bonhoeffer appears in a more favorable post-Holocaust light than the vast majority of his co-religionists. Furthermore, long before he acted on behalf of Jews, Bonhoeffer insightfully analyzed the theological problem that confronted the church in the so-called Aryan paragraph. Almost immediately, he overcame the tendency of Christians in Germany to draw a sharp distinction between baptized and nonbaptized Jews. By September 1933, when he attended a World Alliance conference in Sofia, Bulgaria, Bonhoeffer was expressing the necessity of solidarity with all German Jews, baptized or not (Zerner 1975, 245). Thus, relative to other Christian interpreters of the "Jewish Question" in Nazi Germany, Bonhoeffer stands out for the rapidity of his recognition that the church could not limit its concern to Jewish converts (see Willis 1987, 599–600; and Zerner 1983, 61 ff).

Nevertheless, as the Nazis' anti-Jewish campaign began to unfold in the crucial early months of 1933, Bonhoeffer revealed himself to be more cautious bystander than effective resister. Two pieces of evidence lead us toward this conclusion. The first is Bonhoeffer's decision not to participate in a funeral service for the father of his sister Sabine's husband, who died April 11, 1933. According to Bethge, members of Dietrich's family encouraged him to conduct the funeral for this unbaptized Jew, but he acceded to the wishes of his church superintendent and declined to do so. This decision to distance himself from a Jewish member of his extended family during the first wave of Nazi persecutions is the closest thing in Bonhoeffer's career to classic bystander behavior. Interestingly, this assessment is one Bonhoeffer himself likely would have shared, for in a letter to his brother-in-law written just six months after the event, Bonhoeffer asked: "How could I have been so much afraid at the time? . . . [All] I can do is to ask you to forgive my weakness then. I know now for certain that I ought to have behaved differently" (Bethge 1985, 209). Bonhoeffer's opportunity to atone for his temporary failure of nerve came in 1936 with the passing of his grandmother Julie Tafel Bonhoeffer. At her funeral, Dietrich spoke openly of the woman's deep empathy for German Jews (Zerner 1975, 244).

A second indication of Bonhoeffer's brief identity as a bystander in the Nazi campaign against "non-Aryans" is found in his theological writings during 1933, primarily "The Church and the Jewish Question" (completed on April 15), but also the chapter of "The Bethel Confession" (draft completed August 25) entitled "The Church and the Jews." The former document, which is rightly regarded as a landmark of theologically-based anti-Nazi resistance, openly broaches the prospect of direct action on behalf of the state's victims. According to Bonhoeffer, one possibility for the church's action toward the state in the matter of the Jewish Question

> is not just to bandage the victims under the wheel, but to put a spoke in the wheel itself. Such action would be direct political action, and is only possible and desirable when the church sees the state fail in its function of creating law and order, i.e. when it sees the state unrestrainedly bring about too much or too little law and order. In both these cases it must see the existence of the state, and with it its own existence, threatened. (Bonhoeffer 1965b, 225)

In several respects, however, "The Church and the Jewish Question" lends support to the very bystander posture this passage appears to eschew. First, in focusing on the fate of baptized non-Aryans in the Protestant churches, the tract allows Christians to distance themselves from the majority of German Jews (Gutteridge 1976, 105). This tendency is even clearer in "The Bethel Confession," whose authors assert that "it is the task of the Christians who come from the Gentile world to expose themselves to persecution rather than to surrender, willingly or unwillingly, even in one single respect, their brotherhood with *Jewish Christians* in the church, founded on Word and Sacrament" (Bonhoeffer 1965a, 242, emphasis added).

Second, there is a bystander message implicit in Bonhoeffer's assumption—evident in both "The Church and the Jewish Question" and "The Bethel Confession" section on "The Church and the Jews"—that Christians will naturally perceive Jews' fate through the lens of their rejected Savior. Both documents include passages with which Bonhoeffer's post-Holocaust interpreters have struggled to come to terms and which are crucial for gauging the texts' impact on Christian opinion at the time. For example, at the conclusion of the first section of "The Church and the Jewish Question," Bonhoeffer writes:

*does n't cast a good light on Bonhoeffer!*

Now the measures of the state towards Judaism in addition stand in a quite special context for the church. The church of Christ has never lost sight of the thought that the "chosen people," who nailed the redeemer of the world to the cross, must bear the curse for its action through a long history of suffering . . . But the history of the suffering of this people, loved and punished by God, stands under the sign of the final homecoming of the people of Israel to its God. And this homecoming happens in the conversion of Israel to Christ. . . . From here the Christian church sees the history of the people of Israel with trembling as God's own, free, fearful way with his people. It knows that no nation of the world can be finished with this mysterious people, because God is not yet finished with it. Each new attempt to "solve the Jewish problem" comes to nothing on the saving-historical significance of this people; nevertheless, such attempts must continually be made. This consciousness on the part of the church of the curse that bears down upon this people, raises it far above any cheap moralizing; instead, as it looks at the rejected people, it humbly recognizes itself as a church continually unfaithful to its Lord and looks full of hope to those of the people of Israel who have come home, to those who have come to believe in the one true God in Christ, and knows itself to be bound to them in brotherhood. (Bonhoeffer 1965b, 226)

Alongside this passage from "The Church and the Jewish Question" must be placed the chapter on "The Church and the Jews" from the August 1933 recension of "The Bethel Confession" (Bonhoeffer 1965a, 241–42).

Jews are referred to as murderers. The indictments in both texts do not justify Christian participation in Jewish persecution, but each presents Jewish travail as an integral part of salvation history. "The Bethel Confession" adamantly declares that "no nation can ever be commissioned to avenge on the Jews the murder of Golgotha"; yet its statement that "vengeance is mine says the Lord" encourages Christians to expect that divine vengeance will be manifest in contemporary history (Bonhoeffer 1965a, 241). Similarly, by warning that Christians must "tremble" before Israel's unfolding history, "The Church and the Jewish Question" teaches that Jews will continue to undergo punishment for the crime of deicide.

Both documents, in other words, contain a theological prescription for bystanding. In the German political context of 1933, they could only contribute to an atmosphere in which Christians in Germany who cautiously welcomed the Nazi revolution also assumed the role of bystander. Christians could end up being bystanders when it came to anti-Semitic policies and actions, but could be classified as perpetrators when foreign policy issues, for example, were under consideration. In this sense, the posture toward Jewish suffering assumed in Bonhoeffer's writings from 1933 might best be described as "theological bystanderism"; Christians should expect Jews to suffer in history through a series of punishments instigated by God; yet they were not authorized to participate in executing this punishment. Rather, as they observe God inflicting punishment upon Jews in the historical realm, Christians should maintain fearful humility and participate in quiet self-evaluation.

In terms of social psychology, these sections of Bonhoeffer's writings from 1933 encouraged "just-world thinking," a typical mental habit of bystanders. Bonhoeffer's just-world theology suggests that while Jewish suffering may be tragic, it is to be expected given the Jews' sinful past and God's relentless desire to chasten his chosen people. Of course, the tendency to believe that victims somehow deserve their fate is a natural psychological process. But, as Ervin Staub reminds us, because it is a chief method of devaluing minority groups and making them scapegoats for perceived societal problems, it represents an important step on the path toward genocide. Bystanders, Staub argues, can be moved toward passivity and silence when experts provide them with a definition of reality that normalizes what is going on around them. Such thoughts, in turn, affect behavior (Staub 1989, 18).

Another sense in which Bonhoeffer's writings of 1933 may have encouraged German Protestants in their passivity vis-à-vis Nazi anti-Semitism has been recognized by only a few scholars (Baranowski 1999, 101; Barnes 1999, 115). This is his frequent use of the term *Judenfrage* in "The Church and the Jewish Question." For instance, Bonhoeffer concedes that "without doubt *the Jewish question* is one of the historical problems which our state must deal with, and without doubt the state is justified in adopting new methods here" (Bonhoeffer 1965b, 223, emphasis added). Later, he opines that even if "each new attempt to 'solve the Jewish problem' comes to nothing on the saving-historical significance of this people, such attempts must continually be made" (227).

Because Bonhoeffer did not define or clarify his use of the word *Judenfrage,* we must seek to recover the way this highly charged term would have been understood by his readers. What were the sociopolitical connotations of *Judenfrage* in 1933 Germany? As Paul Lawrence Rose demonstrates, the Jewish Question did not emerge on the stage of German discourse with the Nazi revolution, but had been a pressing concern in German thought since the late eighteenth century. Particularly in the German "revolutionary tradition," Rose maintains, the medieval notion of the Jews as religiously alien was gradually replaced by the conviction that Jewish foreignness could be located in "national character." In the late nineteenth century, this notion of Jewish national character was easily conceptualized in terms of race (Rose 1990). Thus, in the political milieu of 1933 *Judenfrage* connoted both the alien Jew who posed a threat to Germany and the need for concerted action to meet the threat.

As Robert P. Ericksen has shown, for Kittel and other "theologians under Hitler" the *Judenfrage* was intimately tied to a *völkisch* ideology that excluded Jews (Ericksen 1999, 28). Thus, given how little Bonhoeffer and Kittel had in common theologically and politically, it is striking that they relied upon the same language to describe the church's relationship with the Jewish people. Bonhoeffer's hostility to a racial understanding of German Jews and his crusade to oppose adoption of the Aryan paragraph in the Protestant church notwithstanding, he adopted without comment the term favored by pro-Nazi theologians to defend the ideal of an Aryan Christian community. Is this purely coincidence, or is there an invisible continuity in the way these Christian theologians perceived Jews and their fate in the wake of the Nazi revolution? In fact, Bonhoeffer and Kittel appear to share a fundamental theological assumption: As a people uniquely related to God, Jews should behave and believe in certain ways; when they do not, they should expect adversity. At certain points, in fact, Bonhoeffer's analysis of the "Jewish Question" could resemble the Nazis' own. For instance, while "The Bethel Confession" opposes a racial understanding of Jews, it comes dangerously close to endorsing Nazi anti-Semitism when it asserts that no desire for absorption or plan for emigration can remove the Jewish people's "indelible stamp."

Of course, Bonhoeffer's lack of care in invoking the term *Judenfrage* does not prove that he shared the attitudes of Kittel or anyone else toward the fate of Jews. But it did open him to grave misunderstanding in an environment where Nazis and their Christian collaborators also were speaking of the *Judenfrage* as a pressing task of the state, as a social problem that needed to be "solved." In fact, in Bonhoeffer's writings from 1933 the line between bystanding and silent collaboration is often quite thin. Bonhoeffer's use of the highly charged term *Judenfrage,* coupled with his claim that the church exists wherever *Jew* and *German* "stand together under the Word of God" (Bonhoeffer 1965b, 229), gave credence to an anti-Semitic conviction that was widespread during his day, namely, that "Jews" were an alien people whose presence posed a threat to the ethnic Aryans' *Volk.* This message was even clearer in "The Bethel Confession," which stated that God "continues to preserve a 'holy remnant' of Israel after the flesh, which can not be absorbed into another nation by emancipation and assimilation" (Bonhoeffer 1965a, 241). Though clearly intended to oppose the Nazis, this language contained "the very attitudes and prejudices that made the Nazi party successful and the Holocaust possible" (Barnes 1999, 116).

## 3

Clearly, the evidence presented here calls for more serious scholarly consideration of Bonhoeffer's roles as bystander and unwitting collaborator in Nazi anti-Semitism. But it should be noted that his contemporaries fare no better when subjected to similar scrutiny. For example, in his famous Advent sermons of 1933, Cardinal Michael von Faulhaber simultaneously rebuffed Nazi attempts to interfere in the church's life while perpetuating ideas that placed Jews in mortal danger. On one hand, Faulhaber denies the religious significance of racial thinking, reaffirms the Jewishness of Jesus, and defends the sacredness of the Old Testament. On the other hand, he endorses the same expectation of

Jewish suffering that animates Bonhoeffer's early anti-Nazi writings. Furthermore, the cardinal emphasizes that while the church "has stretched forth her protecting hand over the Scriptures of the Old Testament," Christianity does not thereby "become a Jewish religion. These books were not composed by Jews; they are inspired by the Holy Ghost" (Mosse 1966, 258). Faulhaber is especially careful to distinguish between Jews before the appearance of Christ and afterward, when "Israel was dismissed from the service of Revelation" (Mosse 1966, 258).

Faulhaber's views are remarkably reminiscent of Bonhoeffer's mythological description of Jewish travail earlier in 1933. Even when he assumes the relatively sanguine theological outlook of St. Paul, Faulhaber regards Jews *post Christum* as a "mystery," rather than as German citizens who embrace another religion. As has been argued with regard to Bonhoeffer's "The Church and the Jewish Question," Faulhaber's sermons "must be read against the accelerating policy of excluding Jews from German life" (Mosse 1966, 239).

Martin Niemöller, Bonhoeffer's coworker in the German Church Struggle, evinces a similar theological ambivalence toward Jewish fate. Just as Bonhoeffer criticized anti-Jewish sentiments and policies while declaring that the chosen people "must bear the curse for its action [of deicide] through a long history of suffering" (Bonhoeffer 1965b, 226), Niemöller reiterated the church's teaching of contempt for Jews while stressing that "there is no charter which would empower us to supplement God's curse with our hatred" (Niemöller 1938, 195). This excerpt from one of his sermons elucidates Niemöller's perception of Jewish suffering under Nazi rule:

> This is a day [the tenth Sunday after Trinity] which for centuries has been dedicated in the Christian world to the memory of the destruction of Jerusalem and the fate of the Jewish people, and the passage of Scripture provided for this Sunday throws light upon the dark mystery that envelopes the sinister history of this people which can neither live nor die, because it is under a curse which forbids it to do either. We speak of the "Eternal Jew" and conjure up the picture of a restless wanderer who has no home and who cannot find peace . . . [but] we have no license empowering us to supplement God's curse with our hatred. (Gutteridge 1976, 103–4)

This passage is reminiscent of statements by other Christian anti-Nazis during 1933. The term "dark mystery" recalls Faulhaber's Advent sermons, while the "people who can neither live nor die" reminds us of "The Bethel Confession." The difference is that Niemöller's sermon was preached not in 1933, but in 1937.

Thus, the meaning of Bonhoeffer's role as bystander and unwitting collaborator in Nazi anti-Semitism must be clarified by setting it in historical and theological context. During the Nazi era—and after—virtually every German churchman with a public voice was led by ingrained Christian prejudice to speak about Jews in ways that normalized and justified their persecution. If anything sets Bonhoeffer apart from his church contemporaries, it is the conspicuous absence of anti-Jewish rhetoric from his writings after the mid-1930s. By 1938 at the latest, Bonhoeffer recognized the dangers inherent in traditional Christian apprehensions of the Jew. In conversations with his students following Kristallnacht, he is said to have "rejected . . . with extreme sharpness" the notion that the pogrom was a manifestation of an ancient curse on the Jewish people (Bethge 1995b, 62). Thus, before the Holocaust—and before most of his co-religionists—Bonhoeffer recognized that theological apprehensions of the Jewish people possessed the potential to do real harm.

**4**

Even if Bonhoeffer's public statements during 1933 encouraged German Christians to remain passive and silent in the face of Nazism, Dietrich himself could not do so for long. And very naturally Bonhoeffer's roles as resister against Nazism and rescuer of Jews have attracted attention. However, given the paucity of Christian heroes during the Third Reich, perceptions of Bonhoeffer's anti-Nazi activities are susceptible to distortion by myths and romantic projections. Bonhoeffer's enduring popularity is understandably rooted in his bold opposition to Nazi tyranny, which he resisted unto death. But the intimate link in the public imagination between Bonhoeffer and anti-Nazi resistance tends to cast Dietrich in the role of anti-Hitler. If Hitler is the epitome of Evil, then Bonhoeffer becomes a mythic warrior in the service of Good; if Hitler is the consummate anti-Semite, then Bonhoeffer is the philo-Semite par excellence.

Among Christians, Bonhoeffer's celebrated resistance has made him not only a mythic anti-Hitler but a pioneer of post-Holocaust Christianity. In their zeal to remake the church's theology in the shadow of Auschwitz, many Christians have understood Dietrich's martyrdom as a kind of sacrificial death for the redemption of a Christianity corrupted by anti-Judaism. Originally "sacrifice" meant "to render sacred" (Williams 1991, xiii), and in many segments of the Christian world (particularly outside of Germany) this rendering is precisely what has become of Bonhoeffer's legacy (Conway 1982, 45). We must recognize, then, that speaking of Bonhoeffer as a model of resistance to totalitarian rule can reinforce the religious barriers that protect his legacy from vigorous scholarly critique.

We are also likely to underestimate the significance of Bonhoeffer's defiance of National Socialism if we fall prey to the "resistance myth" in which many painful memories of the Nazi era have been repressed. I refer to the popular notions that rebellion against Hitler and the Nazis was widespread, that the majority of Germans were silent victims of Nazi tyranny, that within Germany millions of passive resisters had their activities curtailed by the Nazi police state. From time to time, postwar German culture has been quite receptive to the myth of resistance. In fact, it has even influenced historical scholarship (Koonz 1992, 15). Recognizing the attraction of the resistance myth and the reality it was invented to obscure can illuminate the proper background for understanding Bonhoeffer's role as resister. Given the tendency to project "saints and villains" onto the history of the Third Reich (Giardina 1998), a genuine post-Holocaust portrait of Bonhoeffer will depict his career as resister and rescuer with painstaking accuracy.

## 5

For Bonhoeffer the journey from bystander to resister was quite gradual, as he slowly overcame the elements in his theology that tended toward pacifism and anti-Judaism. His *theological* resistance to the Nazi regime was evident already in the spring of 1933—in his radio address on the "leadership principle" (February), in his essay "The Church and the Jewish Question" (April), and in his work on behalf of the Pastors' Emergency League and Confessing church. Calling this phase in Bonhoeffer's resistance "theological" is not to dispute James Patrick Kelley's claim that "The Church and the Jewish Question" contains a blueprint for what could have been a campaign of serious political resistance by the church. In fact, the image of jamming a spoke in the wheel of state action anticipates Bonhoeffer's own later resistance. But in the early 1930s Dietrich imagined the church as the agent in this sort of resistance.

Bonhoeffer's movement from theological to political resistance was nei-

ther quick nor smooth, but two experiences seem to have been critical in making it possible. First, Dietrich was prepared for direct action during the early
1930s by practicing a "pacifist resistance" that included avoidance of military
service, admonitions against world war, preaching against German rearma-
ment, and working for peace. Second, as he witnessed the Confessing church's
failure to acknowledge the theological either/or he had formulated in the
spring of 1933, Bonhoeffer's faith in theological resistance waned. He left for
London late in 1933, disappointed by his inability to provoke recognition of the
"Jewish Question" at the National Synod meeting in Wittenberg in September.
Upon returning home in 1935, he decided to renew his personal struggle with
the leaders of Germany's Protestant church in the wake of the Nazi Nuremburg
Laws. Bonhoeffer saw the Confessing Synod at Steglitz as one more opportunity to raise the "Jewish Question" in the church. Dietrich was not a delegate to
the synod. He was informed, however, from a reliable source that a resolution
was being drafted on the baptism of Jews that would convey at least an implicit
acceptance of the Nuremberg Laws. He attempted to organize a pressure group
and to encourage a clear statement on the general persecution of the Jews. In
this way he hoped to be "a voice for the voiceless." He felt that this was the occasion when an effective word could and should be said (Gutteridge 1976, 157;
Kelley 1989).

Significantly, it was following the *Bekennende Kirche*'s failure to confront
the issue of Jewish persecution at Steglitz that Bonhoeffer broached with his
students the problem of political resistance (Bethge 1995b, 24). By 1938, when
the Confessing Church's quest for "legalization" led over 85 percent of its members to sign an oath of personal loyalty to the führer, Bonhoeffer had concluded
that there was no longer any hope for effective resistance in the ecclesiastical
realm.

If it is possible to plot a point of no return in Bonhoeffer's progress toward
political resistance, it may have been June 20, 1939—the day he made the fateful decision to return to Germany from New York City, despite the formal offer
of a teaching position at Union Theological Seminary. The crucial importance
of this brief sojourn in New York is suggested by the fact that although Bonhoeffer had already been approached by a group of conspirators, he did not join
them until after his return. Less clear than the timing of Bonhoeffer's determination to enlist in the resistance is its basis. Due to the necessarily private nature of such a decision, it is probably impossible to know just how he arrived at
it. But many Bonhoeffer scholars regard Dietrich's decision to enter the resist-

ance as a long-postponed response to the Nazi persecution of German Jews. This view is supported by personal accounts from those who knew Bonhoeffer and by notations in his Bible following Kristallnacht. Drawing on this evidence, Eberhard Bethge writes that "there is no doubt that Bonhoeffer's primary motivation for entering active political conspiracy was the treatment of the Jews by the Third Reich" (Bethge 1981, 76–77; Peck 1973, 168 ff). Others note that Bonhoeffer's work for the resistance coincided with the heightened persecution of Jews by the Nazi regime. In October 1941 Bonhoeffer collaborated on a report detailing Jewish deportations that was passed to leaders of the Resistance. About the same time, he confessed in his *Ethics* that he was "guilty of cowardly silence at a time when [he] ought to have spoken," and that he had "denied the poorest of his brethren" (Barnes 1999, 124–25).

This is compelling evidence, but it should not be overlooked that the image of Bonhoeffer risking his life in order to save German Jews is sustained in part by the profound need for a hero of Christian conscience in the post-Holocaust world. While the rising tide of Nazi anti-Semitism and the church's failure to stem it were certainly factors in his decision, we may never know exactly what motivated Bonhoeffer to join the German Resistance.

## 6

Bonhoeffer was involved in a number of activities that aided Jewish victims of the Nazi regime. For instance, while in London between 1933 and 1935 Bonhoeffer extended aid to Jewish Christian refugees, and in 1938 he assisted his sister Sabine and her Jewish husband, Gerhard Leibholz, in emigrating to Switzerland (Bosanquet 1968). He also took part in a documented episode of rescue. This was "Operation Seven," a scheme devised by Bonhoeffer's brother-in-law Hans von Dohnanyi and Admiral Canaris of the German *Abwehr*. During August and September of 1942, fourteen German Jews were supplied with false papers and spirited across the border to neutral Switzerland. Bonhoeffer aided the operation by calling on his ecumenical contacts to arrange visas and sponsors for the rescuees (Barnett 1997, 10).

In exploring Bonhoeffer's role as a rescuer of Jews, we face two challenges. On one hand, neither the extent nor impact of his activities should be exaggerated. For instance, many Christians—including some in the Confessing church—engaged in more sustained and more dangerous rescue actions than did Bonhoeffer. Further, Operation Seven was aimed almost exclusively at Jewish-Christians (eleven of fourteen rescuees), prompting the question whether this rescue action "tacitly ... legitimized Nazi efforts against 'real' Jews" (Gushee 1994, 108). Finally, because Holocaust rescue stories can be so compelling, they threaten to distort the context in which they occurred. On the other hand, we should not overlook Dietrich's rescue activities precisely because they have so rarely figured in Bonhoeffer scholarship. This is ironic, because the Nazis themselves regarded Bonhoeffer's role in Operation Seven quite seriously. When the Gestapo arrested him in April 1943, the charge was conspiracy to rescue Jews (Barnett 1997, 10). And despite official reluctance to recognize Bonhoeffer as a "righteous gentile," his actions seem to qualify him for this designation. According to standard definitions, anyone who helped smuggle Jews out of a Nazi-occupied country qualifies as a "rescuer." Similarly, a "righteous gentile" is someone who risked his or her life in a rescue operation, who aided Jews without monetary compensation, and whose deeds can be verified (Oliner and Oliner 1988). Thus, a post-Holocaust perspective on Bonhoeffer will view him in light of the considerable sociological research on rescuers of Jews in Nazi Europe, research that provocatively elucidates Bonhoeffer's decision to become involved in this dangerous game.

From this research has emerged a composite picture of the socialization patterns among persons who later were active rescuers (Gushee 1994). Among the prevalent socializing factors linked to rescue are accepting, affectionate, and communicative parental relationships; child rearing that deemphasizes obedience, avoids gratuitous beating, tends to use reasoning discipline, and does not rely on physical punishment; intense identification with a parent who is a strong moralist; valuing tolerance in childhood; assessing Jews as individuals rather than as members of a group; absence at home of negative stereotypes regarding Jews (but not, interestingly, the presence of positive ones); teaching of values such as "inclusiveness" (or a universal application of moral values), independence, self-reliance, competence, and high self-esteem; and the experience of childhood loss.

Surprisingly, these socialization factors appear to be stronger predictors of rescue behavior than variables such as age, gender, occupation, social class, health, or political affiliation. But socialization alone does not explain altruism. Research indicates that rescue in Nazi Europe was often a function of upbringing combined with favorable situational factors, such as contact with Jewish friends or coworkers and opportunities to take action on behalf of threatened

Jews. While Bonhoeffer cannot be part of a controlled study, he does appear to share many of the *traits* and *experiences* identifiable in other rescuers.

For instance, Bonhoeffer fits the broad socialization profile described in rescue research. He knew childhood loss (an elder brother had been killed in World War I), grew up in an environment of social tolerance and liberal ideas, and developed universalist perceptions while traveling and living outside Germany. As for his family environment, we know that the popular anti-Semitism prevalent in post-World War I Germany was not tolerated in the Bonhoeffer home (Zerner 1975, 239), that his siblings enjoyed close Jewish friendships, and that his family associated "as a matter of course with Jews at the levels of friendship, vocation and education" (Bethge 1981, 50). No doubt the Bonhoeffer children were influenced by the strong moral leadership of their maternal grandmother, Julie Tafel Bonhoeffer, who at age 91 conspicuously violated the boycott of Jewish businesses organized by the SA on April 1, 1933, and, according to one family member, whose "last years were darkened by the distress she felt over the fate of the Jews" (Willis 1987, 600). Kenneth Barnes further elucidates our picture of Bonhoeffer's socialization by noting that Bonhoeffer's Grunewald neighborhood had the highest percentage of Jewish residents of any district in Berlin, a city in which the proportion of Jews was nearly five times greater than in Germany as a whole (Barnes 1999, 110; Rosenbaum 1981, 307). We also know that during his stay in New York City during 1930–31 Bonhoeffer formed a significant friendship with Frank Fisher, an African American seminary student with whom he worshiped and worked in Harlem. During that year, Bonhoeffer developed an interest in black literature and music and was sensitized to racial oppression. Finally, Bonhoeffer gained personal insight on the position of Jews under Nazi rule from his brother-in-law Gerhard Leibholz and his close friend and London roommate Franz Hildebrandt, both of whom were of Jewish origin.

Despite such evidence for the influence of Bonhoeffer's upbringing and formative experiences on his political attitudes, it remains customary to view his path to resistance as an intensely personal affair, the journey of a man bravely struggling to overcome his background. One recent analyst of Dietrich's resistance writes that "at Bonhoeffer's cradle, in his family, in his confessional and national traditions there was no preformed inclination toward resistance" (Mengus 1992, 204). But the significance of Bonhoeffer's socialization cannot be exhausted by observing that his family enjoyed a comfortable social location in Weimar Germany. A more insightful assessment of the role of Bonhoeffer's family in his decision to resist Nazism comes from his "non-Aryan" friend Franz Hildebrandt:

> In the midst of the general capitulation on the part of the German intelligentsia, the Bonhoeffer family, his parents, brothers, sisters and the old grandmother, stood with unclouded vision and unshaken will; their house in Berlin-Grunewald, soon my second home by adoption and grace, was an oasis of freedom, fresh air and good humor. (Zerner 1975, 244; see also Goldberg 1986, 4; and Rasmussen 1990, chapter 1)

This firsthand perspective on the ethos that pervaded the Bonhoeffer home should caution us against concluding that Dietrich had no preparation for rescue or resistance because the Bonhoeffers lacked a tradition of political radicalism. The facts are that Dietrich's extended family brought him both specific *knowledge* of Nazi anti-Jewish measures and the *opportunity* to combat them, which came through his family's contacts with the German resistance. Renate Bonhoeffer, Dietrich's niece, remembers that partly because of Sabine's marriage to Gerhard Leibholz, a law professor at Göttingen, "the Jewish question was the dominant theme in family conversations and with it all other political questions were connected" (Robertson 1989, 122). When these favorable situational factors are combined with our admittedly limited knowledge of Dietrich's childhood socialization, it is difficult to sustain the image of an isolated, lone resister motivated only by personal courage.

To date, the most comprehensive study of rescue during the Holocaust is Samuel P. and Pearl M. Oliner's *The Altruistic Personality: Rescuers of Jews in Nazi Europe* (1988). The Oliners' central conclusion—based on extensive interviews with over two hundred rescuers—challenges scholarly and popular notions of the character "type" most likely to act altruistically in situations of crisis. The paradigm that has reigned virtually since Theodor Adorno's study of the authoritarian personality in 1950 regards autonomy and independence as the traits that make people least susceptible to Fascism and most prone to resistance. Nechama Tec (1986), for example, designated social "marginality" as the chief predictor of rescue behavior. Other researchers have targeted individuality, self-esteem, and separateness as key characteristics of the rescuer personality. Of course, this model of moral courage has inherent attraction, particularly for those affected by the American myth of the lonely and marginal hero.

Eschewing this popular conception of the heroic ideal, the Oliners (1988, 257) have argued for a paradigm shift in our understanding of altruism. In contrast to the perception of rescuers as autonomous, adventurous loners, they have drawn a portrait of community-embedded persons who are led through socialization and experience to empathize with others.

Clearly, this paradigm shift has implications for a post-Holocaust understanding of Bonhoeffer. In popular images of Bonhoeffer the resister and rescuer, the general appeal of the "John Wayne" model of moral courage is combined with the specific attraction of Bonhoeffer the Christian saint and martyr. But these forces can easily distort our picture of the man. It is true that Bonhoeffer's stand on the "Jewish Question" virtually isolated him even in the Confessing church, and that as a result he was compelled, as he put it, "to go for a while into the desert." Yet the exilic existence that circumstances forced upon him should not obscure the fact that from the time of his first public address following Hitler's appointment as chancellor to his fateful involvement in a plot on the führer's life, Bonhoeffer worked in concert with others (Kelley 1989, 81). Nor should we overlook evidence that throughout this period Dietrich received direction, stimulation, and inspiration from family members (Smith and Zimmerman 1966) and friends, from ecumenical contacts abroad, and from participation in a community of resistance. When these aspects of Bonhoeffer's life are kept in view, he begins to resemble other rescuers of Jews, 80 percent of whom in the Oliners' sample expressed a sense of belonging in their communities. The Oliners' substitution of caring empathy for adventurous autonomy as the defining characteristic of the altruistic personality represents a challenge for students of Bonhoeffer. This challenge can be expressed in a series of questions: Has the tendency to link moral courage with independence led us to portray Bonhoeffer as a moral "lone ranger" who discovered the resources to resist political tyranny in the quiet autonomy of his own soul? Has this portrayal led us to ignore the fact that friendship and family were major themes in Bonhoeffer's theology, or that throughout his life he was nurtured by the traditions of church, by ecumenical relationships (Barnett 1995), by his role in a large family, and by his experience as a fraternal twin? Have we obscured these aspects of Bonhoeffer's life through our need to identify a freestanding moral hero untainted by the forces of evil so pervasive in Nazi Germany? The transformation of Bonhoeffer into a kind of "Protestant saint" may itself well be a comment on the paucity of Protestant heroes from the Nazi era. Finally, if Bonhoeffer's career under the Nazis were approached with the assumption that "moral decisions arise as much out of affiliation as through autonomous reasoning" (Oliner and Oliner 1988, 258), how might our image of the man be different? The Oliners conclude their study by noting that the sort of courage displayed by rescuers "is not only the province of the independent and intellectually superior thinkers but . . . is available to all through the virtues of connectedness, commitment, and the quality of relationships developed in ordinary human interactions" (Oliner and Oliner 1988, 260).

## 7

Several interpreters have concluded that, as far as Bonhoeffer's response to Nazism is concerned, his actions were better than his theology (Zerner 1983, 64–65). This conclusion is particularly apt when we consider Bonhoeffer's activities on behalf of Jews in light of his initial theological response to Jewish suffering. And although Bonhoeffer was not alone in combating Nazism with anti-Judaism, it is not enough to call him "the best of the German Gentiles." If we are to arrive at a genuine post-Holocaust perspective on Bonhoeffer's life and legacy, we must give serious consideration to his theological instincts with regard to Jewish suffering. But such consideration is difficult when interpreters of Bonhoeffer vehemently disagree about how the crucial essay "The Church and the Jewish Question" should be read. As Barnes notes, "of all Bonhoeffer's writings, this short essay has been perhaps the most scrutinized, by both his hagiographers, who wish to find in this essay the basis of a strong defense of the Jews, and his detractors, who find the essay anti-Jewish" (Barnes 1999, 114). Barnes explains these varying assessments with the charge that Bonhoeffer "contradicts himself throughout the essay." But more important than a lack of consistency is the essay's deep ambivalence toward Jewish life, an ambivalence rooted in the Christian theological tradition that casts Jews as a divine witness-people.

We encounter reflections on the witness-people tradition in "The Church and the Jewish Question." The first reflection on the witness-people tradition is its *language:* An aura of mythic unreality surrounds Bonhoeffer's description of the "chosen people," a personified theological abstraction (Zerner 1975, 240) whose meaning is to be gauged solely on this people's "saving-historical significance." Second, the passage's *style* sets it off from the rest of the tract, which is characterized by precise and sequential argumentation. Third, the passage evinces a paradoxical *structure:* The reprobationist and preservationist dimensions of witness-people theology that reach in parallel lines back to Augustine are juxtaposed in Bonhoeffer's description of "this people, loved and punished by God" (Haynes 1995, chapter 1). Jews are God's chosen, but murdered God's Messiah and suffer under a divine curse as a result; they are scattered and insecure, but will be brought home by their God. Finally, this paradoxical presentation of Jewish destiny resonates with an *ambivalence* toward Jews that is a leitmotif of the witness-people tradition. This ambivalence is represented by the crucial "but" that functions as a verbal hinge.

Bonhoeffer's reliance on these time-tested ideas is understandable when we recall that the essay was composed in hasty response to the first wave of Nazi anti-Jewish persecutions, particularly the state-organized boycott of Jewish businesses on April 1, 1933. As Eberhard Bethge notes, "in this situation of crisis [Bonhoeffer] searched about, more spontaneously than carefully, for a means of quick reaction, unprepared as he was for the rapidly escalating pressures on all sides" (Bethge 1981, 63). In this moment of acute social chaos, Bonhoeffer plumbed the depths of the Christian imagination in order to comprehend the mystery of Jewish existence. As he strained to comprehend God's way with the Jew, he followed the lead of Christian thinkers since St. Paul (and including Luther, who Germanized the witness-people myth and transmitted its ambivalence into the German anti-Semitic tradition), invoking notions that had been relied upon for centuries to explain the travail of Jews and to assure Christians that their suffering was a mysterious sign of God's providence. Not surprisingly, in the wake of Kristallnacht these ideas were repeated in the discussions of Bonhoeffer's own seminary students (Bethge 1981, 74–75; Zerner 1975, 245).

Nearly every scholar who has written on "Bonhoeffer and the Jews" recognizes that this section of "The Church and the Jewish Question" is crucial for gauging Bonhoeffer's post-Holocaust stature. But some have too quickly labeled Bonhoeffer's words "anti-Semitic" (Barnes 1999, 114, 116), while others, aware that this tract is deeply embarrassing to his reputation as a friend of the Jews, have hastily excused or downplayed them. One scholar dismisses the passage in question as "medieval," with no further explanation. Another characterizes Bonhoeffer's invocation of the "curse that bears down on this people" as "unfortunate" (Robertson 1967a). One scholar contends that it is "definitely not the central theme of the paper" (Bethge 1970); another argues that it is "overshadowed" (Willis 1987) by other elements in the text. Some interpreters attempt to blunt the passage's force by noting that similar formulations are absent in Bonhoeffer's later writings; others by assigning it to an early "phase of Bonhoeffer's developing attitude toward the Jews" (Peck 1973, 167), or by reminding us that these words were intended as a warning to the church. One interpreter acknowledges that "The Church and the Jewish Question" contains "all the ingredients of traditional Christian Anti-Semitism," but avers that these are "morally . . . neutralized" by Bonhoeffer's discussion of unjust state actions (Willis 1987, 605, 607). Yet another scholar sanguinely perceives in the tract "at least some first hints of a less exclusively anti-Semitic understanding of the relationship between the church and Israel" (Kelley 1989, 87).

Diverse as these interpretive glosses are, each encourages us to view witness-people theology as an excrescence of Bonhoeffer's argument in "The Church and the Jewish Question." However, none of these authors offers good reasons for doing so, and they ignore the evidence that this passage is pivotal to Bonhoeffer's thinking about the "Jewish Question" and its implications for the church. Further, the passage is destined to influence how the essay is understood, since the mythic themes it strikes possess an unconscious emotional power for the Christian reader. The passage's resonance in the Christian imagination simply will not allow it to be submerged or displaced by other parts of the essay. Rather, it threatens to distort the way Christian ears hear the rest of Bonhoeffer's argument. The authorial voice may speak in favor of the rights of Jews, but for the Christian reader this voice is neutralized by mythological speculation on the divine necessity of Jewish suffering. Thus, to refer to Bonhoeffer's theological outburst as a series of lamentable "views" or "statements" ignores the unconscious level at which such ideas are communicated.

For all these reasons, we must face the fact that this famous passage at the heart of "The Church and the Jewish Question" cannot be improved by scholarly spin-control. Rather, a post-Holocaust perspective on Bonhoeffer will regard it as compelling evidence of Bonhoeffer's brief role as theological bystander and unwitting collaborator with Nazi _Judenhass._

# 9

# Supersessionism Without Contempt

## The Holocaust Evangelism of Corrie ten Boom

LAWRENCE BARON

1

WITH THE POSSIBLE EXCEPTIONS of Dietrich Bonhoeffer, Oskar Schindler, and Raoul Wallenberg, Corrie ten Boom (1892-1983) is probably the best known "righteous gentile" of the Holocaust. *The Hiding Place,* her account of how her family helped Jews in wartime Holland and then themselves experienced betrayal and internment in German concentration camps, has sold over four and one-half million copies (ten Boom 1971, 1996). Although it was originally published thirty years ago, it continues to outsell every book about the rescue of Jews in Europe during the Second World War except for Anne Frank's *The Diary of a Young Girl* (Frank 1953) and Lois Lowry's *Number the Stars,* a children's book about the rescue of Jews in Denmark (Lowry 1989).

The book's spiritual message about how Corrie ten Boom maintained her faith in Jesus despite the deaths of her father and sister in captivity has made *The Hiding Place* a perennial favorite among Evangelical Christians. In 1997 it became the only Holocaust memoir ever to make the top 10 list of best-selling Christian books in the United States (Gamble 1997, 51–53). *The Hiding Place* also inspired a popular feature film of the same title produced and distributed by Billy Graham's World Wide Pictures in 1975 (Graham 1997, 513–14) and a comic book directed at children (Hartley 1973). Amazon.com currently carries seventy-eight books and audio tapes by or about Corrie ten Boom. Many of the biographies about Corrie ten Boom are aimed at juvenile audiences and present her as a role model of Christian faith and moral courage for today's youth (Benge and Benge 1999; Baez 1989; Watson 1982; White 1983). Another gauge of ten Boom's continuing influence can be found on the 128 Internet websites relating her life and writings to contemporary ethical, political, and religious issues.

In sharp contrast to her fame among Evangelical Christians, Corrie ten Boom has received relatively scant attention in the scholarly literature about gentile rescuers of Jews during the Holocaust (Rittner et al. 2000, 169). Mordecai Paldiel, the director of Yad Vashem's Department of Righteous Gentiles, does not mention her in the hundreds of biographical sketches of rescuers that he compiled for his book *The Path of the Righteous* (Paldiel 1993). He tellingly does include a paragraph about ten Boom in *Sheltering the Jews,* which was published by a Lutheran press (Paldiel 1996, 169). Of the major studies of rescuers of Jews, only David Gushee's *The Righteous Gentiles of the Holocaust: A Christian Interpretation* engages in any analysis of Corrie ten Boom's religious motives for saving Jews (Gushee 1994, 121–24, 143–44, 171). Otherwise, there have been only a few scholarly articles in English that have taken ten Boom's theology seriously (Ariel 1991, 63–78; Baron 1993, 143–48; Blumenthal 1985, 80–88).

The obvious reason for the discrepancy between ten Boom's positive reception among Evangelical Christians and the neglect of her among Holocaust scholars is the unabashed Christian proselytism that was the driving purpose behind her writings and ministry. Much of the scholarship concerning the reaction of European Christians to the Holocaust has focused on the anti-Semitic legacy of the "teaching of contempt" as evidenced in the history of traditional Christian beliefs, policies, and writings concerning Jews and Judaism. At the core of this teaching stands the doctrine of Christian supersessionism, which claims that the covenant with the Gentiles enacted through the crucifixion of Jesus superseded the Israelite covenant with God. Since Judaism allegedly had degenerated into Pharisaic legalism and temple ritualism, the Jews as a people failed to recognize Jesus as the Messiah predicted by their own prophets and therefore conspired with the Romans in his arrest and execution. The subsequent exile and suffering of the Jews were interpreted as Divine punishments that would cease only with their acceptance of Jesus as the Messiah for whom they were waiting (Bratton 1969; Cohn-Sherbok 1992; Gager 1983; Hay 1950; Isaac 1964; Littell 1975; Parkes 1934; Ruether 1972; Williamson 1982).

Consequently, many post-Holocaust Christian and Jewish thinkers have advocated that Christianity renounce the doctrine of supersessionism and missionary campaigns to convert Jews. As the late Catholic thinker Harry James Cargas put it, "Attempts by Christians to convert Jews to their faith must not only be abandoned but also discouraged by the preachers in their churches. Behind every missionary attempt is the usually unstated belief that we have the total truth: you have almost none" (Cargas 1996, 48–49). Rabbi Eliezer Berkovits rejected post-Holocaust Christian-Jewish dialogue by declaring that "one does not enter into a dialogue when one is convinced from the beginning that one is in possession of all the truth and one's partner in the dialogue is in error (Berkovits 1973, 44–46)."

## 2

In this regard Corrie ten Boom came from a family that actively had proselytized Jews. In 1844 her grandfather Willem ten Boom had started a fellowship group that prayed for the Jews, whom he called "God's ancient people" (ten Boom 1976, 15). When her father, Casper ten Boom, ran a shop in the Jewish quarter of Amsterdam, he studied the Torah and Talmud with his Jewish friends and tried to explain to them "the fulfillment of the prophesies of the Old Testament in the New Testament" (ten Boom 1976, 18; ten Boom 1978b, 133). After Casper relocated his store to Haarlem, he still made business trips to Amsterdam, where his encounters with Jewish wholesalers usually evolved into religious debates, with everybody, according to Corrie, "arguing, comparing, interrupting, contradicting—reveling in each other's company" (ten Boom 1971 29–30). Corrie's brother, Willem ten Boom, headed the Dutch Reformed Church's Mission to the Jews. Yet as far she knew, he had never converted a Jew (ten Boom 1971, 20).

Although the ten Booms encouraged the Jews who found refuge in their home to observe Jewish holidays (ten Boom 1971, 112–13), they regularly held Bible study groups with their guests that sometimes led to sharp disagreements over how to interpret scriptural passages:

> It began with a Bible study conducted by Willem ten Boom. Eusi criticized his Christian interpretation of Old Testament texts and offered different interpretations current in Talmudic and general Jewish tradition. Given the circumstances, it was inevitable that both sides would feel frustrated. When the Bible study was finished we went upstairs to the boys' room and Eusi sulked. 'See what I mean,' he said. 'Haven't I said this all along. This shows how

dependent we are on Christian charity. We can't even stand up at such teaching and walk out of the room without appearing discourteous.'(Poley 1993, 76)

Yet conversion was never a precondition for the shelter the ten Boom family gave to these Jews. A member of the Resistance hidden by the ten Booms reported that they respected the convictions of the people they hid and "never abused the integrity of their guests by attempting to convert them." According to him, "They had many animated discussions to be sure, but they considered their daily life to be sufficient example of their faith in Christ" (Poley 1993, 26; Carlson 1983, 80–81).

What is striking about Corrie's supersessionist beliefs is that they are not predicated on a denigration of Judaism or Jewry. The most anti-Judaic statement I have found in her writings is a quotation from a speech by a converted Jew named Da Costa who had influenced her grandfather. It reads: "It is true that Israel missed God's target and was, for a time, set aside and dispersed among the nations. But the day will come when they will fall at the feet of their Messiah in true repentance and live!" (ten Boom 1978a, 32) The most negative passage about Jews she met during her internment occurs in her prison letters. She refers to a Jewish woman with whom she shared a prison cell: "I have told her in detail about the redeeming death of the Savior. She does not accept it. Although she does pray, it is without life. She has no awareness of sin and spends her time reminiscing about all the wealth she had accrued and reproaching herself for not having managed things differently. She is bitter and dwells upon every unkindness of the guards" (ten Boom 1975, 35).

More typical of ten Boom's views on the relationship of Jews to Jesus is the following reply she made to a Jewish boy who told her that as a Jew he could never believe in Jesus:

Then you do not understand that with the Jew (Jesus) in your heart—you are a double Jew. . . . On the divine side He was God's Son. On the human side He was a Jew. When you accept Him, you do not become a Gentile. You become even more Jewish than before. You will be a completed Jew. (ten Boom 1978b, 186)

Of course, this reply implies that Jews are incomplete without Jesus. Before being offended by this viewpoint, we should keep in mind that Corrie ten

Boom believed that every person, regardless of religious or racial origin, was a lost soul if he or she did not consciously feel the Holy Spirit touch their lives and acknowledge Jesus as his or her personal savior. She never targeted Jews per se for proselytization. Her postwar missionary work was devoted to preaching to people throughout the world, particularly atheists in Communist countries and non-Christians in Third World countries in Africa and Asia (ten Boom 1978b, 63–131, 145–77).

Indeed, expressions of philo-Semitism recur far more frequently than anti-Semitic ones in ten Boom's works. She recalls her father often telling her that "love for the Jews" had been "spoon-fed" to him as a child by her grandfather (ten Boom 1978a, 32–33). The ten Boom family sympathized with the early attempts of Zionist settlers to establish a Jewish state in Palestine because the ingathering of the Jews served as a sign of the Second Coming of Christ (Carlson 1983, 23). Her brother Willem had attended a seminary in Germany from 1927 until 1930 and wrote his dissertation on the disturbing rise of racial anti-Semitism during the Weimar Republic. In the following decade, he raised money to build a nursing home for elderly Jews that increasingly became a sanctuary for Jews of all ages fleeing persecution in Germany (ten Boom 1971, 19–20; ten Boom 1976, 89). After Germany invaded the Netherlands, Corrie and her father witnessed a roundup of Jews that prompted Casper to remark, "I pity the poor Germans, Corrie. They have touched the apple of God's eye" (ten Boom 1971, 68).

Aware that her brother had been hiding Jews in his own house and at the nursing home since the beginning of the German occupation, Corrie and the rest of her family soon followed his example. The rabbi of Haarlem entrusted Casper with his collection of Judaica books for the duration of the war. In November 1941 Corrie and her sister Betsie shepherded a Jewish furrier away from a Gestapo raid on his shop and arranged for him to meet his wife safely in Amsterdam. Corrie started to make pickups and deliveries for her father's Jewish customers. As she got to know them better, she feared for their safety and made this pledge: "Lord Jesus, I offer myself for Your people. In any way. Any place. Any time" (ten Boom 1971, 68–73). In late May 1942, when a Jewish woman sought refuge in the ten Boom house, Casper assured her, "In this household, God's people are always welcome" (ten Boom 1971, 76–77). From this first rescue to their betrayal and arrest in February 1944, the ten Booms helped approximately eighty Jews to go into hiding (Moore 1997, 179). Responding to a pastor who refused to hide a Jewish baby, Casper summed up his family's commitment to the Jews with this rebuke: "You say we could lose our lives for this child. I would consider that the greatest honor that could come to my family" (ten Boom 1971, 93–95).

## 3

The ten Booms adhered to a distinctive strain of Dutch Calvinism that had retained an acute sense of Christianity's spiritual and genealogical kinship with Judaism and the Jews. Calvinism generally has held a "more benevolent attitude towards Jews owing to its higher view of the Hebrew Bible and the place of the Law in Christian life" (Williamson 1982, 102–3). David Gushee observes that although Calvin believed that the Jews must seek redemption in Jesus Christ, he also preached that God's election "remains with the Jewish people even as the Gentiles are adopted into the covenant" (Gushee 1994, 122–25). Dutch Calvinists had a long tradition of identifying with biblical Israel because both considered themselves "chosen" nations commanded to order their societies according to God's laws as revealed in the Bible (Groenheis 1981, 118–33). Under the German occupation, the most fundamentalist Calvinist denominations, which constituted only 8 percent of the Dutch population, accounted for 25 percent of the rescues of Jews in the Netherlands (Moore 1997, 162–67). Even though a quarter of the Orthodox Calvinist rescuers interviewed for Sam and Pearl Oliner's book *The Altruistic Personality* expressed anti-Semitic sentiments, they nevertheless privileged the philo-Semitic elements of their tradition when Jews were in harm's way (Baron 1995; Oliner and Oliner 1988).

Corrie ten Boom's family belonged to the Evangelical wing of the mainstream Dutch Reformed Church, and their views of Jews closely resembled those of the schismatic fundamentalist Calvinist denominations in the Netherlands. When asked by a reporter from the *Jerusalem Post* why she loved the Jews, Corrie characteristically replied:

> There are three reasons. First I have to thank you Jews for two great blessings in my life, a book, bursting with good news: the Tanach, the Old Testament, and the fulfillment of the Tanach, the New Testament, written by Jews. Only Luke was not a Jew, but converted by a Jew. Second, my greatest friend and Savior, who is my security and joy in all circumstances, was a Jew. . . . The love for you Jews is in my blood since my grand-father prayed for the peace of Jerusalem. (Carlson 1983, 176)

David Gushee has noted that for some fundamentalist Christians like the ten Booms, "saving Jews constituted a kind of intra-group rescue" because they considered Jews "a special kind of religious kin, fellow believers in the God of Abraham and Sarah, Isaac and Rebekah, Jakob, Leah, and Rachel—brothers and sisters in faith" (Gushee 1994, 121–24). Jacobus Schoneveld has traced the origins of such sentiments in Dutch Calvinism to its relatively "favorable attitude towards the Mosaic Law" and its emphasis on "the concept of covenant," which replicated the Jewish model of the "collective and communal aspects" of political and religious life. He recognizes that this philo-Semitism often co-existed with Christian triumphalism and evangelism (Schoeneveld 1989, 337–39).

Ten Boom's Christianization of the Holocaust has limited the appeal of her story among scholars of the Shoah in particular and Jewish audiences in general. Just as she understood her decision to help Jews as a test of her Christian morality, she perceived her internment in Scheveningen, Vught, and Ravensbrück as a crucible to test her faith. As David Blumenthal has asserted, for Corrie, "to live in the camps, then, is to see one's own life as a Passion" (Blumenthal 1985, 85). Corrie and her sister Betsie achieved serenity by finding "heaven in the midst of hell" (ten Boom 1978b, 28). This blessing in disguise manifested itself as the opportunity to preach to inmates who either had lost their faith or never believed in Jesus at all. Corrie felt that bringing the Gospel to her fellow prisoners was the divine reason for her imprisonment in the concentration camps:

> Yet in the German camp, with all its horror, I found many prisoners who had never heard of Jesus Christ. If God had not used my sister Betsie and me to bring them to Him, they would never have heard of Him. . . . They were worth all our suffering. (ten Boom 1978b, 11–12)

In one of her prison letters, ten Boom penned her most often quoted passage about how she found God by not succumbing to despair in the camps: "I was certain of one thing—that Jesus would never leave us nor forsake us and that for a Child of God, no pit could be so deep that Jesus was not deeper still" (ten Boom 1975, 10). Blumenthal attributes Corrie's ability to maintain her faith to the circumstances of her incarceration. She truly was a martyr for her actions and convictions, unlike the millions of European Jews who were imprisoned and murdered because of their ancestry (Blumenthal 1985, 87–88).

Moreover, Corrie regarded her wartime experiences as foreshadowing "a time of tribulation" when all Christians would be persecuted by the Antichrist (ten Boom 1975, 185–90).

It is equally difficult for Holocaust scholars to share Corrie ten Boom's willingness to forgive her Nazi captors. After her release from Ravensbrück, she wrote to the man who had betrayed her family:

> The harm you planned was turned into good for me by God. I came nearer to Him. A severe punishment is awaiting you. I have prayed for you, that the Lord may accept you if you will repent. I have forgiven you everything. God will also forgive you everything, if you ask him. (ten Boom 1975, 81)

In the dramatic concluding passage of *The Hiding Place,* Corrie describes her meeting with a former guard from Ravensbrück. He thanked her for preaching that God would wash away his sins and offered his hand to her in a gesture of reconciliation. Corrie struggled with her blind hatred for this man who had tormented both her and her sister, but then she finally called on Jesus to give her the strength to shake the man's hand and forgive him. She drew the following lesson from this incident: "And so I discovered that it is not on our forgiveness any more than on our goodness that the world's healing hinges, but on His. When He tells us to love our enemies, He gives, along with the command, the love itself" (ten Boom 1971, 215).

David Blumenthal contrasts this Christian doctrine of forgiveness with the Jewish imperative to seek earthly justice: "The Jew is commanded to be angry at the injustice of human to human, to seek to rectify it, never to forgive it" (Blumenthal 1985, 88). The gist of Blumenthal's remark is reflected in Simon Wiesenthal's *The Sunflower.* In this book, a Jewish concentration camp inmate is called to the deathbed of an SS man who confessed that he sincerely regretted the atrocities he had committed and wanted to be forgiven by a Jew before he died. The Jewish inmate decided to withhold forgiveness because he felt that he could not serve as a proxy for the many Jews who had been killed by the SS man. This viewpoint is echoed by most of the Jewish respondents who offer their opinions in the symposium section of *The Sunflower* on what the appropriate response of the inmate should have been, whereas many of the Christians contributors to the symposium understand forgiveness as a divine virtue relieving the forgiver of bitterness rather than exonerating the sinner for the crimes he had committed. As Father Theodore Hesburgh puts it, "If asked to

forgive, by anyone for anything, I would forgive because God would forgive"
(Wiesenthal 1997, 163–64).

This binary opposition between the Jewish and Christian concepts of forgiveness overly simplifies the beliefs of both groups on this issue. Between Rosh
Hashanah and Yom Kippur, observant Jews are obligated to seek forgiveness
from those they have wronged during the year and to expect their supplications
for forgiveness to be granted, if they have truly atoned for their sins and would
not commit such sins again if faced with the same situation (Teluskin 1994,
345–355; Klein 1997). Of course, an individual Jew cannot forgive German war
criminals for their crimes against other Jews. Jewish outrage over the Holocaust hardly constitutes the totality of Jewish ethics and faith (Goldberg 1995)
and obscures the role forgiveness plays in Judaism.

Corrie ten Boom's evolution from a victim hating her victimizers to a
saintly figure forgiving their transgressions went through several stages. As her
letter to the man who betrayed her family indicated, she fully expected the secular courts to mete out "severe punishment" to him even if his misdeeds were
forgiven (ten Boom 1975, 81). She believed that the Christian ideal of forgiveness highlighted the injustices men were capable of committing against each
other by providing a sharp contrast between human vengeance and divine
mercy:

> I saw the faults of the German people and the horrors of present regimes
> more clearly, and felt them more keenly, perhaps, than many others. I suffered
> daily their effects on my person. I had never before so learned to know the
> Lord Jesus as a tender loving Friend, who never forsakes us or casts us off
> when we are bad, but rather helps us to gain the mastery over sin. (ten Boom
> 1954, 154)

She did not want the Holocaust to be forgotten. Otherwise why would she
have written *The Hiding Place* and spent her ministry bearing witness to what
happened to the Jews in Holland and to her family for helping them? In 1959
she visited Ravensbrück to pay homage to the memory of the 96,000 women
who perished there along with her sister (ten Boom 1971, 219).

Yet as ten Boom's career as an evangelical motivational speaker and writer
burgeoned, her concept of forgiveness sometimes overshadowed her commitment to memory. She recalled keeping the letters of former friends who had
taken advantage of her as reminders of the wrongs they had done even though

she claimed she had forgiven them. Then she realized that she was deluding herself if she preserved the evidence of their misbehaviors. After burning their letters, she comments, "The forgiveness of Jesus not only takes away our sins, it makes them as if they had never been" (ten Boom 1978b, 181–83). In this passage ten Boom's ideal of Christian forgiveness could easily be misused to justify forgetting the Holocaust. In countries guilty of implementing or abetting policies of genocide, Christian tropes of forgiveness reinforce denial or forgetfulness (von Kellenbach n.d.).

## 4

What is good for an individual's peace of mind may not be good for society as a whole. Harvard law professor Martha Minow has enumerated a variety of responses to help overcome the personal and collective bitterness engendered by genocide and widespread atrocities: forgiveness can help heal the individual's soul; historians and fact-finding commissions establish what happened; monuments, museums, and memorial services prevent the events from being forgotten; trials punish the perpetrators; and reparations compensate, if only financially and symbolically, for the damage that has been done (Minow 1998).

It is instructive to compare ten Boom's reaction to Nazi anti-Semitism to that of other Christian contemporaries who condemned anti-Semitism. In 1938 Pope Pius XI commissioned several Catholic theologians to draft a denunciation of Nazi anti-Semitism. Although it was not published until recently, the so-called "Hidden Encyclical" reveals that these theologians were still ensconced in the teaching of contempt about Jews even as they criticized

While Corrie ten Boom's evangelical fervor strikes me as politically incorrect following the losses sustained by Jews in the Holocaust, it has taught me that it is reductionist to equate Christian supersessionism with anti-Semitism. When she visited Israel in the 1960s, Corrie was saddened "to find that many Jews equated Christianity with Hitlerism" (Carlson 1983, 175). Yet it was precisely Corrie's immersion in biblical texts that enabled her to appreciate the filial relationship of Christianity and Christians to Judaism and Jews. She never perceived the Jews as a people whose sins merited either eternal damnation or constant missionary work. She warned her co-religionists about ever presuming that "What a sad mistake we sometimes make when we think that God cares only about Christians. . . . Although God desires that all people become Christians, he does not love one group more than another" (ten Boom 1978b, 110).

It is instructive to compare ten Boom's reaction to Nazi anti-Semitism to that of other Christian contemporaries who condemned anti-Semitism. In 1938 Pope Pius XI commissioned several Catholic theologians to draft a denunciation of Nazi anti-Semitism. Although it was not published until recently, the so-called "Hidden Encyclical" reveals that these theologians were still ensconced in the teaching of contempt about Jews even as they criticized the numerous human rights abuses the Germans had committed against the Jewish people. Thus, they accused the Jews of putting the Savior to death "in collusion with the pagan authorities," of being "blinded by a vision of material domination and gain," and of having "called down upon their own heads a Divine malediction, doomed, as it were, to perpetually wander over the face of the earth," but "never allowed to perish." They warned against the "spiritual dangers" of contact with Jews whose "hatred of the Christian religion had driven" some of them "to ally themselves with, or actively promote revolutionary movements that aim to destroy society and to obliterate from the minds of men the knowledge, reverence, and love of God." The draft reiterated the traditional Christian and modern stereotypes of Jews while rejecting persecution as a means to defend Christian values against Jewish religious and secular sins (Passelecq and Suchecky 1997, 246–59).

Corrie ten Boom's benevolent, albeit supersessionist, stance toward the Jews and Judaism more closely resembles that of the Jehovah's Witnesses. As an evangelical group, the Witnesses tried to convert all nonbelievers, including Jews, before the Second Coming of Christ (Weiss 1996, 313). The Witnesses felt a spiritual kinship toward the Jews as the People of the Old Testament even though the Gospels implicated Jewish leaders in the killing of Christ. The Witnesses believed that Christ died for mankind's sins and that there was no retroactive Jewish guilt associated with the Crucifixion. In 1940 their German newspaper *Das Goldene Zeitalter* stated unequivocally that "the present generation of Jews is in no way responsible for whatever the Pharisees and others committed nineteen hundred years ago" (Chu and Liebster n.d., 18). The Witnesses supported the Zionist movement for eschatological reasons and opposed all forms of racism because they believed in the equality of all human beings as God's creation (Garbe 1998, 1–2). The Witnesses, like Corrie ten Boom, regarded Hitler as a demonic leader whose doctrines had to be challenged in defense of basic Christian principles (Helmreich 1979, 392–97).

Corrie ten Boom and the Witnesses should serve as reminders that Jews can dialogue even with those who seek their conversion as long as they do so with friendly persuasion and acts of compassion rather than with rancor and recrimination against a people presumed guilty of deicide and satanic plots. To be sure, there are Evangelical Christians who are certain that "God does not hear Jewish prayers" or that the anti-Christ will be a Jew. Christian evangelicals can cite literal interpretations from the New Testament to vilify the Jews and Judaism. A recent poll of people who identify themselves as members of the Christian Right indicates that approximately one-third of them disagree with the statement that Jews remain God's Chosen People compared to almost two-thirds of Gentiles who do not identify themselves as members of the Christian Right. At the same time, almost 20 percent of the former concur with the charge that Jews are guilty of killing Christ compared to less than 10 percent of the latter (Smith 1999, 250–52).

Yet one sees Corrie ten Boom's living legacy in figures like Billy Graham, who has refrained from participating in Evangelical campaigns that specifically target Jews (Graham 1997, 417–21), or Douglas Young, who declares on his website *Bridges for Peace* that the "root cause of anti-Semitism is satanic and anti-God" and counsels Christians to "rise up and speak up on behalf of Israel and the Jewish people" (Young 1997). In a recent editorial, Richard Mouw of the Fuller Theological Seminary remarked that "Corrie ten Boom looms large in my gallery of special saints" because "she was willing to risk her life to work for the physical safety (of Jews), even if those efforts did not afford opportunities to lead them to Christ." Mouw is particularly sensitive to the shadow that the Shoah has cast on Christian-Jewish relations and frankly admits:

> We must also learn about the suffering of the Jewish people. Evangelicals need to think more deeply about what it means to Evangelize Jews after the Holocaust. Much has happened in Jewish-Christian relations since the New Testament was written. The Christian record during that two thousand years of history is not an admirable one. Indeed, Christians have committed atrocious deeds against Jews. We cannot simply quote Paul—who wrote when the church was a minority religion struggling to clarify both continuities and differences with a Jewish majority—without recognizing that we do so from this side of Auschwitz. . . . None of this cancels our obligation to evangelize, but it does highlight an obligation to avoid unnecessary offense and to understand the challenges we face. (Mouw 1997, 12–13)

Why should Jews take an Evangelist like Corrie ten Boom seriously? David Gushee provides a convincing reason for doing so in his study of religiously motivated Christian rescuers of Jews when he concludes: "Given the desperate importance of neighbor-love in a world full of suffering and needy neighbors, all paths that *genuinely lead Christians in love's direction* should be accorded legitimacy and warmly welcomed" (Gushee 1994, 172; see also Rausch 1984, 1991, 1993).

# 10

# Irene Harand's Campaign Against Nazi Anti-Semitism in Vienna, 1933—1938

## The Catholic Context

GERSHON GREENBERG

*For Joshua Haberman, with gratitude*

## 1

THE OUTSPOKEN OPPONENT of Nazism and anti-Semitism Irene Harand (1900–1975), awarded the Righteous Gentile award in 1968 by Yad Vashem, expressed her views in monographs, in articles, and in public lectures locally, where her audiences were sprinkled with Nazis poised for violent confrontation, and across Europe. She founded the Harandbewegung: Weltverband gegen Rassenhass with conferences and offices in central and Eastern Europe. Some Nazis alleged that she was financed by Jews and allied with Jewish-financed Catholics opposed to *Volk* and *Führer,* and complained that *Sein Kampf* defamed Nazi Germany and the graced führer while falsely accusing Nazis of inciting war and mass murder. Hans Schopper degraded her as the "*armen irren* Irene Harand," traced her support to a Jew by the name of "Wolf," and ridiculed her attempt to be the "apostle of understanding between Jews and Christians" (1941, 27; Correspondence held by U.S. Holocaust Memorial Museum Archives).

According to her religious weltanschauung (ideology), the anti-Semitism represented by the swastika was irreconcilable with Christianity's Jewish origins, its cross, and its absolute principle of love-of-neighbor (*Nächstenliebe*). She rejected those Catholics who advocated raw triumphalism and undermined *Nächstenliebe* for groundless and false racial, economic, and national-chauvinistic concerns. She drew support from those with humanistic concerns, with appreciation for the character and contribution of scriptural Judaism, and with commitment to principles of justice and morality. In doing so, however, she turned her eyes from their own coexisting commitments to Christian missionizing, triumphalism, and Catholic-Nazi cooperation.

Harand received a secular education, but was raised a Catholic by her Roman Catholic father and Lutheran mother and was married in a Catholic ceremony. Her opposition to anti-Semitism followed a meeting with a Jewish attorney of Vienna, Moritz Zalman, then representing an impoverished Catholic nobleman pro bono in proceedings against his son at a time when Viennese Jews were hated because of their race and religion. Following a parade of Nazi youths in Vienna shouting *Juda verrecke!* they founded the Oesterreichische Volkspartei to move the Christian Social Party (CSP), founded by Dr. Karl Lueger and then led by Dr. Ignaz Seipel, toward Christian ideals. The CSP advocated a nonracial form of anti-Semitism, whereby Austrians could protect themselves from pernicious Jewish influences by segregating Jews into a minority entity with its own schools, doctors, and judicial system (Körber 1939, 265–69; Schopper 1941; Reichschrifttumskammer 1935 and 1938; Haag 1981).

In March 1933 Harand published *So? Oder So? Die Wahrheit über den Antisemitismus: 3. Flugschrift der Oesterreichischen Volkspartei,* a twenty-three-page treatise opposed to Austrian hatred of Jews. She rejected defamatory lies about the Talmud in the writings of Rohling and his advocates and praised the objections raised by the likes of Delitzsch. She denounced the *Protocols of the Elders of Zion:* "If someone wants to undermine the commandment of *Nächstenliebe* by inciting hatred and contempt, then for God's sake the least they can do is not come up with such lies"—and accusations that Jews were Bolsheviks, capitalists, Marxists, and Freemasons; that they were cowards during World War I and criminals. She also attacked German racism. The text enumerates Jewish contributions to medicine, science, art, and literature. Some 100,000 copies were printed, many of which she distributed personally outside the Vienna opera house (Harand 1933; Rohling 1872 and 1883; Delitzsch 1881, 1883a, and 1883b).

In reaction to Streicher's periodical *Der Stürmer,* Harand published *Gerechtigkeit: Gegen Rassenhass und Menschennot,* from September 6, 1933, to

March 10, 1938. With the message that anti-Semitism violated Christian morality and that the pagan movement of Nazism had to be stopped lest it destroy European civilization, it was translated into French, Czech, and Hungarian and distributed as well in Scandinavia, Poland, Yugoslavia, Romania; it had 28,000 subscribers. At this time she replaced the Oesterreichische Volkspartei with the Weltverband gegen Rassenhass und Menschennot. In 1935 Harand lectured in Denmark, Norway, and Sweden as well as helped establish support groups in Warsaw, Riga, Helsinki, Geneva, and Zurich.

In 1936 she published the 348-page *Sein Kampf: Antwort an Hitler* (completed June 1935), to convince Christians of the dishonesty of Nazi teachings and to explain the dangers of German National Socialism while assuring the swastika's victims that some people would not acquiesce to the Third Reich's terror, but would struggle until the victims were redeemed from their suffering. Expanding upon *So? Oder So?,* Harand discredited lies about Jewish usury and the Talmud's alleged contempt for non-Jews. Toward the end of 1936 she traveled to New York to enlist Jewish and Protestant support. Her contacts in the Protestant world included John Haynes Holmes (minister of the Community Church, New York), the American Christian Committee for German Refugees (led by Harry Emerson Fosdick), the Emergency Committee in Aid of Political Refugees from Nazism—to whom she wrote that once anti-Semitism destroyed Jews it would go after other groups, and was liable to be more damaging to Christians than to Jews—and Edward Russell of the Palestine Federation of America. Her Jewish contacts included the B'nai B'rith, the American Jewish Committee, and the Anti-Defamation League—which distributed *Sein Kampf* to American libraries during the war. Harand and her husband were in London during the *Anschluss* in 1938. In June 1938 they emigrated to New York via Canada (Hausner 1974; Haag 1981; Pauley 1987 and 1992).

## 2

To Harand, two mutually exclusive mindsets had defined themselves in Europe, one symbolized by the cross, the other by the swastika. The cross symbolized a readiness for self-sacrifice for the sake of one's fellow man, made possible by Christ's love for his fellow man. The four-hooked, vicious symbol of the swastika meant the rise to power in Germany based upon lies, hatred, and the release of bestial instincts. Having gained power, the swastika elevated deceit to the rank of a guiding principle (Hausner 1974, 116–19, 302–3). In "Heilige Arbeit," an unpublished lecture-text that the RSHA (Reichssicherheitshauptamt) eventually seized, Harand spoke of the Nazis' relentless lies to a public tolerant of an endless repetition of lies but not of truths. Violating Jesus' paradigmatic truthfulness in the prophetic tradition (Zechariah 9:16–17), they promulgated mythic falsehoods about blood-division between peoples, about Aryan blood flowing in some veins and Jewish in others, as well as about capitalizing on centuries of anti-Semitism and destructive instincts. The blood of the Jewish people, expressed with lamentations, was useless; the blood of the Aryan alone, expressed in iron will, had value. Worse, Nazi lies became narcotics against wounds from which the world was bleeding to death, and which needed desperately to be treated. Against them, Harand wrote, one must be ready to shed one's own blood (*"Heilige Arbeit"*). In a second unpublished text, "Junge Menschen-Unsere Zukunft," Harand condemned Aryan discrimination against others. Were there, she asked, even ten youths without hatred left among the Hitler Jugend and Bund deutscher Mädel, to save the generation as once ten righteous would have spared Sodom from God's wrath? (*"Junge Menschen"*).

The swastika replaced the centrality of the human soul and spirit with that of blood and racial origin. It denied human love and justice, regarded compassion and tolerance as weaknesses unworthy of Aryans, and validated criminal acts in the drive to dominate. It diverted the mind from seeking proper solutions to socioeconomic world problems to focusing instead on cruel and bloody confrontations. Further, it promoted an ideology of violent means to salvation, as embodied by the millennial Third Reich with its total domination of individual words and deeds. Finally, it preached a myth of blood and soil, whereby only the pure and noble Aryan race had a right to life and the Jews were to be exterminated. To secure *Lebensraum,* other nations would be conquered violently, oppressed, and exterminated by the Germans.

The swastika, for Harand, constituted a pagan religion with its own pope, apostles, rituals, pilgrimages, and holy scriptures. Its leader was an idol adored by his cult, for whom his word was absolute law. It stood for barbarism and decline against culture and progress; for violence, injustice, robbery, and bloodshed against love. While the realm of Catholic Christianity was of Christ's word, the mystery of spirit and blood, and the divinization of the Son of Man, that of the anti-Christ was of the creed of the swastika, the blood of the Aryan nation, and the divinization of the führer. In the first the individual could possibly realize himself spiritually and transcend himself into the realm of divine experience; in the second the human soul and its freedom, conscience, and quest for perfection were dominated (Hausner 1974, 116–19, 302–3).

**3**

It followed from the divided universe that Catholicism had to oppose anti-Semitism for the sake of its Christian identity. The *Gerechtigkeit* masthead proclaimed in bold letters: "I fight against anti-Semitism, because it disgraces our Christianity." Harand told Oscar Leonard of B'nai B'rith during her New York visit, "I am fighting not so much in behalf of the Jews, as to save Christians from becoming beasts" (Leonard 1937).

Beyond the cosmic either/or, there was the particular fact that Jesus was Jewish. The assault against the Jew was a sin against Christ, for insofar as He presented himself as a human being, He was a Jew as were the first apostles. Jesus was as much a Semite as Moses, and no Aryan. She cited the pope's August 1933 observation (transmitted by the Central News Agency) that not only was Jesus Jewish, but that He bound Himself to the Old Testament (Matthew 5:17). She estimated that the Old Testament was cited countless times in the New Testament, and observed that Catholic priests recited the Psalms. The Old Testament seeped into Catholic ritual. The eucharist originated with the bread and wine that Melchisedec brought to Abraham (Genesis 14:18) and the sacrificial intent of the binding of Isaac (*Akeidah*); liturgy included scriptural references (*"Es ist ein Ros entsprungen."* [Isaiah 35:1]). Wedding ceremonies included the phrase *"Es segne Euch der Gott Abraham, Isaak, und Jakobs."* To attack the Old Testament was to attack Christianity—as indeed did happen with Alfred Rosenberg's *Myth of the Twentieth Century.*

Harand invoked against *Der Mythus des XX. Jahrhunderts* the "Christian commandment to love the Jew" (Matthew 6:43–44). All humans shared a common spiritual identity, making racial and physical characteristics irrelevant. The fact that a Jew attended a temple rather than a church, venerated prophets rather than saints, did not change the fact that he or she was to be treated as a human being just as any Christian. There was no greater satisfaction for the soul than surrendering one's own needs for those of the other, and the greater the sacrifice, the greater the soul's reward. In Germany, however, youth were being trained for egoism, that is, to worship heredity (*Stamme*) and blood, and to choke off any feeling for the distress of the other. Everything was to be sacrificed to the idol of power. The feelings of compassion and sacrifice-for-the-other were regarded as absurd weaknesses to be abandoned in the name of becoming a willful and free German. Nazi Germany's values rejected *Nächstenliebe* (Güdemann 1890) and replaced it with the fear and terror of concentration camps, leaving Jews without civil rights and forcing them to become beggars. Harand warned that if the National Socialist Party became as powerful as intended and conquered others it would apply its treatment of Jews and Catholics as worthless to all those who did not blindly subject themselves. In essence, not to follow Jesus' preaching of *Nächstenliebe,* to separate external behavior from inner piety and religious awe, was to deny His religion. Not to oppose anti-Semitism in the name of *Nächstenliebe* was to abandon one's Christianity (Harand 1933, 2, 14–15; 1935e, 13, 34–35, 74, 79–80, 303–5; 1935c, 1936g, 1936h, 1936i).

In this vein, a writer for *Gerechtigkeit* cited the nineteenth-century Catholic prayer included in Joseph S. Bloch's refutation of the Catholic theologian from Munich, August Rohling, which condemned Christian oppressors who glorified in Israel's misery as a testimony to Jesus' triumph. For Jesus taught that all men were brothers, and instead of gloating over Jewish suffering, Christians should seek to ease it. The prayer declared:

> My God, I have learned from Jesus that all men are brothers. Therefore I will honor the human nature and human rights which we all share. The [Jews'] misery and civil oppression will inspire me to console them and alleviate their suffering. By sharing in their destiny, I will share in their recovery from the terrible blow of the ancient destruction. (Alwe 1936; Bloch 1922, 609–10; Brunner 1804, 236)

Harand criticized earlier Catholic writers who supported anti-Semitism and thereby compromised their Christianity. Rohling falsely accused Jews of violating the principle of *Nächstenliebe.* His *Der Talmudjude* (1872), drawing from Johannes Eisenmenger's discredited *Entdecktes Judentum* (1711), alleged that Jews considered themselves part of the divine substance and Christians as idolaters unworthy of *Nächstenliebe.* In 1883 Rohling alleged that Jews were obliged by their religion to exploit non-Jews, even ruin their lives, honor, and property. He had Catholic defenders, but was properly opposed by such Christian scholars as Delitzsch and such Jewish scholars as Löwy (1882), and ended up disgraced. Drawing from the rabbinical sources cited by Bloch (1922) and

Kopp (1886), Harand observed that Jewish alienation, expressed not toward Christians but to other non-Jews, never meant that non-Jews were to be treated dishonestly. She was offended by the fact that Rohling's *Der Talmudjude* continued to be taken seriously. There were, indeed, seventeen editions published as of 1922. In *Zur Wiener Judenfrage* (1936) Georg Glockemeier drew from it to allege that Jews regarded unborn non-Jews as animals, all non-Jews as thieves, murderers, and prone to incest, and the Jewish oath to a Christian as not binding. It followed for Glockemeier—in the spirit of Streicher's *Der Stürmer*—that the cleft created by Jews between themselves and the rest of the world, racial-religious in nature, was deeper even than the cleft of blood drawn by Germans. Jewish influence therefore had to be blocked off, and Jews confined to a minority sphere (Rohling 1872 and 1883; Ecker 1921; Kopp 1886; Delitzsch 1881, 1883a, 1883b; Bloch 1922; Gugenheimer 1883; Lewin 1884; Schubert 1977; Harand 1936h; Glockemeier 1936; Pauley 1992, 213–14; Heer 1970, 272).

Jesuit Father Georg Bichlmair directed the Paulus Werke (Opus Sancti Pauli), founded in 1934 in Vienna to promote Jewish-Christian understanding and to convert Jews. Its nominal head was Theodor Cardinal Innitzer, Archbishop of Vienna; and its journal, *Die Erfüllung* (The Fulfillment—that is, the Christian fulfillment of Judaism) was edited by the converted Jew Johannes M. Oesterreicher. Paulus Werke was dissolved in 1938 by the Gestapo, and Bichlmair was arrested by the Nazis on November 10, 1939, for his work on the Hilfsstelle der Caritas für nichtarische Christen (or "K" movement, named after the social worker Manuela Kalmansegg), a society for the relief and education, professional training, and emigration of non-Aryan (that is, Jewish-born) Christians under the personal protection of Innitzer.

Upon the occasion of its moving to new offices on February 13, 1936, Bichlmair, in response to Cardinal Innitzer's invocation, declared: "At a time when racial hatred and idolatry of race are celebrating their triumph, it is valuable to emphasize that we, who draw from Austria's ancient culture which adhered to Christ's admonition that all humans are one, take a different standpoint." On March 18, 1936, he addressed Katholische Aktion of Vienna on "Der Christ und der Jude." The interest in the lecture was so great, Harand reported, that it was repeated the next day, because the CSP's *Reichspost* (which subsequently published it) advertised it as an anti-Semitic presentation, and anti-Semitism was now fashionable. Bichlmair explained that the Jewish question was originally a religious matter, then a social and legal issue, and now a national and *völkische* problem. Although some Jews contended that they were not a particular entity (*Volksgemeinschaft, Nation,* or *Rasse*) because they had neither common language nor culture, others (Zionists and Orthodox) believed they were, because for Christians and Germans the Jews were an entity. Originally, he explained, Jews were selected by God for the religious reasons of their pure belief in Him and His morality, rather than for racial or biological traits or national character. But since they were chosen to serve as the instrument to prepare for the Redeemer, when they crucified their Messiah they lost their religious edge. They became a spiritually void, homeless corpse carrying itself amidst the nations, whose sole value was to witness the terrible mistake. Israel was left a racial-biological entity, alienated from the spiritual dimension that was its raison d'être. Only baptism and entry into the mystical Christ and the visible church could displace the terrible legacy with pure religious spirit. Given the danger of such an entity, Jews had to be removed from public positions of responsibility. Bichlmair distinguished self-defense against a dangerous *Volk,* a moral obligation of the Christian German, from racial hatred, even as he identified Jews as a *Rasse* with inherited traits that needed to be cordoned off. This self-defense did not violate *Nächstenliebe,* which did not require a Christian to surrender his rights or compromise his obligation of self-love. The Christian's right to protect himself was the primary issue (*Rechtsfrage*) (Bichlmair 1936a and 1936b; Zeller 1936; Weinzierl 1969).

Harand caught the ambiguity and the hypocrisy. In February Bichlmair said that Nazi racial laws were ethically untenable, and in March he described the racial-national character of the Jews as dangerous for Christians. She also rejected his definition of the Jewish question as a *Rechtsfrage* rather than one of *Nächstenliebe.* Harand did not consider the Jews dangerous, but even if they were, for her *Nächstenliebe* was to be absolute. She disapproved of Bichlmair's bringing up Jewish guilt for the crucifixion, so typical of Catholic anti-Semites; the fact remained that the Roman governor arranged it and his soldiers carried it out. Harand also cited Bichlmair's earlier "Christen und Juden," in which he himself criticized Christians for not recognizing the positive contribution Jews made as the chosen means of granting the world the Savior and for stressing the ridiculous and burdensome elements of the Talmud, but ignoring its religious and ethical context. In his March address, he was doing just that himself. She referred to a summer 1933 papal declaration that German persecution of the Jews reflected an incapacity for civilized behavior, that Jesus, His mother, her family, and the apostles were of Jewish heritage, and that Christians had no basis to claim superiority over the Jews (Harand 1936c, 1936e, 1936g; Editor 1936; Heer 1970; Pauley 1992, 150–74).

Bichlmair's views were reprinted by Staatsrat Leopold Kunschak, leader of the Christian Social Worker's Association, in its *Mitteilungen des Freiheitsbundes*. In his own address three days earlier to the Freiheitsbund: Wehrorganization der christlicher Arbeiterschaft he declared himself not a racial but a social anti-Semite with disrespect for the assimilationist but respect for the believing Jew. He regarded Jewish presence as destructive and sought its removal. The Jewish question would have to be resolved, if not in a timely way, rationally and humanely, then in an untimely way, irrationally and animalistically. To Harand, Kunschak was evidence of the need for Christians to promote *Nächstenliebe* (Harand 1936f; Pauley 1992, 121, 158–59; Reimann 1967, 242–48; Blenk 1960).

In May 1936 Harand responded to *Kampf der Jugend für Sozialreform* by "Pugnator," published by the Sozialen Arbeiterkreis des Reichsbundes der katholischen Jugend Oesterreichs. Following Glockemeier and Kunschak, Pugnator accused Jews of being motivated by usury, dishonesty, and ambition, and of threatening to destroy Christian-German/Austrian societal and economic life. Echoing Bangha and Bichlmair, Pugnator invoked the theme of self-defense against the principle of *Nächstenliebe*, alleging that Christian-German Austrians had to protect themselves because the Jews were encircling them: "Does it contradict *Nächstenliebe* for me to oppose my opposer?" He added that this reaction would come directly from the Austrians and not via the Third Reich. One did not have to seek out a blacksmith, he said, if one were a blacksmith oneself. Harand responded by saying that if a blacksmith were being sought, then the church's should be found in the pope, who in March 1928 had condemned anti-Semitism for its hatred of God's chosen people. Or Pugnator should turn to the words of Innitzer and Faulhaber, or to the pages of the Catholic periodical *Sturm über Oesterreich*, which opposed making racial doctrine into a pillar of Austrian political ideology as was so for the Third Reich (Harand 1936g; Pugnator 1936a).

In essence, Harand objected to the view of Bichlmair and Pugnator, that *Nächstenliebe* ought to be subject to matters of the Austrian Christians' rights and protection. For her *Nächstenliebe* was an absolute category. Moreover she did not accept the fact that the Jews were a threat, never having accepted the triumphalist position that Christianity succeeded Judaism, that Judaism had to surrender, and that, having failed to do so, Judaism was spoiled.

**4**

Other Catholic figures were also a source of support for Harand. The Austrian noblemen Heinrich Johann Maria Graf von Coudenhove-Kalergi and his son Richard Nikolaus were the founders of the Paneuropa movement in Vienna, seeking a united Europe. Harand cited the elder's *Das Wesen des Antisemitismus* to refute *Mein Kampf*. In *So? Oder So?* she rejected allegations about Jewish cowardice by suggesting that Jewish suffering and martyrdom for the sake of mankind resembled Christ's, drawing from his historical data. In *Sein Kampf* she refuted accusations that Jews had no sense of ideals or sacrifice. In the face of persecution, they remained faithful to their ancestral creed. They chose instead to suffer contempt, ghetto imprisonment, the Jew-badge, restriction of civil rights, poverty, torment, torture, and, ultimately, painful death. Citing *Das Wesen*, she said that while it would have been wise to cling to faith within and embrace Christianity formally, only some did. Their steadfastness, as Coudenhove-Kalergi wrote, contained great heroism—"such a supernatural, divine greatness, such a majesty of character, that I cannot help bowing low to those martyrs with reverence and unbounded admiration; and exclaiming, instead of 'Jew, Jew, hep, hep, hep': 'Judah, Judah, hip, hip, hurrah' " (Harand 1933, 10–12; Harand 1935e, 129–31; Coudenhove-Kalergi 1932, 165–66, 175–76, 199; Coudenhove-Kalergi 1935).

Bela S. (or P. Adelbert) Bangha was educated at the University of Innsbruck, joined the Jesuits in 1895, served as general secretary of the Marianischen Kongregationen der Gesellschaft Jesu in Rome, and then moved to Budapest, where he published *Magyar Kultura*. Harand (1935e) cited his passage in "Katholizismus und Judentum" (1934) about boycotts against Jews. Such "injustice and harsh oppression of an entire people, including the innocent, is absolutely irreconcilable with Christian conscience. An un-Christian resolution of the Jewish question is of itself already an impossible resolution" (Bangha 1934, 76).

Harand did not bring forward the less than pious context for Bangha's statement. His view about Judaism's post-crucifixion role in history anticipated Bichlmair's triumphalism—as well as Hudal's and Oesterreicher's. By rejecting Christ, Bangha felt, Jews rejected the most beautiful treasure of their religious doctrine, namely the authentic belief in the Messiah. Christians had made great spiritual strides in education and institutions and not because of any racial superiority. Jews, burdened by their ancestors' neglect, however, had become morally inferior. By their heredity, Jews lacked the fullness of supernatural light that the Gospel poured down upon Christians. "Anyone who looks with pride upon the inborn ethical inferiority of the Jews should quietly ask himself: If I were born a Jew, would my ethics be any better? Might I indeed not be worse than the worst Jew?" (1934, 53). A boycott was indeed desirable "to essentially repel the dominance of the Jewish spirit and its influence on spiritual and economic life as well as for Christians to be more conscious than before of protecting their religious, ethical and maternal value" (1934, 76). But a boycott would be impotent because so many Christians were co-opted by Jewish views and even rejected anti-Semitism, and because Jews had so much control of the world economy and, through that, of a large part of politics, press, and cultural life (Harand 1936h; Hovorka 1936; Bangha 1934, 9–125; Heer 1970, 338–39).

When Archbishop of Vienna Theodor Cardinal Innitzer was rector of the University of Vienna he stopped assaults upon Jewish students by threatening to close the university for a year. In "Die sozialen Verhältnisse in Palästina zur Zeit Jesu Christi" in 1932, cited by Harand (Harand 1936c; 1935e, 87), he refuted the claim that Jews were by heredity incapable of manual labor, justifying denigration of their civil status. Ancient Jews lived from agriculture and cattle breeding, and at the time of Jesus they practiced varied modes of manual labor. Jesus Himself was a carpenter. In the July 1934 inaugural issue, he wrote that *Die Erfüllung's* goal was to mediate between Jews and Christians in terms of the religious perspective about Jewish existence, to serve the peace that came from God. At the February 13, 1936, ceremony of the Paulus Werkes, he stated that the movement's aim was to quell racial hatred and idolatry by returning to the ancient Austrian way of following Christ's admonition to treat all people, including Jews, as human beings.

Harand sent Innitzer a copy of *Sein Kampf* soon after publication. In a handwritten note of September 9, 1935, he thanked her for the "interesting and informative" work, and expressed "infinite sadness" about the conditions in the Third Reich described therein. For example, Harand wrote of the "unspeakable torments and humiliations" against German Jewry, "achieved primarily through the incitement of the instinct of hatred against the Jews," and of how the swastika "does not even recoil from mass murder, when it worked to secure the positions it achieved" (1935e, 5). Innitzer asked, "When will it become different?" Without explaining, he said he wanted to write more but could not. He did say that the book's last paragraph—"The swastika constitutes a great danger for mankind. It is the greatest danger of the twentieth century. If we wish to deal with it, we must use those weapons which are strange to it: Idealism and the courage to sacrifice, reason and love, truth and *Gerechtigkeit*"—should become a rallying cry for all non-Nazis. He closed by asking Harand not to publicize his note.

Harand did not deal with the fact that for Innitzer the Catholics had to work constructively with National Socialism to avoid tragedy. Indeed, on March 18, 1938, three days after meeting with Hitler, Innitzer would declare his support for the *Anschluss* (Harand 1935e, 86–91, and 1936c; Körber 1939, 269; Hudal 1976, 136n; Pauley 1992, 298–300; Reimann 1967; Heer 1970; Weinzierl 1985, 95–112).

Harand praised Archbishop of Munich Michael Cardinal Faulhaber for his "deep moral religiosity" and "admirable courage in these, the hardest days of his life." She cited a pulpit sermon three times, in which he stated that when he had stepped forth against racial hatred, people wanted to stone him, and his life was in great danger (1935e, 18–19, 67–68, 305; 1936b and 1936g). On January 4, 1934, he had rejected the importance of blood relationships in the name of the spiritual faith distinct to the New Testament (Galatians 3:28).

Harand also cited Faulhaber's Advent sermon (1934) in which he declared that anyone who sought to diminish Judaism by claiming that the Old Testament was not divine revelation would have then to agree that, given the quality of scripture, the Jews who produced it had to be the most gifted race in history. She contrasted Faulhaber with the Protestant Swiss theologian Adolf Schlatter, who was out to raise the stature of the *Bekenntniskirche* in Hitler's eyes by accusing Jews of trying to frustrate public Christian life and by suggesting that Jews should be grateful to the Nazis for giving them ghettos. A truthful man, Faulhaber knew that one served Christ not by stoning Jews but by helping them—which is why, Harand observed, the Nazis hated him.

Harand did not cite the 1936 sermon in which Faulhaber hailed Pope Pius XI's friendship with the Third Reich—and attacked a German newspaper which, on January 1, 1936, published the "spiteful falsehood" that the pope was half Jewish because his mother was a Dutch Jewess. "Such a lie is clearly calculated to expose the Pope to mockery in Germany." According to Theodore S. Hamerow, Faulhaber was conflicted between Christian universalism and denominational self-interest, between transcendental faith and religious expediency. On the one side, Faulhaber spoke of the fact that before Christ's death the people of Israel had been the bearers of revelation. The Old Testament was sacred, its words inspired by God's spirit, its contents the building stones of God's kingdom. In a letter to the New Testament scholar Alois Wurm he condemned government anti-Semitism as "so un-Christian that every Christian, not only every priest, would have to stand up against it," and he wrote Professor Theodor Steinbüchel in Giessen that "we cannot deny [Jews] every right in the German fatherland without destroying the foundation in natural law of our own love of the fatherland." On the other, in public declarations he distinguished pre-Christian Old Testament Judaism and post-Christian Jewish issues of politics and morality. The church, he said, did not oppose German efforts "to keep the special character of a people as pure as possible" or "to deepen the sense of a people's community through reference to its community of blood" (Faulhaber 1934; Heer 1970, 272–369; Hamerow 1997).

Austrian Bishop Alois Hudal served as rector of the German national church in Rome, Santa Maria dell'Anima. Harand pointed out that as Bichlmair spoke on March 18, 1936, against the Jews, Hudal stated that the stream of Judaism contributed a metaphysical sense, a spiritual horizon expressed in Psalms and Prophets, to the Christian religion of spirit. The Jews were the first recipients of revelation, and their revealed Old Testament prepared the way for Christ. To tear the Old Testament away from the New, he observed, would leave the Christian Gospel a "bloodless utopia" (1936, 94–123). Hudal sought to remove blood from the debate. He rejected Rosenberg's view that religious truth had a biological and racial basis. Religious truth was spiritual, and did not change according to blood. Christianity sought to bring all races to the single Christ and a single moral consciousness, a supernatural *Blutsgemeinschaft,* that is, a community in which blood was sublimated into spirit. When he told the pope that the title of his forthcoming *Die geistigen Grundlagen des National Sozialismus* was suggested by Giovanni Gentile's *Grundlagen des Fascismus* (1936), the pope responded, "That's your first mistake. There's nothing of spirit in this movement. It's massive materialism." Hudal sought the triumph of supernatural religion over racial naturalism and materialism; the Christian community of faith allowed for no Aryan paragraph (1935; 1936). He told the pope that if Nazism were enlightened religiously it could respond to the threat of nihilism coming from eastern Europe. The ideas of nationalism and socialism were inherently good, but had to be injected with

Christianity lest they end up as wild barbarism, pitiless state-collectivism that tyrannized the masses, and with a Caesar-type leader who dominated all the parties. When Hitler received a copy of *Die Grundlagen* he expressed the hope that the relationship between Nazism and the Catholic church would improve in the future, although Hudal's proposed compromise of confining racial teaching to the biological-racial sphere and leaving it out of a spiritual-cultural environment was rejected by the Nazis. The two strains coexisted, because Hudal's appreciation for Judaism was tied to its being sublimated into and transcended by Christian spirituality. Accordingly, he criticized Judaism for not comprehending that its value lay in preparing the way for Christianity. Because of that failure, once their state ended Jews had no place and became a wandering source of disquiet among the nations. Thus, he regarded Rohling as an outstanding scholar of Jewish history—who had the misfortune of being before his time in struggling against the Talmudic representation of Christianity and dominance by Judaism. He also supported Austria's need to protect itself from Jewish influence and advocated confining it. In the end, the Bichlmair whom Harand attacked and the Hudal whom she praised had much in common (Harand 1936c and 1936d; Volk 1978, 193; Liebmann 1988a and 1988b; Hudal 1935; 1936, 74; 1976, 118, 137, 159).

5

Thus, in her quest for support Harand was prepared to selectively highlight some statements and to leave others in the shadow. In the case of Bangha, when Jews turned from Christ they became morally inferior. He advocated a boycott against them to confine their influence and withdrew only because it was not realistic. Harand avoided his triumphalism. She praised Innitzer for his opposition to the swastika and its destructive impact, but avoided his readiness to find a way to cooperate with and support Fatherland-nationalism. She praised Faulhaber's stance against racial hatred in the name of spiritual Christianity and his appreciation for the Old Testament, but overlooked his appreciation for the purity of the German blood community and his readiness to support cooperation between the Catholic church and Nazism. She appreciated Hudal's rejection of blood-based religion in the name of spirituality, but avoided the triumphalism and intent to confine Jewish influence as well as Hudal's interest in finding a way to cooperate with Nazism, even if on Christianity's terms. Overall, Harand took signs of antiracism and appreciation for Hebrew scripture and lifted them out of the respective contexts: Christian spiritual triumphalism, efforts to confine Jewish influence, and commitments to cooperation between Catholicism and National Socialism. The absence of contextual debate might explain the absence of dialogue—with the exception of Innitzer—between the Christian leaders and Harand's movement.

In the case of Oesterreicher, Harand was more discriminating. But the division this involved between his humanism and his Christian triumphalism and mission was not realistic. Johannes M. Oesterreicher of Vienna, a Jew who converted to Catholicism and was ordained a priest on July 17, 1927, edited *Die Erfüllung* from 1934 to 1938. He voiced opposition to anti-Semitism in a variety of contexts. He criticized proposals to limit Jewish influence in public life by declaring Jews a separate minority, segregated and with limited rights. Such proposals insisted that Jews should have their own schools and be excluded from the army, the police, the judiciary and the parliament. A *numerus clausus* should be in force for university admission, and participation in the professions had to be proportional to their number. This proposal was intended, anti-Semites insisted, to find a rational and legal solution to the Jewish problem, lest it be resolved by unrestrained brutality. Oesterreicher rejected the idea of a minority entity. Rights were a matter of achievement, not of racial or blood identity. Instead, the humane spirit had to be promoted as Jacques Maritain had done in his work on theocentric humanism (Maritain 1936). Oesterreicher acknowledged that Jews had sinned in the past against Europeans, but there was nothing like the injustice and suffering being wrought against them now in the name of Germany (Oesterreicher 1936e; Pauley 1992, 159–60).

Oesterreicher appreciated Faulhaber's statements in *Judentum, Christentum, Germanentum. Adventspredigten* (1933) on behalf of the spiritual values of the ancient Hebrews, which, for Oesterreicher, were subsequently transferred to Christ the Messiah. The religious values of the Hebrews of the pre-Christian period surpassed those of all others of the time. The one and transcendent God descended in revelation from His infinite heights and through His commandments spoke to man. Faulhaber's descriptions of the eternal religious, ethical, and social values of the God-inspired Old Testament, Judaism's gift to the world, were words "for the time, but not out of the time, words of a prophet" (Oesterreicher 1934/1935).

Oesterreicher objected to Hudal's belief that the state could in an emergency exclude Jews to protect its *Volkstum* from being overwhelmed by foreign influence. Without denying the state's right to protect itself from destructive influence, Hudal's implied justification of the Nuremberg Laws was irreconcilable with Christianity. As the church (and Hudal) opposed sterilization because it cut off the human capacity and the choice to procreate, it must also oppose the defamation of the Jews as a group, thereby cutting off their humanity. Indicating his stress on the matter as a purely religious one, Oesterreicher differed with Hudal's observation that 586 BCE, when the First Temple was destroyed and the state ended, was the key to understanding Judaism. The turning point was rather 70 CE, fulfilling Jesus' promise of punishment for disbelief. The second destruction belonged to the era of Christianity whereby 586 BCE was an event internal to Israel, and 70 CE was a world event with implications as well beyond the ephemeral and for salvation (Oesterreicher 1936d; Hudal 1936, 94).

Harand appreciated Oesterreicher's essay "Hominem non Habeo," which rejected the Nuremberg Laws. He did so, he said, in the name of *Gerechtigkeit,* for it was unjust to brand Jews as sex-criminals; in the name of the spirit, for the Laws violated the creation of man in the image of God; in the name of the Gospel, for they fostered racial superiority and thereby violated Christ's message of love, which eliminated racial division; and in the name of the church, for prohibition of marriage between Jews and Aryans undermined the church's administration of sacraments without discrimination. Moreover, insofar as the Laws struck at the very human being of German Jews, beyond politics and economics, it threatened humanity as such. Harand made it clear that she rejected *Die Erfüllung*'s solution to the Jewish question, namely conversion. But she lauded Oesterreicher for urging believing Christians to see Jews as human beings, as brothers, who in their own way served God. God loved the human being and did not discriminate between the Aryan or Jew who entered the kingdom of God or who was the neighbor with the right to *Nächstenliebe* (Oesterreicher 1935a; Harand 1936a; Weinzierl 1981).

By separating *Die Erfüllung*'s mission of conversion from Oesterreicher's pleas for treatment of Jews as human beings, Harand imposed a division that would have been impossible for Oesterreicher. For him, the humanity of the Jew, the spiritual reality that preempted racial division, existed for conversion to Christ. In his attacks on Gaston Ritter (1933) and Christian Loge (1934) he stated his agreement about Israel's great guilt. But the guilt had to be forgiven, not attacked with falsehoods. Instead of demanding that Jews know themselves, the authors should promote *Nächstenliebe:* "The one who still does not fully love Christ, the more fully does Christ love him" (Pope Callistus II).

Oesterreicher understood the Christian anger at the Jews' stubborn, thousand-year-long rejection of Christ. But the anger must be transferred into love. For him, the guilt was Jewish, and the love was Christian (Weinzierl 1985; Ritter 1933; Loge 1934; Oesterreicher 1935b, 1935c, 1936a).

In June 1936 Oesterreicher condemned the Jew-hatred breaking out in Austria, which invoked God's name to promote the base instinct of hatred, threatening the inner existence of the Christian more than the outer life of the Jew. For example, the view attributed to Bichlmair and Kunschak was that anti-Semitism was reflective of Christ, who knew Jews best and rejected them. Oesterreicher pointed out that on March 25, 1928, the Holy Office declared that the Catholic Church was to pray for the Jews, who bore the divine promise until they became blinded and Christ became its bearer. In Christian love, the Holy See condemned the anti-Semitic hatred of the people once chosen by God (1936b).

Despite the personal gratitude Oesterreicher felt he owed to him, he criticized Bichlmair's March 18, 1936, address. The Jewish question had not become a national, racial problem; it remained a religious matter, that of redemption. Jews were not a *Volk* like the Germans, but rather a religious community—namely the old Israel vis-à-vis the new Israel, that is, the church. The issue was their un-Christian presence, and that could not be resolved socially, politically, or professionally. Second, if Bichlmair wished to posit *Rechtsfrage* against *Nächstenliebe,* then *Gerechtigkeit* had to be applied to the Jews as well. Whatever injustice may have been committed by an individual Jew, Jews were not to be collectively persecuted. Moreover, the Jew had the right (*Recht*) to expect *Nächstenliebe* from the Christian as a Christian (1936b).

While Harand wished to set aside Oesterreicher's commitment to conversion and bring forth his devotion to humanistic-Christian principles, such an approach would not have suited Oesterreicher. He objected to those who sought minority status for Jews, drew racial divisions, did not appreciate the greatness of Hebrew scripture, advocated persecuting the Jews, and dredged up false accusations about them. But his humanism and love were inextricably bound up with his belief in Jewish sin and Christian redemption. He was no less triumphalist than Bichlmair or Hudal, even if his approach was one of reconciliation rather than alienation. His objection to the Nuremburg Laws was seamlessly connected to his expectation that Jews would convert. His humanism was theological, and his theology was one of Christian triumphalism.

**6**

Harand's efforts were generated by her Catholic principles. Within the Jewish world, her viewpoint was perceived and appreciated. In Sweden, Arnold Kalisch said that her bold attempt to eliminate anti-Semitism was guided by her Christian religiosity and its *Menschenliebe*. He appreciated the opposition she drew between Christianity and the German religion of self-idolatry and anti-Semitism (1935). A writer for *Israelitische Wochenblatt* felt that the impact of *Sein Kampf* was strengthened by the fact that it came from a pious Catholic (Harand 1935d).

In 1947 Harand was recognized by the leading ultra-Orthodox historian of the Holocaust, Moshe Prager, who wrote that this Christian woman was the only one intelligent enough to reveal the essence of the Nazi revolt. She warned that the campaign against the Jews would be the stepping-stone for terror against all mankind, that the swastika would not recoil from mass murder, that Hitler's war against the Jews was not only intended to humiliate the Jews and make them suffer, or to persecute Catholics and Christians faithful to Christ, but to dominate the whole world. She knew that the war against the Jews placed all of Christian civilization in danger (1947). On October 16, 1968, Harand received the Righteous Gentile award from Yad Vashem at the Israeli Consulate in New York. In his letter of recommendation, the Eichmann prosecutor Gideon Hausner wrote that he remembered Harand from the days he served as an emissary of the Akiva Youth Movement and Hehaluts in Poland, 1934–35, and that she was the symbol of human conscience, who had struggled almost alone against Nazism. She warned the world and the citizens of Austria against the danger of surrender to the Nazi deceit. Hausner knew that in the Vienna swarming with Nazis, she was risking her life.

But Harand's Catholic impetus evoked little support from the major Catholic figures of her day. Her Catholic principles did not take root among the Catholic leadership, which may be attributable to the fact that there was little common ground. Her commitment to *Nächstenliebe* was absolute. For Bichlmair it was conditioned by the perceived rights of the Christian—as it was for Roth and Bangha. Her appreciation for Hebrew scripture was shared by Faulhaber and Oesterreicher, but Faulhaber was interested in finding a modus vivendi for the church and the Reich, while Oesterreicher's appreciation implied conversion by Jews to Christianity. She shared Hudal's turn away from blood racism to matters of the spirit, but Hudal's spirituality did not preclude his belief that Jews were a failed people. Ultimately, the Catholic leaders were committed to Christian triumphalism: With the advent of Christ, Jews were to concede to Christianity. Not having done so, they became a sinful, pitiable, and ultimately dangerous entity. Harand believed in *Nächstenliebe* as a Christian principle devoid of triumphalism; she believed that the principle was so absolute that Jews did not have to become Christians to deserve it.

# 11

# Representations of the Nazi Past in the German Protestant Church in Early 1945

MATTHEW D. HOCKENOS

1

IN THE MONTHS immediately prior to and following Germany's uncondi-tional surrender in early May 1945, the predominant mood among leaders of the German Confessing church was one of uncritical complacency. "You should have seen this self-satisfied church at Treysa," Martin Niemöller wrote disparagingly in November 1945, referring to the August 1945 Treysa Confer-ence, the first national gathering of Protestant church leaders after the war (EZA, 2/35, 162). With the exception of Pastor Martin Niemöller, Swiss Re-formed theologian Karl Barth, and a small group of critical and reform-minded colleagues from the councils of brethren, church leaders at Treysa alleged that given the Nazi state's unrelenting persecution of the church, the Confessing church had indeed acted commendably.

Established authorities in the German Protestant (Evangelical) church founded the Confessing church in 1934 to defend the traditional doctrine and organization of the regional churches (*Landeskirchen*) against the theological heresies and organizational restructuring of the German Christians (*Deutsche Christen*) during the Nazi period. The German Christians wanted to integrate the twenty-eight regional Protestant churches into a united German Evangeli-cal Reich church under the leadership of a Reich bishop, who would be subor-dinate to Hitler. Theologically, the German Christians advocated the integration of Christian dogma with National Socialist doctrine. Quickly rising to prominence in the early 1930s, with initial support from the Nazis, the German Christians gained control of many *Landeskirchen* by the end of 1933 (Bergen 1996; Conway 1968; Scholder 1972 and 1985).

From its inception, intense feuding took place within the Confessing church. On one side, conservative church leaders and theologians, such as Bishop August Marahrens, Bishop Hans Meiser, and Hermann Sasse as well as moderate conservatives including Bishop Theophil Wurm, showed a willingness to compromise with the Nazi state and the German Christians in order to protect their regional churches from complete takeover. On the other side, Karl Barth, Hermann Diem, and Martin Niemöller led the opposition against German Christian and Nazi intervention in religious affairs. After the Nazi defeat and diminution of the German Christians, a number of churchmen initially associated with Niemöller and the councils of brethren, such as Hans Asmussen and Helmut Thielicke, took increasingly conservative stances both politically and theologically in opposition to the criticisms made by Barth, Diem, and Niemöller regarding the Confessing church's resistance record. Although a tiny minority of German Christians continued to maintain regional and national leadership positions in the postwar period, the bulk of the church's postwar leaders came from the ranks of the internally divided Confessing church and reflected these divisions (Barnett 1992; Gerlach 2000; Helmreich 1979).

In their pastoral letters, private correspondence, sermons, and public statements in early 1945, Confessing church leaders overwhelmingly emphasized the church's united opposition to the pro-Nazi German Christian movement, its hard-fought liberation from the totalitarian grip of the Nazis, and its churchly role in alleviating the mental, physical, emotional, and spiritual anguish brought on by Nazi rule, the Allied aerial bombardment of German cities, and the displacement of tens of thousands of Germans from the eastern territories. During this time, widely proclaimed to be "the hour of the church," self-pity and self-praise were interwoven with predictions that the church would rise again from the rubble like a phoenix and re-Christianize the German people (Besier 1994, 42–43; Jürgensen 1976, 265–76). Niemöller and a small number of churchmen from the councils of brethren countered the postwar church's self-congratulatory stand with highly critical lectures and stinging public statements. They acted as the conscience of the church and, as a consequence, many of their orthodox Lutheran colleagues from the conservative-nationalist wing of the Confessing church treated them as pariahs.

The intensity of the struggle among Confessing church leaders in putting forth their competing interpretations of the church's legacy under Nazism indicates that they understood all too well the significant impact the dominant interpretation would have on the church's immediate and long-term future.

Several strategies employed by select Confessing church leaders in the spring and summer of 1945 to construct official histories of Germany's recent past emerged. These histories tried to create a harmony with their visions of the church for the second half of the twentieth century. By analyzing sermons, pastoral letters, public declarations, and private letters written by leading churchmen, it is possible to reconstruct the political agendas and theological convictions underlying their representations of the past and visions of the future. How did they publicly represent the Church Struggle (*Kirchenkampf*), including the disputes within the Confessing church, and the behavior of the church under the Nazis? What goals did these churchmen expect to achieve by interpreting the past as they did? Who or what did they blame for the Nazis' coming to power, the millions of people killed in the Second World War, and Germany's devastation? And finally, what changes in the church, if any, did Protestant leaders envisage in light of the experience of the past decade?

As one might expect given the antagonisms during the Nazi era, Confessing churchmen clashed over how to answer these questions in the spring and summer of 1945. Most notable among the competing responses were *Word to the Congregations,* an official church statement supported by a broad spectrum of churchmen at the Treysa Conference, and *Word to the Pastors,* a statement drafted by the Reich Council of Brethren, which conservative church leaders at Treysa rejected (Greschat 1994; Greschat 1982, 77–78 and 74–76). An analysis of these and other responses illuminates the competing political and theological agendas within the Confessing church. Pastor Hans Asmussen, Bishop Theophil Wurm, and theologian Helmut Thielicke favored a positive depiction of the church's resistance record and saw little need for fundamental changes. The position taken by Barth and Niemöller, in contrast, emphasized the church's shared responsibility for Nazi rule as well as the need for practical changes in church organization and a rethinking of the church's dogma. Although many Confessing church leaders participated in these debates, the statements of a select few who are representative of larger groups within the Confessing church stand out.

**2**

The strategy of the conservative majority, including Asmussen, Thielicke, and Wurm, entailed four interlocking components: stressing the conservative, churchly nature of their resistance; using purposefully vague and obfuscating religious terminology to explain the rise of Nazism; insisting that the Confessing church had taken a united stance against Nazism; and reminding the world that Germans had suffered horrendous treatment under both the Nazis and the Allies.

Their objective in 1945 was to unify the church around a legacy of what they termed "conservative churchly resistance," which describes how these churchmen conceived and portrayed their actions under Nazi rule. It was a myth they created to assuage their consciences and to cleanse an unimpressive resistance record. Like all myths, conservative churchly resistance was one part fact and many parts fiction. They insisted that in keeping with the church's apolitical, God-given commission to preach the gospel and administer the sacraments, their opposition to Nazism took place outside the political sphere. Their resistance, so the argument went, was not against Nazi politics per se but rather against Nazi and German Christian encroachments on church life and doctrine. Thus, their quarrel with the German Christians and their Nazi supporters over church proclamations and governance took place within the jurisdiction of the church. Many in the Confessing church believed that their ecclesiastical and spiritual resistance, that is, resisting a complete takeover of the church by the German Christians and Nazis and continuing to preach the Word of God as always, was the responsible and appropriate reaction to Nazism for churchmen.

The dearth of public and/or political stands by conservative churchmen against Nazism was not, as the myth of conservative churchly resistance implies, because they were men of the cloth. Rather, their infrequent public denunciations of the Nazis' illegal, immoral, and racist political activities were, in part, because they shared much of the Nazis' nationalist, anti-Communist, and anti-Semitic political agenda. They did not, however, support the systematic extermination of Jews and others deemed expendable by the Nazis, and there were courageous individuals in the church who took a stand against particular Nazi policies, particularly the euthanasia program. Nevertheless, the vocal support the Nazis received from enthusiastic church leaders, both from the pulpit and in the press, easily debunks the myth that pious pressures drove churchmen to express their resistance conservatively and within the walls of the church.

Significantly, Martin Luther's doctrine of two kingdoms provided churchmen with a convenient theological trope for supporting their claim to have maintained a strict separation of religious and political spheres. While most Confessing churchmen, especially those from the intact churches, such as Wurm, rarely tried to assert a legacy of political resistance because that assertion would imply a failure to keep the spiritual and earthly kingdoms separate, they instead insinuated that their conservative churchly resistance had politically detrimental effects for the Nazi regime. Most conservatives, however, were careful not to draw attention to the church's politics during the Nazi period for fear of drawing attention to their initial enthusiasm for Hitler and their failure to speak out except when the church was under attack. Conservatives may have been content with their accommodating and compromising behavior under the Nazis, but they did not expect the Allies to agree or understand. Thus, they created the myth of conservative churchly resistance and defended it vigorously.

Conservatives sought to construct the identity of the postwar church around its resistance to the politicization of the religious sphere by the German Christians, on the one hand, and the so-called radicals in the Confessing church, on the other. Supposedly, between political radicals on both the left and right sat the conservatives, who eschewed politics. They argued that as creatures of the religious sphere, they had not contributed to the rise and maintenance of Nazi rule, which were political phenomena.

The myth of conservative churchly resistance also allowed them to argue that they rejected Nazism without providing evidence of acts of resistance other than being faithful to Jesus Christ or defending the church's traditional hierarchical structure. Church leaders made the construction of the myth considerably easier by defining resistance as taking place in the religious sphere but having political implications. In doing so, vague references of loyalty to Jesus Christ, such as continuing to preach the gospel as usual, became heroic acts of resistance.

The use of grandiose and purposefully vague religious imagery and terminology was the second interlocking piece in the conservatives' explanations for the rise of National Socialism, the barbarity of the Second World War, and Germany's collapse in 1945. The Lutheran law-gospel dualism was implicit in this tendency to shy away from concrete explanations. Conservatives com-

monly sought to explain Germany's defeat, destruction, and misery as a consequence of God's anger at his disobedient children. "God's angry judgment has
broken out over us all," began Treysa's *Word to the Congregations* (Greschat
1982, 77). This type of apocalyptic imagery suggested that human beings were
responsible for the postwar catastrophe only in the sense of having earned
God's wrath. Now, so the argument went in spring and summer of 1945, they
could expect God's blessing and forgiveness because, according to the orthodox Lutheran understanding of the law and gospel, God's mercy always followed his wrath.

The final components of the conservative interpretation were an emphasis
on unity and German suffering, both essential to the Confessing church's
legacy if it hoped to emerge from twelve years of Nazi rule as a vital moral and
political force in Germany's immediate and long-term future. Part of the complex motivation behind the construction of an official church history that emphasized united and sustained resistance was power politics. Church leaders
sought to guarantee themselves a leading role in the vital decisions about German reconstruction by convincing the occupation forces, the foreign churches
in the ecumenical movement, and the German population itself that the Confessing church—as a whole, not just certain individuals—had suffered great
hardship for its opposition to the Nazis' inhumane and anti-Christian policies.

Treysa's *Word to the Congregations,* for instance, focused on the church's resistance, real and contrived, its captivity in the Nazi state, and its recent liberation from the shackles of Nazism. Although the Treysa statement alluded
briefly to the Confessing church's intermittent timidity, this allusion was overshadowed by numerous descriptions of men and women from all confessions
who "took a stand against injustice" (Greschat 1982, 77). We are told that when
the church took its responsibilities seriously, it criticized concentration camps,
condemned the murder of Jews and the sick, and sought to protect youth from
National Socialist propaganda. In this statement, which church leaders intended to read to and circulate among their congregations, they maintained
that the repression by the Gestapo was so intense that it silenced the church's
voice. Only when the war was over and the Nazis defeated could the church
openly declare "what was prayed and planned behind walls and in seclusion"
(Greschat 1982, 77). The implication here is that it was too dangerous for
church leaders to voice openly their opposition to the Nazis, so privately they
prayed for a Nazi defeat and planned for a future in which Christian virtues
would be given a prominent place. Church leaders who found it difficult to de-

fend claims of resistance with the fact of their silence often pointed to silent prayers as proof of both Nazi repression and the church's resistance.

Hans Asmussen, a Lutheran pastor from Altona (near Hamburg) and president of the church chancellery after August 1945, took a similar tack in a June 1945 letter to the archbishop of Canterbury, in which he undertook to reestablish the ecumenical connections that had been severed when the war began (Greschat 1982, 63–68). Pastor Asmussen assured the archbishop that the Confessing church's silence and turning inward (*Verinnerlichung)* during the war years was due neither to agreement with Hitler's war aims nor to a spiritual flight from the reality of the times, as some Anglicans had charged, but was rather the result of severe repression by the Nazi state. Forced to toe the National Socialist party line or relinquish the public sphere to Nazi authorities, according to Asmussen, the Confessing church grudgingly chose the latter and sought to make the best of it by enriching the Confessing church through intense self-reflection and prayer. Indeed, Asmussen emphasized that the church's *Verinnerlichung* had the salutary effect of molding a degree of spiritual cohesiveness previously unknown in the Protestant churches, thereby enhancing the church's witness and implicitly its conservative churchly resistance (Greschat 1982, 64).

Asmussen sought in his letter to counter a barrage of foreign radio broadcasts, many from Britain, which were lumping all Germans together as collectively guilty for the crimes committed under Nazi rule. If Germans were to receive a sympathetic hearing from any corner abroad, German churchmen believed it would come from foreign churches. Therefore it was imperative to convince foreign church leaders that German clergymen vigorously combated Nazism while never politicizing Christ's message.

The Lutheran bishop of Württemberg, Theophil Wurm, also called attention to Nazi repression, confessional unity, and the church's opposition to Nazism in his spring 1945 statement "To Christianity Abroad" (Greschat 1982, 68–70). Like Asmussen, Wurm insisted that communication between the German church and churches abroad was impossible during the war because of the state's all-encompassing control and that now, in spring 1945, he was taking the first opportunity to express the German church's desire to declare its solidarity with Christians outside Germany. Wurm asked Christians abroad to refrain from believing that because no protest from within Germany was heard that all Germans were pro-Nazi (Greschat 1982, 68). Those who did speak out, Wurm contended, ended up in concentration camps.

Except in the vague sense of not having been Christian enough, church leaders at Treysa shied away from acknowledging that it was the church's long history of nationalism and loyalty to the state that had laid the groundwork for the church's unquestioning attitude toward the rise and sustained rule of National Socialism. To do otherwise would have implied that the church needed to undergo fundamental changes to make certain that it would not accommodate anti-Christian forces again. Moreover, a thorough reckoning with the church's past would not only disrupt church unity and increase despair in the congregations but would also alienate the congregation from its leadership. Church leaders knew only too well how sensitive their people were to the imputation of guilt or responsibility in the wake of the appalling scenes of the liberation of Nazi concentration and extermination camps by the Allies. The church did not want to discourage former or potential members by being too stern a judge.

In view of the all-too-frequent blanket accusations by the occupying forces, church leaders contrived to make the church the "spokesman" or "champion" of the German people, to use the words of Pastor Halfmann, a leading Lutheran from Schleswig-Holstein (Jürgensen 1976, 263). As the self-selected spokesmen for the defeated and demoralized population, many clergymen took advantage of the opportunity to win the trust of the population by appeasing them. Despite the apparent contradiction in identifying the church with the victory against Hitler *and* the defeated German people, church leaders persisted with their mission. They wanted to secure support from the Allies in order to have a voice in Germany's future, on the one hand, and to claim the role of spokesmen for the German people, on the other. As the statements analyzed in this essay demonstrate, these spokesmen attempted to counter accusations of collective guilt by stressing the severe hardship endured by the German people at the hands of both the Nazis and the Allies.

Thus, ecclesiastical politics account, in part, for the lack of criticism leveled against Lutheran theology and the hierarchical organization of the Lutheran *Landeskirchen,* both of which help to explain the church's accommodation to Nazism. When conservatives discussed blame specifically, it was usually directed at the former top-ranking Nazis. For instance, in Bishop Wurm's statement "To Christianity Abroad" he wrote, "We do not refuse to share the guilt which leading men in the party and state have heaped on our people" (Greschat 1982, 68). The implication is clear: as good Christians we must bear the guilt, but we are not guilty.

Wurm, like many others, blamed the reparation burdens and mass unemployment caused by the Versailles Treaty at the end of World War I for creating the conditions in Germany that allowed the Nazis to come to power. These conditions led to a mood of despair and in turn to extreme nationalism and the rise of Nazism (Greschat 1982, 68). He acknowledged and condemned the suffering of other people, namely, the captivity and mass murder of German and Polish Jews as well as the atrocities carried out by military commando units against the populations in German-occupied territories. But his emphasis was on the suffering and hardship endured by Germans as a consequence of National Socialism and, more recently, by the violations of law and lack of mercifulness on the part of the Allies (Greschat 1982, 69). The church's conduct during the twelve years of Nazi rule never came up for criticism. The primary message Wurm wanted to convey to Christians abroad was that the German people also suffered and that Germans were not the only ones guilty of unchristian behavior.

Wurm asked Christians abroad not to perceive the Nazi atrocities as representative of the German character. "Every people has its Jacobins, who under certain conditions attain power," he told them (Greschat 1982, 68). By associating Nazis with Jacobins, Wurm accomplished two corresponding goals of the conservatives. First, he linked Nazism to Enlightenment thought and de-Christianization, both characteristic of Jacobinism. In so doing, he uncoupled Nazism from Germany's conservative traditions and tied it to mass politics and secularization, two modern trends that conservative Lutherans found highly objectionable. Conservatives like Wurm and Asmussen interpreted Nazism and all its horrors as an outgrowth of the French Revolution and the subsequent Terror, not Prusso-German militarism and nationalism.

As *Word to the Congregations* and these letters demonstrate, conservative Confessing church leaders were eager to explain that their wartime silence was not voluntary. At a time when the Allies were publicizing the full extent of German atrocities in the eastern territories, Wurm and Asmussen clearly saw a need to remind the world that Germans were suffering as well. This suffering, *Word to the Congregations* suggested, could have been lessened had more Christians throughout Europe taken their responsibility as Christians seriously by speaking out against all injustices that made a mockery of God's commandments—the gassing of Jews *and* the bombing of German cities. Germans, so the argument suggested, had an excuse for not publicly condemning Nazi policy, namely the terror tactics of the Nazi secret police. The Allies and Christians abroad, however, had no excuse for their silence regarding the atrocities committed against Germans in the last years of the war. Those Christians who ignored their responsibility were guilty of disloyalty to God and should, the statement advised, reassume Christian responsibility—understood broadly and vaguely as obedience to God.

From the very beginning, conservative clergymen circumvented the real issues of human agency and responsibility in favor of references to European secularization and the wrath of God to explain the rise of Nazism and its consequences. Germany's destroyed cities were not, they claimed, the result of German nationalism and territorial aggression but rather God's response to men and women for worshipping and serving "the creature more than the creator" (Vollnhals 1988, 167).

In "To Christianity Abroad," Bishop Wurm contended that the brutal acts perpetrated by both Germans and the Allies in World War II were the consequence of *Gottesentfremdung* (estrangement from God), *Christusfeindschaft* (enmity toward Christ), rampant *Mammonismus* (greed), and coarse *Materialismus* (materialism) (Söhlmann 1946, 20). By emphasizing what he saw as the redirection in post-World War I Europe from religious-centered worldviews toward secularized human-centered ones, Wurm obscured the particularities of National Socialism and ultimately the specificity of Nazi atrocities. In Wurm's view, all of Europe was guilty of turning away from Christ. By claiming that the victorious powers were guilty of the same violations of human decency for which the world was correctly reproaching the National Socialist regime, Wurm equated the Allies with the Nazis (Greschat 1982, 69).

Helmut Thielicke, a renowned Lutheran theologian preaching in Stuttgart in 1944–45, stated explicitly that Nazism must be understood in terms of its antireligious roots (Besier et al. 1989, 205). Like Wurm, he blamed the secularization of the modern world: "National Socialism is the last and most fearful product of secularization. Secularization means that man escapes from God's hand into the most fearful hands of men. It is the mystery of man emancipated from God that has broken out in Germany. Germany has had to live out this mystery in the presence of the other peoples, and suffer exemplary suffering. That may have been its tragic mission" (Besier et al. 1989, 204). The salutary aspect of this strategy for conservatives was that it relieved Germans from the burden of accountability for specific crimes but held them accountable and guilty for abandoning God. Consequently, the only penance necessary in 1945 was to return to the fold of the church and devote oneself to Christ.

At the same time, conservatives admitted and universalized guilt. As Christians, they insisted, we are guilty before God, but then, of course, so is everyone. Thielicke even went so far as to imply in the above passage that Germany's uniqueness was not that the Nazis came to power in Germany and managed to stay in power until the Allies removed them; rather, Germany's uniqueness was in its exemplary degree of suffering, which apparently was a part of the tragic mission assigned to Germany by God.

Even the otherwise critical and unambiguous statement of guilt and repentance, the *Word to the Pastors,* which was issued by the leaders of the councils of brethren and rejected by many conservatives at Treysa (although not by Asmussen, who helped draft it), suggested that the catastrophe and chaos wrought by National Socialism was brought on by demonic forces. "Demonic was the power which in the last few years drove the German people to atrocities before which we and the entire world shudder with horror. Apocalyptic were the manifestations of total war" (Greschat 1982, 74). Asmussen reasoned that not only had the political doctrine of National Socialism seduced Germans away from their Christian beliefs and values, but had also served as a substitute for their Christian faith. In his letter to the archbishop of Canterbury, Asmussen again referred to the satanical forces at work in the Nazi movement, which subverted the natural gifts of reason and insight in many Germans (Greschat 1982, 65 and 67). The Nazis' seductive lure, he reasoned, was successful because man's self-confidence and hubris led him to forget that God was the creator and man His creation.

Certainly it was appropriate for church leaders like Asmussen, Thielicke, and Wurm to employ explanations in keeping with the basic premises of Christian thought. However, by avoiding a discussion about Germany's widespread support inside and outside the church for Nazi domestic and foreign policy, the majority in the Confessing church failed to hold human beings and institutions, such as the church itself, responsible for their concrete actions or inaction. Furthermore, references to their betrayal of Christianity served to divert attention from their actual role, whether it was one of anguished silence or professional complicity.

Conservatives considered the construction of an official history—one that included resistance, unity, and German privation—a precondition for a number of objectives: to generate respect from the occupation forces; to attain an influential role in the reconstruction of German institutions, especially those that affected the church's future; to achieve prestige and leadership among ordinary Germans; and to preserve their positions as leaders of one of Germany's most influential institutions. When the small but extremely influential critical minority in the Confessing church put forth a competing interpretation of the legacy of the Nazi period—emphasizing the church's shared responsibility for National Socialism, the church's divisiveness in the *Kirchenkampf*, and the hardship that Germans inflicted on others—these reform-minded critics impeded, but never completely scuttled, the conservative majority's attempt to refound the church on a myth of conservative churchly resistance.

References to "demonic" and "apocalyptic" in *Word to the Pastors* annoyed some of the radical Confessing church clergy, such as Martin Niemöller and Karl Barth, who wanted to see a more forthright statement of the origins and consequences of National Socialism. In a letter to Niemöller in late September 1945, Barth, a highly controversial Swiss Reformed theologian and a critic of German Lutheranism who had taught theology in Germany from 1921 to 1935, encouraged Niemöller to urge the German church to provide the foreign delegation of ecumenical leaders visiting Stuttgart with a frank statement of German responsibility for the chaos and destruction that had engulfed Europe. Ridiculing conservative rationalizations, Barth advised Niemöller against "Asmussensche Theologie" and any references to the devil, demons, original sin, and the guilt of the other (Ludwig 1971, 319).

Earlier, in a lecture in January 1945, Barth warned his Swiss audience to keep a watchful eye on the German manipulation of religious rhetoric. "We must reckon with the religious profundity of the Germans, which all too willingly avoids the acknowledgment of their own concrete guilt by pointing out the great truth that before God in the last resort all men and nations are alike guilty and alike in need of forgiveness for their sins: thus the bold conclusion is drawn that a particular German repentance is obviously unnecessary and absolutely uncalled for" (Barth 1947, 106). Although Barth wanted every German to admit responsibility, he did not believe that Germans as a people were collectively guilty. He believed that comparatively few Germans had taken part in the crimes themselves. But all Germans were responsible because they directly or indirectly participated through political indifference or errors of judgment (Barth 1947, 38–39).

In an April 1945 essay written at the request of the *Manchester Evening News* and patronizingly entitled "How Can the Germans Be Cured?", Barth likened Germany to a very sick patient (Barth 1947, 3–20). Although all the nations of Europe were also likened to sick patients, Barth told the British that "some patients suffer from more serious diseases than others" (Barth 1947, 83). By distinguishing Germany from the rest of Europe, Barth separated himself from those church leaders, German and non-German apologists, who maintained that the secularization of the Western world in the past century was to blame for the rise of Hitler and the present state of affairs across Europe. Barth singled out what he saw as Germany's unique history to explain the origins of National Socialism. His focus on German history was a determining factor in his disagreements with conservative churchmen, in particular Hans Asmussen, who in 1934 had collaborated with Barth in writing the *Barmen Declaration* (Besier 1994, 121–42).

Barth's interpretation of German history was similar to the classic *Sonderweg* thesis. In a series of lectures to Swiss audiences in January and February 1945 entitled "The Germans and Ourselves," he traced a direct line in German history from the Prussian military tradition to Hitler. "The achievement of Frederick the Great and Bismarck could not be brought to a more logical conclusion nor to more complete destruction than it has been done by Adolf Hitler.... We have to reckon with the possibility that the great majority of Germans even now scarcely realize...what a responsibility they assumed when they supported first Bismarck, then Wilhelm II, and last of all, Adolf Hitler" (Barth 1947, 83).

Significantly, Barth applied the same logic to explain why the German Christian movement appealed to so many German Lutherans. Just as the *Sonderweg* thesis explained Hitler and Nazism by focusing on the German people's historical legacy of supporting charismatic authoritarian leaders, Barth looked to the history of Lutheranism to explain the church's failure to declare explicitly the anti-Christian nature of Nazism and the German Christians. He maintained that German Lutheranism paved the way for the German paganism and nationalism of the German Christians in the 1930s. As early as 1939, in an open letter to French Protestants, he wrote, "[Germany] suffers from...Martin Luther's error on the relation between law and gospel, between the temporal and spiritual order and power. This error has established, confirmed, and idealized the natural paganism of the German people, instead of limiting and restraining it" (Barth 1941). Here and elsewhere Barth asserted that Luther's doctrine of two kingdoms, the law-gospel dualism, and the orders of creation were responsible, in part, for the Lutherans' easy accommodation with German Christians and Nazis.

This type of thinking, as well as statements by Niemöller and others, prompted Hans Asmussen to respond with an essay entitled "Does Luther Belong Before the Nuremberg Court?" (Asmussen 1947). Clearly, conservatives were piqued that radicals were charging the church with having done too little and blaming the church's complacency and complicity on orthodox Lutheran theology and the church's hierarchical structure. They accepted Treysa's *Word to the Congregations* because it did not acknowledge that the history, organizational structure, and theology of the church played a leading role in creating the conditions that led to the successful rise and sustained rule of the Nazis. For conservatives, it was the absence—not the presence—of orthodox Lutheranism that was to blame.

Not only did the critics within the Confessing church embrace a genuine desire to seek out the historical causes of the church's errant judgments, particularly in the church's theology, structure, and relation to the state, they also wanted to make the changes necessary to ensure that this error would never happen again. Although Barth and Niemöller were successful in provoking the conservatives and in initiating a public discussion about the church's acquiescence during the Nazi era, they never succeeded in making the fundamental changes in the church that they believed were necessary to make sure that the church did not compromise with another political ideology, such as Fascism, in the future.

In his speech at the Treysa Conference, Niemöller also sought a concrete explanation for all that had transpired in Germany and in particular within the church from 1933 to 1945. As a *"Behördenkirche"* (a church beholden to the state), Niemöller contended, the church never considered that it had a responsibility to its brethren or the public to pass critical judgment on the Nazi state and its policies. Rather than lay blame on a few Nazis or a general trend like secularization, Niemöller faulted the structure of the Lutheran churches and their traditional subordination to the state.

Niemöller challenged the conservative Lutheran interpretation by emphasizing the responsibility of church leaders to openly criticize the state when its policies clash fundamentally with church doctrine. Although not citing the orthodox interpretation of Luther's doctrine of two kingdoms in his Treysa address, Niemöller directly challenged this central pillar of orthodox Lutheranism elsewhere. He was especially forthright in a January 1946 address to the Confessing church in Frankfurt when, in what sounded like a passage borrowed from Barth, Niemöller said, "An error, which for a long time had a place in the Evangelical [Protestant] church, consisted in the belief that the

Evangelical church does not have anything to do with public life" (Niemöller 1946, 12). The claims of God and the church, Niemöller asserted, encompass all areas of life, including the spiritual and the political worlds. Niemöller did not advocate that the church involve itself in politics by offering its official support for specific candidates in an election, but rather that Christians abide by Christian principles in the public sphere. Of course, conservatives such as Bishop Wurm did not dispute this advocacy. The disagreement between Niemöller and Wurm lay in how to define Christian values and responsibility.

By public or Christian responsibility, Niemöller meant that the church was responsible for more than simply preaching the gospel and administering the sacraments as stated in the seventh article of the Augsburg Confession. It should fall to the church, Niemöller insisted, to criticize the state publicly when it failed to ensure each citizen basic human rights. And for that reason, Niemöller declared, the church could not be indifferent to the form of the state nor to its basic principles. Niemöller even went so far as to argue that Christianity and democracy had a special affinity, one that did not exist between Christianity and conservative authoritarianism (Niemöller 1946, 12). He attributed the church's failure to take this responsibility seriously to the orthodox Lutheran misinterpretation of Luther's doctrine of two kingdoms, which was based on a traditional understanding of the law-gospel dualism.

The Berlin Council of Brethren's July 1945 *Word to the Pastors and Congregations* also provided a clear confession of the church's failure to live up to its responsibilities: "The pastors and parish leaders who avoided the struggle must be reproached for their failure, which caused the church and the people disaster and guilt. Often human fear outweighed the responsibility for the church, state, and people. Churchmen hid behind the words of the Bible in order to hide their submission to worldly powers. Only by submitting to the totalitarian claims of the state was it possible for the state to repress the church's public role" (Söhlmann 1946, 139–40).

After heaping blame on the church establishment for failing to take a stand, the Berlin Council of Brethren's statement went on to challenge the frequently stated claim that the Confessing church was a resistance church. "Unfortunately," the text continued, "the Confessing church is not without guilt. To be sure many brothers and sisters witnessed in word and deed, but through lack of unanimity, through lack of courage in thought and deed, through falsely insisting on old ways, through our own failure and weakness, we spoiled the holy things God had entrusted us with. Compared with all these things we only suffered and resisted a little. We cannot be reproached with having been too radical. On the contrary, we reproach ourselves for having been silent when we should have spoken" (Söhlmann 1946, 139–40).

Perhaps no churchman provided a more forthright and refreshingly simple explanation than Lutheran pastor Gottlieb Funcke of Münster. In precisely the spirit called for by Barth and Niemöller, he explained why God had unleashed his wrath and, not incidentally, why Hitler was so popular: "Because the majority [of Germans] cheered on the leadership of the Third Reich or actually gave it free rein as long as it seemed to offer successful results" (Greschat 1982, 70). Funcke maintained that although many of the wartime atrocities against Germans, Poles, Russians, and Jews were relatively unknown until 1945, the inhumane treatment of German Jews had been known for a long time and that for this, "we are all guilty" (Greschat 1982, 70).

## 3

A major concern for most conservative churchmen in 1945 was to unify the church around a legacy of conservative churchly resistance to the German Christians and Nazism. Myths of unity and resistance were essential for the church to emerge from the twelve years of Nazi rule as an influential spiritual and political force. To provide the church with the necessary leverage to realize this goal, Protestant leaders sought to reinterpret the recent past—and in particular their accommodations to the National Socialist cause—in a favorable light.

The majority of Confessing church leaders, especially conservatives from the intact Lutheran churches who emerged in 1945 to resume church leadership, portrayed themselves to the occupation forces, the foreign churches, and the German people as leaders of the resistance to Nazism. Conservatives believed that their defense of the church against the encroachments of German Christians and the Nazi state was the appropriate response for churchmen whose primary task, regardless of the political context, was to preach the gospel and administer the sacraments. In short, for conservative church leaders, resistance to Nazism was synonymous with defending the church—and they did defend the church vigorously.

They maintained publicly that despite great suffering and hardship they had persevered in their defense of the church against the incursions of the Nazi state and the German Christians. Indeed, they would have done more, so the argument went, had it not endangered the laity. They rejected any suggestion that Luther's doctrine of two kingdoms, the law-gospel dualism, or the orders of creation were in any way responsible for the church's acquiescence and accommodation. In fact, conservatives frequently referred to the separation of the spiritual and worldly realms and the inevitability of God's mercy following his wrath as a means to explain and defend their action and inaction.

To be fair, this portrayal of the Confessing church was not without some truth. Yet, it intentionally exaggerated the Confessing church's resistance to the Nazi regime while virtually ignoring the weakness and inconsistency of its responses, which at times took the form of complicity, at other times complacency, and only rarely public opposition.

In stark contrast, the leaders of the councils of brethren explicitly pointed to organizational and theological defects in the church that they traced back to the close relationship between church and state. The hegemony of the church's bureaucratic control over God's Word proved that the church's problems went deeper than merely Nazi repression. Consequently, the Reich Council of Brethren admonished, "That is why it is not enough to simply overcome the destruction wrought by National Socialism. Our task goes further. A new church order must be created based on God's leadership" (Greschat 1982, 75). By acknowledging that structural and theological flaws in the church led to its accommodating stance toward Nazism, they recognized the need for fundamental changes in the church's organization, leadership, and dogma.

# 12

# Liturgy and the Holocaust

How Do We Worship in an Age of Genocide?

JOHN T. PAWLIKOWSKI

MY INTEREST in the topic of liturgy and the Holocaust has been instigated by the writings of three scholars in particular. They are the liturgist David Power, my mentor in social ethics Reinhold Niebuhr, and the historian George Mosse. At the 1983 meeting of the North American Academy of Liturgy, Power warned that "The greatest temptation threatening liturgical reform is that of a retreat into the past, or a retreat into abstract universalism. It is one to which Churches succumb when they find themselves doomed to silence by the inability even to face, let alone make any sense of, current reality. Can we in truth celebrate Eucharist after the Nazi Holocaust and in fact of an imminent nuclear holocaust, and in a world half populated by refugees, in the same way as we did before the occurrence of such horrors?" (Power 1983, 328).

And it was an intense study of Niebuhr's classic work *The Nature and Destiny of Man* (1964) while a student at the University of Chicago that brought me to the realization of what Niebuhr termed the "vitalistic" side of the human person. Niebuhr used the term *vitalistic* to cover the various areas of human consciousness not directly controlled by the rational faculty. It includes the faculty of feeling, the human sexual drive, and the faculty of memory and myth-making, among others. Some trends in Catholic morality were suspicious of this dimension of humanity, locating ethics primarily in people's rational capacity. We have in fact seen a resurgence of this belief in recent years in Catholic circles, a prime example being the viewpoint that generally dominates John Paul II's *Veritatis Splendor* (Pawlikowski 1995, 177–93). Niebuhr insisted that reason was just as capable of generating human sinfulness as the vitalistic powers. More importantly, he stressed that no authentic and effective human ethics could be developed without the constructive involvement of vitalistic energies. The Holocaust has shown the enduring wisdom of this Niebuhrian perspective.

The regeneration of the vitalistic side of humanity, albeit in highly destructive directions, stood at the heart of the Nazi enterprise. The historian J. L. Talmon once described Nazi ideology as the denial of any "final station of redemption in history," which gave birth to a cult of power and vitality as ends in themselves (Talmon 1973, 22–24). The Nazis became aware of the tremendous power of this vitalistic dimension. No scholar has made this point as clearly as the historian George Mosse, who spent considerable time examining the impact of the Nazi public liturgies during his scholarly career. While it verges on the obscene to give the Nazis credit for anything, Mosse's writings demonstrate that the Nazi leadership was extremely perceptive in recognizing the influence of symbolism in human life (Mosse 1977). Contemporary Holocaust scholar Irving Greenberg also acknowledged the importance of this aspect of Nazism. Reflecting on the failure of Enlightenment-based liberalism to provide an effective moral counterweight to the Nazi manipulation of human vitalism shows the inadequacy of any exclusively rational-based morality after the Shoah. Greenberg makes this point quite strongly: "How naive the nineteenth-century polemic with religion appears to be in retrospect; how simple Feuerbach, Nietzsche, and many others. The entire structure of autonomous logic and sovereign human reason now takes on a sinister character. . . . For Germany was one of the most 'advanced' Western countries—at the heart of the academic, scientific, and technological enterprise. All the talk about 'atavism' cannot obscure the way in which such behavior is the outgrowth of democratic and modern values, as well as pagan gods" (Greenberg 1977, 17).

One of the convictions that has continued to deepen within me as I have studied the Holocaust these many years under the tutelage of Holocaust scholars such as Mosse and Greenberg and within a framework of reflection provided by the likes of Power and Niebuhr is that moral sensitivity remains an indispensable prelude to moral reasoning. We ethicists can provide the necessary clarifications of human response mandated by such sensitivity. Such clarifications are absolutely essential if religious experience is not to degenerate into religious fanaticism. But, as an ethicist, I cannot create the sensitivity itself. Mere appeals to reason, authority, and/or natural law will prove ineffective by themselves. Such sensitivity will reemerge only through a new awareness of

God's intimate link with humankind, in suffering and joy, through symbolic experience. Nothing short of this awareness will suffice in light of the Holocaust.

Let me say at this point that I view the Holocaust as the culmination of a long-term process in which a sense of God's personal relationship with people had been gradually lessening. Gerardus van der Leeuw pointed to one aspect of this reality in his comments about the breakdown between dance and religion in modern culture. Dance has not surrendered its appeal in our world, but it has largely shed its sacral character. It appears to have become entirely "recreational," but in fact there may be more to its continuing appeal than we fully appreciate. The result of this breakdown has been the closure of one of the primary channels for the experience of God's relationship to people. "Primitive man," says van der Leeuw, "views the dance as a most serious affair, with religious significance. It sets into motion powers which are holy to man; it touches on all levels of life and raises it to a higher level. All other meanings are included in the religious" (Leeuw 1973, 35). He remained convinced that the religious dimensions of dance will reemerge as we again become conscious of the unity of body and soul. A similar phenomenon can be seen in contemporary art. Rarely do prominent art museums exhibit contemporary religious art. What religious art there is on display tends to be premodern. Art has not lost its connection to value as much as dance, but it remains another example of the separation of vitalistic creativity and religion.

As Western society has moved through the centuries, it has gradually, though somewhat subtly, closed off more and more avenues to the personal encounter with God. We in the West have often critiqued the atheism of Marxist societies. But in practice we in the West may not be far behind. The Third Reich provides a challenging window on this breakdown. On one hand, its political ideology was highly methodological and calculating. On the other hand, it clearly saw the importance of ritualistic expression, but in a way that eschewed any understanding of moral honing whether from religiously or more generally humane moral impulses. There was no outside control on the generation of vitalistic energies that created an immense sense of power. The Holocaust thus represents another example of the process that van der Leeuw described in his analysis of the separation of dance and religion.

I see an urgent need to counter the growing one-dimensionality in Western society in the midst of a growing awareness of human power and freedom through the development of a new moral sensitivity. This moral sensitivity must be engendered by a symbolic encounter with the Creator God who speaks to us in a new compelling way (Pawlikowski 1996). Strange as it may seem, the Holocaust provides us with some help in this regard. For if the Holocaust reveals one permanent quality of human life, it is the enduring presence of, the ongoing need for, symbolic communication. Mothers often sang to their children in the camps up till the door of the gas chambers. Camp music and camp song were vital to survival in the camps as well as a source of defiance to the evil all around the prisoners (Hirsch 1997, 157). But we must be clear. The experience of the vitalistic in our life is no guarantee of goodness. Didier Pollefeyt, an ethicist from Leuven who has done important work in Holocaust studies, has asserted that creativity does not automatically generate goodness, because sometimes aesthetics and crimes coincide (Pollefeyt 1997). Clearly public ritual played a central role in the implementation of Nazi ideology. That is why the text and structure of liturgy become so significant.

Many experiences of prayer and meditation may be vitalistically energizing. But they remain neutral in terms of social commitment, because there is no directional text connected with them. Regrettably, in the West, ritual has often been relegated almost exclusively to the realm of play and recreation. Yet it is in the power inherent in this vitalistic side of humanity that liturgy has the greatest potential for channeling men and women into constructive moral commitment.

In light of the Holocaust we can no longer afford to give scant attention to the vitalistic dimension of humanity, to reduce it simply to the realm of play and recreation. The development of moral reasoning remains crucial, but it is no substitute for the healing of the destructive tendencies in humanity's vitalistic side, which requires a symbolic encounter with a loving God.

The discussion of the centrality of the vitalistic dimension of the human person brings to the fore another key issue: Where do we locate divine activity in the world today? An important Holocaust scholar, the late Arthur Cohen, hinted that divine involvement in human affairs may be more subtle than we once thought (Cohen 1981). The Holocaust has rendered any belief about direct divine intervention in history obsolete. But we are not left simply with a deist version of the divine. Where we must look is the nexus of human consciousness and affectivity, the realm of the vitalistic. That is why Cohen's approach to post-Holocaust theodicy provides an added critical dimension to the otherwise brilliant analyses of other Holocaust scholars such as Emil Fackenheim, Irving Greenberg, and David Blumenthal. God retains the potential for profound influence on human history. But that influence comes primarily through divine involvement with human consciousness, with the healing of destructive tendencies, and with the strengthening of creative, vitalistic energies. Humanity is the agent of God in human history. People are the link between God and history. But if we understand the intimate bond between human consciousness and the shaping of the political, cultural, and economic configurations of human history, we will come to appreciate that though God's involvement in human history in light of the Holocaust needs to be understood as mediated, it remains crucial and profoundly real; it remains basic to any comprehensive theory of morality.

For me it is the liturgy or sacred ritual, call it what you will, that has the greatest potential for making God's presence available to the human community in a way that will channel constructive moral commitment. My colleague in the ecumenical cluster of theological schools at the University of Chicago, Professor Robert Moore, a psychologist by professional training, has used the term "ritual containment" to describe this inherent power of worship. Sacred ritual, especially if it is linked to long-standing traditions such as Judaism and Christianity, has the inherent possibility of preventing destructive expressions of vitalistic energy of the kind we witnessed in Nazi Germany. Some liturgists, such as my former colleague at Catholic Theological Union Kathleen Hughes, have cautioned against making the liturgy overly moralistic in tone (Hughes and Francis 1991, 52). Up to a point I agree with her. With rare exception I would support the notion that particular moral issues should not be superimposed on the liturgy. But having said this, I remain convinced that sacred ritual must set out a certain overarching moral framework for focusing the energies hopefully released by the experience of God in the course of ritual participation. This framework relates directly to the aspect of "ritual containment" about which Robert Moore has spoken.

For sacred ritual to provide the necessary moral framework for vitalistic energies, its text, structure, and gestures must emphasize the following themes. The first is a fundamental sense of community. In a seminal article some years ago Msgr. John Egan emphasized the importance of this stress on community in the liturgy, going back to Virgil Michel's root metaphor of the body of Christ: "We do not stand alone before God, but as a community of people vitally and organically bound to one another in Christ. In the social apostolate the doctrine of the mystical body affirmed the fundamental truth that the human person is created as a social being, a being whose existence and growth is defined and developed in interaction with other human beings" (Egan 1983, 9).

The development of a sense of human co-creational responsibility for the earth is likewise vital for "ritual containment." The post-Holocaust, divine-human relationship will need to be one in which there is a clear recognition of God's utter and inescapable dependence upon the human community in the process of creational salvation. The God whom we used to invoke in the liturgy to intervene and correct the ills of the world died in the ashes of the Holocaust. God will not intervene to stop such perversions of authentic human freedom whether during the Holocaust or in more recent instances such as Rwanda and Bosnia. The Holocaust and these succeeding genocides have taught us that God will not, perhaps even cannot, effect the full redemption of that part of divine power he has graciously shared with humankind unless human beings assume their appointed role of co-creators. This co-creatorship theme has been highlighted in Catholic social documents from the U.S. and Canadian bishops as well as in Pope John Paul II's encyclical *Laborem Exercens*.

I must acknowledge that some of my ethics colleagues have challenged such a co-creationship orientation. Stanley Hauerwas has argued against my position, insisting that in light of the Holocaust we need to assert human limitation rather than human power to regain a proper sense of humility (Hauerwas 1981, 34). I have to say that on the whole he has not persuaded me. In fact, failing to take seriously the depth of our new responsibility may well lead to further catastrophes. But we do share some commonality in our analysis. For me the assertion of co-creatorship must be done in the context of a newly heightened sense of humility, a clear recognition that any measure of co-creatorship we enjoy is not self-generative but a gift of God, coupled with a forthright recognition of the other side of this power: the destructive tendencies that surfaced so prominently during the Nazi era. The fear and paternalism that have frequently characterized the God-human person relationship in the past is fast eroding. But the new relationship being born cannot be made fully whole until the human community develops a profound sense of dependence on the ultimate Creator of all human power. Without this sense of dependence, the potential for goodness and love inherent in the new consciousness will become a reality that is one long nightmare of hate and destruction. The Nazi ideologues believed that they had acquired total power over the life process. They, and they alone, would decide its future course without any moral evaluation of their endeavors. We know the human disaster such a perspective created.

A proper incorporation of a sense of human dependency, of a sense of humility, into sacred ritual is critical for creational survival. Here is where Hauerwas and I profoundly agree. But so powerful is the sense of co-creatorship that Lutheran theologian Philip Hefner has termed it absolutely decisive (Hefner 1993). Somehow we must bring to the fore in liturgical celebration the enhanced power of humanity and, subsequently, the responsibility for creation that is now a reality. Older terms such as *stewardship* are simply too weak in my judgment.

Another aspect of this same awareness is a genuine belief in the goodness of the earth. Some Holocaust scholars such as Richard Rubenstein look to the philosophy of Nietzsche as providing roots, albeit indirect, for Nazi philosophy. The Catholic Holocaust commentator Frederich Heer shares this perspective with Rubenstein, interpreting Nazi philosophy as in part a reaction to the anti-world sentiment buried deep in the Christian consciousness. Heer quotes fellow commentator Karl Erlingagen, who has asked: "Could not Nietzsche's cry, 'Remain faithful to the earth,' be interpreted as the cry of protest of a misunderstood and mistreated world, and be echoed in its truest sense by the Christian? . . . The contempt for the world of which we speak goes far beyond contempt for the material and the basely sensual; it extends to the purest realms of the spirit" (Heer 1970, 401). Clearly, as George Mosse has shown in his research, the Nazi public ritual was meant in part to overcome this negativity. Somehow the liturgy needs to make people aware of the fundamental compatibility of earthliness and spirituality if the quest for authentic earthly existence is to avoid the destructive paths taken by Nazi philosophy.

Let me mention three additional themes that need exposure in the liturgy if we are to achieve the goal of "ritual containment." The first is what Jürgen Moltmann in his volume *The Crucified God* (1974) has asserted as a comprehensive Christology based on the Holocaust experience (Pawlikowski 1998, 345–68) and has termed the "vulnerability of God." Only a modification of God's omnipotence, through participation in human suffering and dependence on the human community, will finally curb the combination of pride and power that has proven so destructive in the course of human history. If God can be dependent, so can humanity. "Vulnerability" can in fact be a mark of its "godliness." Such sacred imagery flies in the face of Nazi assertions of unlimited human power as the sign of human greatness.

There is also a need for the liturgy to image Jesus' central emphasis on reconciliation even to the point that my colleague Donald Senior has called "enemy love" (Senior 1983, 163). This emphasis must be done within a context of a clear acknowledgment of Jesus' confrontational side as well.

Finally, we need to build into sacred ritual some sense of the importance of lament. David Power and others have stressed the need to resurrect an understanding of the power of lament to heal and control emotions in times of mass human destruction such as the Holocaust, Rwanda, and the global AIDS epidemic (Power and Lumbala 1993; Berenbaum 1996). Uncontrolled vitalistic energies in such settings can easily lead to further death and destruction through retaliation. Yet the pain of the experience must be released. Lament can play a crucial role in releasing, yet containing, such energies.

We should address one other dimension of the liturgy-ethics link in light of the Holocaust. Increasingly, I have been intrigued with the role of symbolism in forging social cohesion and in providing society with public values. As we examine the Holocaust, we begin to detect how purely rational ideals were totally ineffective in combating the upsurge of Nazism. Here lies the fundamental flaw in classic liberalism. To their "credit," if I may use that term, the Nazis recognized that symbols are extremely important in determining the public values of a society. They were quite aware that symbols bind people in ways that ideas alone cannot. They understood that their ideology would have fallen on arid ground without their public liturgies. They understood that acts of celebration strengthen resolve in ways that mere discussion cannot. So public ritual became vital for the implementation of the Nazi scheme for society.

As we examine the public life of the American republic today, the question haunts me. Are we not faced with a situation that in some ways parallels that of Germany at the time of the Nazi ascendancy? Some years ago Rollo May offered reflections on the meaning of symbols that may have an application for the public state of America's soul and that may help illuminate a proper response to this question. He wrote: "I would suggest that the difference between a 'sign' and a genuine 'symbol' lies at this point: when a word retains its original power to grasp us, it is still a symbol, but when this is lost it deteriorates into being only a sign, and by the same token when a myth loses its power to demand some stand from us, it has become only a tale" (May 1966, 17).

The question before us is whether the symbols of transcendence that have undergirded American public morality are now collapsing in the process of becoming signs and tales with no power to grasp us. Was this not in part the dilemma of the Weimer era in pre-Nazi Germany? The success of the Nazis in presenting new symbols through their public rituals to an alienated and frustrated society may contain a vital lesson for those of us identified with liberal Christianity and liberal Judaism. People need symbols. If we simply join with those who oppose all public symbols, then we may in effect be paving the way for the triumph of religious symbolism motivated by religious fanaticism.

A central challenge before the mainline churches today is the creation of new symbols of transcendence for American society and the clarification of the proper limits of such symbols in terms of their specific religious content. It is a challenge that we have not yet adequately addressed. If the challenge is to be met, however, it is my conviction that liturgists will have to consider assuming a significantly new role. They will need to step beyond denominational boundaries to look at what current symbols in society might be reinvigorated and what new ones might be developed. There is no other group on the current American scene with the creative potential to deal with this reality. Certainly Hollywood and certain other sectors of the public media have the creative potential for this role, but on the whole show few signs of interest in such an undertaking. And our universities frequently study ancient myth and ritual and analyze social symbols from a sociological perspective. But virtually nowhere is there attention in any great measure to the creation and maintenance of symbolic bondings in contemporary America that acknowledge our dependence on a Creator God while clearly asserting our newly realized co-creational responsibilities. It would be my plea that liturgists explore more deeply, in an interreligious context to be sure, this aspect of their calling.

In the frontispiece to his *Holocaust Kingdom,* Alexander Donat quotes from Revelation 6:8: "And I looked, and behold a pale horse: and his name that sat on him was Death, and Hell followed with him. And power was given unto them over the fourth part of the earth, to kill with sword, and with hunger, and with death, and with the beasts of the earth." Unless we can recreate a new dynamic sense of a God-human person relationship through symbolic experience and thus shape a new moral sensibility within humankind, we have little chance of preventing the horse from riding through our lands once more as it did during the Holocaust. Our cooperative calling today is truly death-defying.

REFERENCES

INDEX

# References

Adam, Karl. 1933. "Deutsches Volkstum und katholisches Christentum." *Theologische Quartalschrift* 114: 40–63.

Adolph, Walter. 1972. *Sie sind nicht vergessen Gestalten aus der jüngsten deutschen Kirchengeschichte.* Berlin: Enka.

———. 1987. *Geheime Aufzeichnungen aus dem nationalsozialistischen Kirchenkampf.* Edited by Ulrich von Hehl. Mainz, Germany: Matthias-Grünewald.

Albrecht, Dieter, ed. 1976. *Katholische Kirche im Dritten Reich. Eine auseinandersetzung zum Verhältnis von Papsttum, Episkopat und deutschen Katholiken zu National-sozialismus 1933–1945.* Mainz, Germany: Matthis-Grünewald.

Alvarez, David, and Robert A. Graham. 1997. *Nothing Sacred. Nazi Espionage Against the Vatican, 1939–1945.* London: Cass.

Alwe. 1936. "Ein Christliches Gebet für Juden." *Gerechtigkeit* 4, no. 151: 2.

Appleby, Scott. 2000. *The Ambivalence of the Sacred: Religion, Violence, and Reconciliation.* New York: Rowman and Littlefield.

Arendt, Hannah. 1977. *Eichmann in Jerusalem: A Report on the Banality of Evil.* New York: Harmondsworth.

Ariel, Yaakov. 1991. "Jewish Suffering and Christian Salvation: The Evangelical-Fundamentalist Holocaust Memoirs." *Holocaust and Genocide Studies* 6, no. 1: 63–78.

Asmussen, Hans. 1947. "Gehört Luther vor den Nürnberger Gericht?" *Nachrichten für die Evangelisch—lutherische Geistlichen in Bayern* 2, nos. 19–20: 123–28.

August, Jochen. 1984. "Die Entwicklung des Arbeitsmarkts in Deutschland in den 30er Jahren und der Masseneinsatz ausländischer Arbeitskräfte während des Zweiten Weltkrieges: Das Fallbeispiel der polnischen zivilen Arbeitskräfte und Kriegsgefangenen 1939/1940." *Archiv für Sozialgeschichte* 24: 305–54.

Baez, Kjersti Hoff. 1989. *Corrie ten Boom.* Uhrichsville, Ohio: Barbour Publishing.

Bangha, Bela S. 1934. "Katholizismus und Judentum." In *Klärung in der Judenfrage,* edited by Nikolaus Hovorka, 9–125. Vienna: Reinhold.

Baranowski, Shelley. 1986. *The Confessing Church, Conservative Elites, and the Nazi State.* Lewiston, N.Y.: Edwin Mellen Press.

———. 1987. "Consent and Dissent: The Confessing Church and Conservative Opposition to National Socialism." *Journal of Modern History* 59: 53–78.

———. 1999. "The Confessing Church and Antisemitism: Protestant Identity, German Nationhood, and the Exclusion of the Jews." In *Betrayal: German Churches and the Holocaust,* edited by Robert Ericksen and Susannah Heschel, 90–109. Minneapolis, Minn.: Fortress Press.

Barnes, Kenneth C. 1999. "Dietrich Bonhoeffer and Hitler's Persecution of the Jews." In *Betrayal: German Churches and the Holocaust,* edited by Robert P. Ericksen and Susannah Heschel, 110–28. Minneapolis, Minn.: Fortress Press.

Barnett, Victoria. 1992. *For the Soul of the People.* Oxford, U.K.: Oxford Univ. Press.

———. 1995. "Dietrich Bonhoeffer's Ecumenical Vision." *The Christian Century,* Apr. 26, 454–57.

———. 1997. "Dietrich Bonhoeffer: An Unfinished Hero." Unpublished manuscript.

———. 1999. *Bystanders: Conscience and Complicity During the Holocaust.* Westport, Conn.: Greenwood Press.

Baron, Lawrence. 1993. "Evangelical Converts, Corrie ten Boom, and the Holocaust: A Response to Yaakov Ariel." *Holocaust and Genocide Studies* 7, no. 1: 143–48.

———. 1995. "Parochialism, Patriotism, and Philo-Semitism: Why Members of the Reformed Churches Rescued Jews During the Holocaust." Unpublished manuscript.

Bärsch, Carl-Eberhard. 1998. *Die politische Religion des Nationalsozialismus. Die religiöse Dimension der NS-Ideologie in den Schriften von Dietrich Eckart, Joesph Goebbels, Alfred Rosenberg und Adolf Hitler.* Munich: Fink.

Barth, Karl. 1941. *The Christian Cause.* New York: Macmillan.

———. 1947. *The Only Way.* New York: Philosophical Library.

Barth, Karl, and Johannes Hamel. 1959. *Christenheit unter marxistische Herrschaft.* Berlin: Siedler Verlag.

Baum, Gregory. 1996. *The Church for Others. Protestant Theology in Communist East Germany.* Grand Rapids, Mich.: W. B. Eerdmans.

Bäumer, Remigius. 1983. "Die theologische Fakultät Freiburg und das Dritte Reich." *Freiburger Diözesan-Archiv* 103: 265–89.

———. 1984. "Die 'Arbeitsgemeinschaft katholischer Deutscher' im Erzbistum Freiburg. Der Versuch eines 'Brückenschlags' zum Nationalsozialismus." *Freiburger Diözesan-Archiv* 104: 281–313.

Bayerisches Gesetz und Verordnungs Blatt. 1940. Mar. 14, no. 7: 37 (folder) Arbeitsämter 880, Staatsarchiv Munich.

Bayerisches Statistisches Landesamt. 1953. *Historisches Gemeindeverzeichnis: Die Einwohnerzahlen der Gemeinden Bayerns in der Zeit von 1840 bis 1952.* Munich: Bayerisches Statistisches Landesamt.

Beckmann, Joachim, ed. 1950. *Kirchliches Jahrbuch: 1945–1948*. Gütersloh, Germany: Chr. Kaiser.

Benge, Janet, and Geoff Benge. 1999. *Corrie ten Boom: Keeper of the Angel's Den*. Seattle, Wash.: Youth with a Mission.

Bentley, James Martin. 1984. *Niemöller*. New York: Free Press.

Berenbaum, Michael. 1996. "Genocide in Rwanda." In *Biblical and Humane: A Festschrift for John F. Priest*, edited by Linda Bennett Elder, David L. Barr, and Elizabeth Struthers Malbon, 291–99. Atlanta, Ga.: Scholars Press.

Bergen, Doris. 1996. *Twisted Cross: The German Christian Movement in the Third Reich*. Chapel Hill: Univ. of North Carolina Press.

Berger, David. 1998. *Natur und Gnade: In systemtatischer Theologie und Religionspäda-gogik von der Mitte des 19. Jahrhunderts bis zur Gegenwart*. Regensburg, Germany: Roderer.

Berkovits, Eliezer. 1973. *Faith After the Holocaust*. New York: KTAV.

Besier, Gerhard. 1994. *Die evangelische Kirche in den Umbrücken des 20. Jahrhunderts*. Neukirchen Veuyn, Germany: Neukirchen Verlag.

———. 1995. *Der SED Staat und die Kirche*. 3 vols. Munich/Berlin, Frankfurt am Main: Propyloaen.

Besier, Gerhard, et al., eds. 1986. *Bekenntnis, Widerstand, Martyrium. Von Barmen 1934 bis Plötzensee 1944*. Göttingen, Germany: Vandenhoeck and Ruprecht.

———. 1989. *Kirche nach der Kapitulation: Die Allianz zwischen Genf, Stuttgart und Bethel*. Stuttgart, Germany: Verlag W. Kohlhammer.

———. 1999. *Nationaler Protestantismus und Ökumenische Bewegung. Kirchliches Handeln im Kalten Krieg (1945–1990)*. Berlin: Duncker and Humblot.

Bethge, Eberhard. 1970. *Dietrich Bonhoeffer. A Biography*. New York: Harper and Row.

———. 1981. "Dietrich Bonhoeffer and the Jews." In *Ethical Responsibility: Bonhoeffer's Legacy to the Churches*, edited by John Godsey and Geffrey Kelly, 43–96. New York: Edwin Mellen Press.

———. 1985. *Dietrich Bonhoeffer: Man of Vision, Man of Courage*. New York: Harper and Row.

———. 1995a. "Unfulfilled Tasks." *Dialog* 34, no. 1: 30–31.

———. 1995b. *Friendship and Resistance: Essays on Dietrich Bonhoeffer*. Grand Rapids, Mich.: Eerdmans.

Bettac, Interim Superintendent Ulrich (Beetz). 1937a. To the Brandenburg Consistory, concerning "Pfarrstellenbesetzungen bei Stadtpatronen," Feb. 12. NE 126/750, Domstiftarchiv Brandenburg.

———. 1937b. To Pastor Günther Harber (Cfehrbellin), Apr. 22. NE 200/734, Domstifarchiv Brandenburg.

————. 1938. To Pastor Knuth (Berlin), July 18. NE 140/814, Domstiftarchiv Brandenburg.

————. 1939a. To Pastor Isleib (Hakenberg), Jan. 10. NE 140/814, Domstiftarchiv Brandenburg.

————. 1939b. To Frau Krüger (Nauen), Apr. 5. NE 703/770, Domstiftarchiv Nauen.

————. 1939c. To Frau Eichler (Leegebruch), Oct. 27. NE 141/835, Domstiftarchiv Brandenburg.

————. 1939d. To the Brandenburg Consistory, Oct. 31. NE 127/751, Domstiftarchiv Brandenburg.

Bichlmair, Georg. 1936a. "Rede bei der Eröffnung des neuen Heimes des Paulus-Werkes in Wien 13 February 1936." *Berichte zur Kultur und Zeitgeschichte* nos. 292/293: 124.

————. 1936b. "Der Christ und der Jude." *Reichspost* 43, no. 78 (Mar. 19).

Blenk, Gustav. 1960. *Leopold Kunschak und seine Zeit*. Vienna: Europa Verlag.

Blessing, Werner K. 1988. "Deutschland in Not, Wir im Glauben: Kirche und Kirchenvolk in einer katholischen Region 1933–1949." In *Von Stalingrad zur Währungsreform: Zur Sozialgeschichte des Umbruchs in Deutschland*, edited by Martin Broszat et al., 3–111. Munich: Oldenbourg.

Bloch, Joseph S. 1922. *Israel und die Völker nach jüdischen Lehre*. Berlin: Benjamin Harz.

Blumenthal, David R. 1985. "Religious Jews and Christians in the Holocaust: A Review Essay." In *Emory Studies on the Holocaust: An Interfaith Inquiry*, edited by David R. Blumenthal, 80–97. Atlanta, Ga.: Emory Univ. Press.

Boberach, Heinz H., ed. 1971. *Berichte des SD und der Gestapo über Kirchen und Kirchenvolk in Deutschland 1934–1944*. Mainz, Germany: Matthias-Grünewald.

————. 1984. *Meldungen aus dem Reich: Die Geheimen Lageberichte des Sicherheitsdienstes der SS, 1938–1945*. Herrsching, Germany: Pawlak.

Bonhoeffer, Dietrich. 1965a. *Ethics*. New York: Simon and Schuster.

————. 1965b. "The Church and the Jewish Question." In *No Rusty Swords: Letters, Lectures, and Notes 1928–1936*, edited by Edwin H. Robertson, 221–29. Translated by Edwin H. Robertson and John Bowden. New York: Harper and Row.

Borg, Daniel. 1966. "Volkskirche, 'Christian State,' and the Weimar Republic." *Church History* 35: 186–206.

————. 1984. *The Old-Prussian Church and the Weimar Republic*. Hanover, N.H.: Univ. Press of New England.

Bosanquet, Mary. 1968. *The Life and Death of Dietrich Bonhoeffer*. New York: Harper and Row.

Bracher, Karl Dietrich. 1983. "Demokratie und Ideologie in Zeitalter der Machtergreifung." *Vierteljahrshefte für Zeitgeschichte*: 1–24.

Brandenburg Consistory. 1938. To the Prussian Supreme Church Council, May 5. 7/12233, Evangelisches Zentralarchiv Berlin.

———. 1940a. To the Prussian Supreme Church Council, Mar. 16. EZA 14/10559, Evangelisches Zentralarchiv Berlin.

———. 1940b. To protesting parishioners in Nauen, May 18. EZA 14/10559, Evangelisches Zentralarchiv Berlin.

———. 1940c. To the Prussian Supreme Church Council, Oct. 8. 14/10559, Evangelisches Zentralarchiv Berlin.

Bratton, Fred Gladstone. 1969. *The Crime of Christendom: Theological Sources of Christian Anti-Semitism.* Boston, Mass.: Beacon Press.

Breuning, Klaus. 1969. *Die Vision des Reiches. Deutscher Katholizismus zwischen Demokratie und Diktatur (1929–1934).* Munich: Hueber.

Brosseder, Johannes. 1988–89. "Möhler's Romantic Idea of the Church: Its Problem in the Present." *Philosophy and Theology* 3: 161–71.

Broszat, Martin. 1981. "Resistenz und Widerstand. Eine Zwischenbilanz des Forschungsprojekts." In *Bayern in der NS-Zeit.* Vol. 4. *Herrschaft und Gesellschaft in Konflikt,* edited by Martin Broszat et al., 697–99. Munich: Oldenbourg.

Browning, Christopher. 1998. *Ordinary Men: Reserve Police Battalion 101 and the Final Solution in Poland.* New York: Harper.

Brunner, Philipp Josef, ed. 1804. *Gebetbuch für aufgeklärte Katholische Christen.* Heilbronn am Neckar, Germany: J. D. Clatz.

Brunotte, Heinz, and Ernst Wolf. 1965–71. *Zur Geschichte des Kirchenkampfes. Gesammelte Aufsätze.* Göttingen, Germany: G. Mohn.

Bucher, Rainer. 1998. *Kirchenbildung in der Moderne. Eine Untersuchung der Konstitutionsprinzipien der deutschen katholischen Kirche im 20. Jahrhundert.* Stuttgart, Germany: Kohlhammer.

Buchheim, Hans. 1953. *Glaubenskrise im Dritten Reich. Drei Kapitel nationalsozialistischer Religionspolitik.* Stuttgart, Germany: Deutsche Verlags-Anstalt.

Burleigh, Michael. 2000. *The Third Reich: A New History.* New York: Hill and Wang.

Cargas, Harry James. 1996. "Christian Preaching After the Holocaust." In *Removing Anti-Judaism from the Pulpit,* edited by Howard Clark Kee and Irvin J. Borowsky, 43–49. New York: Continuum.

Carlson, Carole C. 1983. *Corrie ten Boom: Her Life, Her Faith.* Old Tappan, N.J.: Fleming H. Revell.

Casanova, José. 1994. *Public Religions in the Modern World.* Chicago: Univ. of Chicago Press.

Chadwick, Owen. 1977. "Weizsäcker, the Vatican, and the Jews of Rome." *Journal of Ecclesiastical History* 28, no. 2: 179–99.

Chandler, Andrew, ed. 1998. *The Moral Imperative: New Essays on the Ethics of Resistance in National Socialist Germany, 1933–1945.* New York: Basic Books.

Chu, Jolene, and Simone Liebster. "Jehovah's Witnesses: A Case of Spiritual Resistance." Unpublished manuscript.

Cohen, Arthur. 1981. *The Tremendum: A Theological Interpretation of the Holocaust.* New York: Crossroad.

Cohn-Sherbok, Dan. 1992. *The Crucified Jew: Twenty Centuries of Christian Anti-Semitism.* Grand Rapids, Mich.: William B. Eerdmans.

Conway, John S. 1964. "Historiography of the German Church Struggle." *Journal of Bible and Religion* 32: 221–30.

————. 1968. *The Nazi Persecution of the Churches 1933–1945.* New York: Basic Books.

————. 1982. "The German Church Struggle and Its Aftermath." In *Jews and Christians After the Holocaust,* edited by Abraham J. Peck, 39–52. Philadelphia, Pa.: Fortress Press.

Coppenrath, Albert. 1937. Strafsache, Aug. 17. Reich Justizministerium, R 3001 III g17 555/38, Bundesarchiv, Berlin.

————. 1938. *Unsere St. Matthias Pfarrei im Wandel der Zeiten.* Berlin: Salvator.

————. 1948. *Der westfälische Dickkopf am Winterfeldtplatz. Meine Kanzelvermeldungen und Erlebnisse im Dritten Reich.* 2d ed. Cologne, Germany: J. P. Bachem.

Corni, Gustavo. 1990. *Hitler and the Peasants: Agricultural Policy of the Third Reich, 1930–1939.* New York: Berg.

Cornwell, John. 1999. *Hitler's Pope: The Secret Story of Pius XII.* New York: Viking Press.

Correspondence held by U.S. Holocaust Memorial Museum Archives: RSHA-SD Berlin. Osobi fond #500. RG-11.001M.01, reel 3; and RG-15.007M, reel 49: Between Harand and Ruryniec-Peuth, Oboz Zydowski, Kaminka-Montefiore, Schmalz-Rosenkranz, Waldman, Richard E. Gutstadt, Charles Edward Russell, Francis Henson, Holzer, dated Aug. 1933 through Dec. 1936. Harand, "Junge Menschen-Unsere Zukunft," n.d. (nos. 236–37) and Harand, "Heilige Arbeit," n.d. (nos. 247–49). Yad Vashem Archives: Gideon Hausner to M. Landau, Aug. 15, 1968.

Coudenhove-Kalergi, Heinrich. 1932. *Das Wesen des Antisemitismus.* Vienna: Paneuropa.

————. 1935. *Judenhass von heute.* Vienna: Paneuropa.

Cramer, Pastor (Kremmen). 1933. To Superintendent Graßhoff (Nauen). STN 1335, NE 101/647, Domstiftarchiv Brandenburg.

Dahm, K. W. 1968. "German Protestantism and Politics, 1918–1939." *Journal of Contemporary History* 12: 29–49.

————. 1965. *Pfarrer und Politik: Soziales Position und politische Mentalität des deutschen evangelischen Pfarrstandes zwischen 1918 und 1933.* Köln, Germany: Opladen Westdeutscher Verlag.

Damberg, Wilhelm. 1993. "Kirchengeschichte zwischen Demokratie und Diktatur. Georg Schreiber und Joseph Lortz in Münster 1933–1950." In *Theologische Fakultäten im Nationalsozialismus,* edited by Leonore Siegele-Wenschkewitz and Carsten Nicolaisen, 146–67. Göttingen, Germany: Vandenhoeck and Ruprecht.

Delaney, John J. 1995. "Rural Catholics, Polish Workers, and Nazi Racial Policy in Bavaria, 1939–1945." Ph.D. diss., State Univ. of New York/Univ. at Buffalo.

Delitzsch, Franz T. 1881. *Rohling's Talmudjude beleuchtet.* Leipzig, Germany: Dörffling und Franke.

————. 1883a. *Schachmatt den Blutlügnern Rohling und Justus.* Erlangen, Germany: A. Deichert.

————. 1883b. *Was Aug. Rohling beschworen hat und beschwören will.* Leipzig, Germany: Dörffling und Franke.

Dietrich, Donald. 1987. "Catholic Theologians in Hitler's Reich: Adaptation and Critique." *Journal of Church and State* 19: 19–45.

————. 1988. *Catholic Citizens in the Third Reich: Psycho-Social Principles and Moral Reasoning.* New Brunswick, N.J.: Transaction Publisher.

————. 1995. *God and Humanity in Auschwitz: Jewish-Christian Relations and Sanctioned Murder.* New Brunswick, N.J.: Transaction Publishers.

Eckardt, A. Roy. 1986. *Jews and Christians: Contemporary Meeting.* Bloomington: Indiana Univ. Press.

Ecker, Jakob. 1921. *Der Judenspiegel im Lichte der Wahrheit.* Paderborn, Germany: Bonifacius.

Editor. 1936. "Die Wahrheit: Bichlmair und Kresse." *Jüdische Wochenschrift* 52, no. 14.

Egan, John. 1983. "Getting Liturgy and Justice to Merge." *National Catholic Reporter,* Sept. 30, 9.

Eichmann, Eduard. 1934. *Lehrbuch des Kirchenrechts auf Grund des Codex Iuris Canonici.* Vol. 2. Paderborn, Germany: Ferdinand Schöningh.

"Einspruch gegen die Wahl des Herrn Pfarrer Andrich. . ." Undated. NE 703/770, Domstiftarchiv Brandenburg.

Ericksen, Robert P. 1985. *Theologians under Hitler: Gerhard Kittel, Paul Althaus, Emanuel Hirsch.* New Haven, Conn.: Yale Univ. Press.

Ericksen, Robert P., and Susannah Heschel, eds. 1999. *Betrayal: German Churches and the Holocaust.* Minneapolis, Minn.: Fortress Press.

Eschweiler, Karl. 1933. "Die Kirche im Neuen Reich." *Deutsches Volkstum* 15, 451–58.

*Evang. Sonntagsblatt für den Kirchenkreis Nauen.* 1935–1940. Ki 490, Domstiftarchiv Brandenburg.

EZA (Evangelisches Zentralarchiv in Berlin), Bestand 2, Akte 35, p. 162.

Fangmeier, Jürgen, and Hinrich Stoevesandt, eds. 1981. *Karl Barth, Letters 1961–68.* Translated by Geoffrey W. Bromiley. Edinburgh: T and T Clark.

Faulhaber, Michael. 1934. "Das Alte Testament und seine Erfüllung im Christentum." *Schönere Zukunft* 9, no. 15: 349–58.

Flannery, Edward. 1985. *The Anguish of the Jews: Twenty-Three Centuries of Anti-Semitism.* New York: Paulist Press.

Foreign Service posts of the department of state. 1944–47. RG 84, box 5, National Archives, Washington, D.C.

Forstman, Jack. 1992. *Christian Faith in Dark Times: Theological Conflicts in the Shadow of Hitler.* Louisville, Ky.: Westminster/John Knox Press.

Frank, Anne. 1953. *The Diary of a Young Girl.* Translated by B. M. Mooyaart. New York: Doubleday.

Friedlander, Henry. 1995. *The Origins of Nazi Genocide: From Euthanasia to the Final Solution.* Chapel Hill: Univ. of North Carolina Press.

Friedlander, Saul. 1964. *Pie XII et le IIIe Reich.* Paris: Editions du Seuil.

Gager, John G. 1983. *The Origins of Anti-Semitism: Judaism in Pagan and Christian Antiquity.* New York: Oxford Univ. Press.

Gamble, Rhonda Renee. 1997. "Evangelical Representations of Corrie ten Boom." Masters thesis, San Diego State Univ.

Garbe, Detlef. 1998. "Between Resistance and Martyrdom: Jehovah's Witnesses During the Third Reich." Unpublished manuscript.

Gartenschläger, Pastor Georg (Bötzow). 1933. To Superintendent Graßhoff (Nauen). STN 1427, NE 101/647, Domstiftarchiv Brandenburg.

Gellately, Robert. 1990. *The Gestapo and German Society: Enforcing Racial Policy 1933–1945.* Oxford, U.K.: Clarendon Press.

Gerlach, Wolfgang. 2000. *And the Witnesses Were Silent: The Confessing Church and the Persecution of the Jews.* Lincoln: Univ. of Nebraska Press.

*Germania.* 1935 (circa). Undated newspaper clipping. VI/1 Albert Coppenrath, Diözesanarchiv Berlin.

Gestapo files, 1939–45. Record Group Gestapo Case Files 1058; 5361; 5784; 7251; 7596; 14819; and 15748 in Staatsarchiv Würzburg.

Geyer, Michael. 1994. "Resistance as Ongoing Project: Visions of Order, Obligations to Strangers, and Struggles for Civil Society 1933–1990." In *Resistance Against the Third Reich, 1933–1990.* Chicago: Univ. of Chicago Press.

Geyer, Michael, and John Boyer, eds. 1994. *Resistance Against the Third Reich, 1933–1990.* Chicago: Univ. of Chicago Press.

Giardina, Denise. 1998. *Saints and Villains.* New York: Fawcett.

Gille, Gustav. 1940a. "Predigt gehalten bei der Probeaufstellung am 21. Jan. 1940 in Nauen durch P. Gille." 14/10559, Evangelisches Zentralarchiv Berlin.

———. 1940b. To the Brandenburg Consistory, Oct. 19. 14/10559, Evangelisches Zentralarchiv Berlin.

Glockemeier, Georg. 1936. *Zur Wiener Judenfrage.* Leipzig, Germany: Johannes Günther.

Godsey, John D. 1960. *The Theology of Dietrich Bonhoeffer.* Philadelphia, Pa.: Westminster.

Godsey, John D., and Geoffrey Kelly, eds. 1981. *Ethical Responsibility: Bonhoeffer's Legacy to the Churches.* New York: Edwin Mellen Press.

Goldberg, Michael. 1986. "Bonhoeffer and the Limits of Jewish-Christian Dialogue." *Books and Religion* 14, no. 3: 3–4.

———. 1995. *Why Should Jews Survive: Looking Past the Holocaust Toward a Jewish Future.* New York: Oxford Univ. Press.

Goldhagen, Daniel. 1996. *Hitler's Willing Executioners: Ordinary Germans and the Holocaust.* New York: Alfred A. Knopf.

———. 2002. *A Moral Reckoning: The Role of the Catholic Church in the Holocaust and the Unfulfilled Duty of Repair.* New York: Alfred A. Knopf.

Goritzka, Richard. 1999. *Der Seelsorger Robert Grosche (1888–1967): Dialogische Pastoral zwischen Erstem Weltkrieg und Zweitem Vatikanischem Konzil.* Würzburg, Germany: Echter.

Gotto, Klaus, and Repgen, Konrad. 1990. *Die Katholiken und das Dritte Reich.* Mainz, Germany: Matthias-Grünewald.

Graham, Billy. 1997. *Just As I Am: The Autobiography of Billy Graham.* New York: Harper Collins.

Graßhoff, Superintendent (Nauen). 1933a. To district pastors, Apr. 29. NE 70/736, Domstiftarchiv Brandenburg.

———. 1933b. To the Brandenburg Consistory, Aug. 15. NE 50/825, Domstiftarchiv Brandenburg.

Greenberg, Irving. 1977. "Cloud of Smoke, Pillar of Fire: Judaism, Christianity, and Modernity after the Holocaust." In *Auschwitz: Beginning of a New Era?* edited by Eva Fleischner, 17—25. New York: KTAV.

Greschat, Martin, ed. 1982. *Die Schuld der Kirche: Dokumente und Reflexionen zur Stuttgarter Schulderklärung vom 18./19. Oktober 1945.* Munich: Kaiser.

———. 1993. "Die Bedeutung der Sozialgeschichte für die Kirchengeschichte." *Historische Zeitschrift* 256: 67–103.

———. 1994. *Protestanten in der Zeit: Kirche und Gesellschaft in Deustchland vom Kaiserreich bis zum Gegenwart.* Stuttgart, Germany: W. Kohlhammer.

Groenheis, G. 1981. "Calvinism and National Consciousness: The Dutch People as the New Israel." In *Britain and the Netherlands,* edited by A. C. Duke and K.C.A. Tamse, 118–33. The Hague, Netherlands: Martin Nijhoff.

Grosche, Robert. 1933a. "Die Grundlagen einer christlichen Politik der deutschen Katholiken." *Schildgenossen* 13: 46–52.

———. 1933b. "Der Kampf um den Reichsgedanken im politisch-sozialen Leben der Gegenwart." *Deutsches Volk* 1: 91–99.

———. 1934. "Reich, Staat und Kirche." In *Die Kirche im deutschen Aufbruch,* edited by F. J. Wothe, 26–49. Bergisch-Gladbach, Germany: Heider.

Großmann, Anton. 1984a. "Fremd und Zwangsarbeiter in Bayern 1939–1945." In *Auswanderer—Wanderarbeiter—Gastarbeiter: Bevölkerung, Arbeitsmarkt und Wanderung in Deutschland seit der Mitte des 19. Jahrhunderts.* Vol. 2, edited by Klaus J. Bade, 584–619. Ostfildern, Germany: Scripta Mercaturae.

———. 1984b. "Polen und Sowjetrußen als Arbeiterim Bayern 1939–1945." *Archiv für Sozialgeschichte* 24: 355–7.

Güdemann, Moritz. 1890. *Nächstenliebe.* Vienna: R. Löwit.

Gugenheimer, Joseph. 1883. *Kritische Beleuchtung des in Paderborn 1883 von Dr. Justus (Brimanus) erschiener Judenspiegel.* Vienna: M. Hirschler und Sohn.

Günther, R., et al. 1938. To the Brandenburg Consistory, Mar. 7. 7/12233 and 14/10318, Evangelisches Zentralarchiv Berlin.

Gushee, David P. 1994. *The Righteous Gentiles of the Holocaust: A Christian Interpretation.* Minneapolis, Minn.: Fortress Press.

Gutteridge, Richard. 1976. *The German Evangelical Church and the Jews 1879–1950.* Oxford, U.K.: Basil Blackwell.

Haag, John. 1981. "A Woman's Struggle Against Nazism." *The Wiener Library Bulletin,* n.s., 34, nos. 53/54: 64–72.

Hagmann, Meinrad. 1946. *Der Weg ins Verhängnis: Reichstagswahlergebnisse 1919 bis 1933 besonders aus Bayern.* Munich: Beckstein.

Hallie, Philip. 1979. *Lest Innocent Blood Be Shed. The Story of Le Chambon and How Goodness Happened There.* New York: Harper.

Hamerow, Theodore S. 1997. *On the Road to the Wolf's Lair. German Resistance to Hitler.* Cambridge, Mass.: Harvard Univ. Press.

Hamilton, Richard F. 1982. *Who Voted For Hitler.* Princeton, N.J.: Princeton Univ. Press.

Harand, Irene. 1933. *So? Oder So? Die Wahrheit über den Antisemitismus: 3. Flugschrift der Oesterreichischen Volkspartei* Vienna: I. Harand.

———. 1935a. "Ein Frontsoldat über *Sein Kampf.*" *Gerechtigkeit* 3, no. 113: 3.

———. 1935b. "Der Talmud im Feuer der Jahrhundert." *Gerechtigkeit* 3, no. 115: 3; 3, no. 116: 3; 3, no. 120: 2.

———. 1935c. "Verständigung durch Nächstenliebe." *Gerechtigkeit* 3, no. 116: 1.

———. 1935d. "Sein Kampf: Antwort an Hitler." *Gerechtigkeit* 3, no. 117: 4.

———. 1935e. *Sein Kampf: Antwort an Hitler.* Vienna: I. Harand.

———. 1936a. "John M. Oesterreicher." *Gerechtigkeit* 4, no. 129: 2.

———. 1936b. "Ein Priester, der die deutsche Juden beneidet." *Gerechtigkeit* 4, no. 130: 1.

———. 1936c. "Das Volk mit schlimmen Erbanlagen." *Gerechtigkeit* 4, no. 134: 1–2.

———. 1936d. "Die Stimme des Bishop Hudal." *Gerechtigkeit* 4, no. 134: 3.

———. 1936e. "Der Vortrag Pater Bichlmairs." *Gerechtigkeit* 4, no. 134: 3.

———. 1936f. "Meine Antwort an die Antisemiten." *Gerechtigkeit* 4, no. 138: 1–3.

————. 1936g. "Eindeutig gegen den Antisemitismus." *Gerechtigkeit* 4, no. 140: 1–2.

————. 1936h. "Der Weg zur Menschlichkeit." *Gerechtigkeit* 4, no. 145: 1.

————. 1936i. "Wahre Religiosität." *Gerechtigkeit* 4, no. 155: 1–2.

Harder, Pastor Günther (Fehrbellin). 1933. To Superintendent Graßhoff (Nauen). STN 1577, NE 101/647, Domstiftarchiv Brandenburg.

Hartley, Al. 1973. *The Hiding Place*. Old Tappan, N.J.: Fleming H. Revell.

Hauerwas, Stanley. 1981. "Jews and Christians among the Nations." *Crosscurrents* 31 (spring): 34.

Hausner, Joseph. 1974. "Irene Harand and the Movement Against Racism, Human Misery, and War." Ph.D. diss., Columbia Univ.

Hay, X. Malcom. 1950. *The Foot of Pride: The Pressure of Christendom on the People of Israel for 1900 Years*. Boston, Mass.: Beacon Press.

Haynes, Stephen R. 1995. *Reluctant Witnesses: Jews and the Christian Imagination*. Louisville, Ky.: Westminster/John Knox.

Heer, Friedrich. 1970. *God's First Love*. New York: Weybright and Talley.

Hefner, Philip J. 1993. *The Human Factor: Evolution, Culture, and Religion*. Minneapolis, Minn.: Fortress.

Hehl, Ulrich von. 1985. *Priester unter Hitlers Terror: Eine biographische und statistische Erhebung*. Mainz, Germany: Grünewald.

Heiber, Helmut. 1991. *Universitäten unterm Hakenkreuz*. Part 1. Munich: K. G. Saur.

Heilbronner, Oded. 1998. "Catholic Resistance in the Third Reich." *Contemporary European History* 7: 409–14.

Heim, Manfred. 1997. "Die Theologische Fakultät der Universität München in der NS-Zeit." *Münchener Theologischen Zeitschrift* 48: 371–87.

Heinzmann, Richard. 1987 "Die Identität des Christentums im Umbruch des 20. Jahrhunderts." *Münchener Theologische Zeitschrift* 38: 115–33.

Helmreich, Ernst Christian. 1979. *The German Churches Under Hitler: Background, Struggle, Epilogue*. Detroit, Mich.: Wayne State Univ. Press.

Herbert, Ulrich. 1990. *A History of Foreign Labor in Germany, 1890—1980*. Ann Arbor: Univ. of Michigan Press.

————. 1997. *Enforced Foreign Labor in Germany Under the Third Reich*. New York: Cambridge Univ. Press.

Herczl, Moshe Y. 1993. *Christianity and the Holocaust of Hungarian Jewry*. Translated by Joel Lerner. New York: New York Univ. Press.

Hering, Rainer. 1990. *Theologische Wissenschaft und "Drittes Reich."* Pfaffenweiler, Germany: Centaurus Verlagsgesellschaft.

Himes, Michael J. 1997. "Divinizing the Church." In *The Legacy of the Tübingen School*, edited by Donald J. Dietrich and Michael J. Himes, 95–110. New York: Crossroad.

Hirsch, David H. 1997. "Camp Music and Camp Songs: Szymon Laks and Aleksander

Kulisiewicz." In *Confronting the Holocaust: A Mandate for the Twenty-first Century,* edited by G. Jan Colijn and Marcia Sachs Littell, 157–68. Lanham/New York/Oxford: Univ. Press of America.

Hlond, H. E. 1941. *The Persecution of the Catholic Church in German-Occupied Poland. Reports Presented by Primate of Poland to Pope Pius XII, Vatican Broadcasts, and Other Reliable Evidence.* Preface by H.E.A. Cardinal Hinsley. New York: Longmans Green.

Hoffmann, Peter. 1988. *The History of German Resistance, 1933–1945.* Cambridge: Harvard Univ. Press.

Höpfl, Bernhard. 1997. *Katholische Laien im nationalsozialistischen Bayern: Verweigerung und Widerstand zwischen 1933–1945.* Paderborn, Germany: Ferdinand Schöningh.

Horn, Daniel. 1979. "The Struggle for Catholic Youth in Hitler's Germany: An Assessment." *Catholic Historical Review* 65, no. 4: 561–82.

Hovorka, Nikolaus, ed. 1936. *Klärung in der Judenfrage.* Vienna: Reihnold.

Hudal, Alois. 1935. *Rom, Christentum und Deutsches Volk.* Innsbruck, Austria: Tyroli.

———. 1936. *Die Grundlagen des Nationalsozialismus.* Leipzig, Germany: J. Günther.

———. 1976. *Römische Tagebucher.* Graz, Austria: Stocker.

Hughes, H. Kathleen, and Mark Francis. 1991. *Living No Longer for Ourselves: Liturgy and Justice in the Nineties.* Collegeville, Minn.: Liturgical Press.

Hughes, Philip E. 1966. *Creative Minds in Contemporary Theology.* Grand Rapids, Mich.: Eerdmans.

Hürten, Heinz. 1992. *Deutsche Katholiken 1918–1945.* Paderborn, Germany: Ferdinand Schöningh.

Isaac, Jules. 1964. *The Teaching of Contempt: Christian Roots of Anti-Semitism.* Translated by Helen Weaver. New York: Holt, Rinehart, and Winston.

Isleib, Pastor Konrad (Hakenberg). 1939. To Acting Superintendent Bettac (Beetz), Jan. 7. NE 140/814, Domstiftarchiv Brandenburg.

Jacobs, Manfred. 1983. "Kirche, Weltanschauung, Politik. Die evangelischen Kirchen und die Option zwischen den zweiten und dritten Reich." *Vierteljahreshefte für Zeitgeschichte* 31, no. 1: 108–35.

Janta, Alexander. 1944. *I Lied to Live.* New York: Roy.

Jauch, Ernst Alfred. 1997. "Albert Coppenrath (1883–1960)." In *Mitbauer des Bistums Berlin. 50 Jahre Geschichte in Charakterbildern,* edited by Wolfgang Knauft, 93–110. Berlin: Morus.

John Paul II. 1993. *Veritatis Splendor.* Boston: St. Paul Books and Media.

Johnson, Eric. 1999. *Nazi Terror: The Gestapo, Jews, and Ordinary Germans.* New York: Basic Books.

Jucovy, Jon. 1985. "The Bavarian Peasantry under National Socialist Rule, 1933–1945." Ph.D. diss., City Univ. of New York.

Junghanns, Albert. 1980. "Der Freiburger Dogmatiker Engelbert Krebs (1881–1950)." Ph.D. diss., Univ. of Freiburg im Breisgau, Germany.

Jürgensen, Kurt. ed. 1976. *Die Stunde der Kirche: Die Ev.-Luth. Landeskirche Schleswig-Holsteins in den ersten Jahren nach dem Zweiten Weltkrieg.* Neumünster, Germany: Karl Wachholtz Verlag.

Kaiser, Jochen-Christoph. 1985. *Frauen in der Kirche. Evangelische Frauenverbände in Spannungsfeld von Kirche und Gesellschaft, 1890–1945: Quellen und Materialen.* Düsseldorf, Germany: Schwann.

Kalisch, Arnold. 1935. "Irene Harand's Kampf." *Judisk Tidskrift,* no. 9.

Katz, Jacob. 1980. *From Prejudice to Destruction: Anti-Semitism, 1700–1933.* Cambridge, Mass.: Harvard Univ. Press.

Kelley, James Patrick. 1989. " 'The Best of the German Gentiles': Dietrich Bonhoeffer and the Rights of Jews in Hitler's Germany." In *Remembering for the Future.* Vol. 1. Edited by Yehuda Bauer, 80–92. Oxford, U.K.: Pergamon.

Kershaw, Ian. 1983. *Popular Opinion and Political Dissent in the Third Reich, Bavaria 1933–1945.* New York: Oxford Univ. Press.

———. 1985. "Widerstand ohne Volk?" In *Der Widerstand gegen den Nationalsozialismus: Die deutsche Gesellschaft und der Widerstand Gegen Hitler,* edited by Jürgen Schmädecke and Peter Steinbach, 793–95. Munich: Piper.

———. 1993. *The Nazi Dictatorship. Problems and Perspectives of Interpretation.* 3d ed. London: Edward Arnold.

King, William McGuire. 1982. "Prelude to the German Church Struggle: Otto Dibelius and the Century of the Church." *Journal of Church and State* 24: 53–71.

Kitchen, Martin. 1995. *Nazi Germany at War.* New York: Longman.

Klan, J. S. 1987. "Luther's Resistance Teaching and the German Church Struggle under Hitler." *Journal of Religious History* 14: 432–43.

Klein, Charles. 1997. *How to Forgive When You Can't Forget.* New York: Berkley Books.

Koonz, Claudia. 1992. "Ethical Dilemmas and Nazi Eugenics: Single Issue Dissent in Religious Contexts." In *Resistance Against the Third Reich 1933–1990,* edited by Michael Geyer and John W. Boyer, 15–38. Chicago: Univ. of Chicago Press.

Kopp, Josef. 1886. *Zur Judenfrage nach den Akten des Prozesses Rohling-Bloch.* Leipzig, Germany: J. Klinkhardt.

Körber, Robert. 1939. *Rassesieg in Wien der Grenzfeste des Reiches.* Vienna: W. Braumüller.

Krebs, Engelbert. 1913. "Hirscher und die Wiedergebuhrt des katholischen Lebens in Deutschland." *Freiburger Diözesanarchiv* 41: 170–86.

———. 1915. "Vom Segen des Krieges." *Theologie und Glaube* 7: 21–26.

———. 1917. "Die Wertprobleme und ihre Behandlung in der katholischen Dogmatik." *Oberrheinische Pastoralblatt* 19: 215–25, 247–55.

———. 1917–18. "Cardinal Merciers offentliches Wirken." *Hochland* 15: 188–205, 332–48.

———. 1922a. "Vom Priestertum der Frau." *Hochland* 19: 196–215.

———. 1922b. "Katholische Studenten und Juden." *Bädische Beobachter,* May 26.

———. 1923. *Dogma und Leben.* Vol. 1, rev. ed. Paderborn, Germany: Bonifacius.

———. 1924. *Die Kirche und das neue Europa.* Freiburg, Germany: Herder.

———. 1925. *Dogma und Leben.* Vol. 2. Paderborn, Germany: Bonifacius.

———. 1927a. "The Primitive Church and Judaism." *Thought* 1: 658–75.

———. 1927b. *A Little Book on Christian Charity.* Translated by Isabel Garahan. St. Louis, Mo.: B. Herder.

———. 1928. *Um die Erde.* Paderborn, Germany: Bonafacius.

———. 1933a. "Gedanken zum Reichskonkordat." *Freiburger Tagespost,* no. 173.

———. 1933b. "Die Aufgabe der Universität im neuen Reich." *Freiburger Tagespost,* no. 173.

———. 1933c. *Vom Wesen der Authorität im Lichte des christlichen Glaubens.* Freiburg, Germany: Waibel.

———. 1933d. "Judentum und Christentum." *Lexikon für Theologie und Kirche* 5: 678–79.

———. 1934. *Jesuitischer und deutscher Geist.* Freiburg, Germany: Waibel.

———. 1934–35. "Möhlers Athanasius." *Hochland* 32, no. 2: 385–98.

———. 1935. "Arteigenes Christentum." *Stimmen der Zeit* 129: 81–93.

Kreidler, Hans. 1988. *Eine Theologie des Lebens, Grundzüge im theologischen Denken Karl Adams.* Mainz, Germany: Matthias-Grünewald.

"Kreiskirchentag in Nauen." 1933. NE 300/590, Domstiftarchiv Brandenburg.

Krieg, Robert A. 1992. *Karl Adam: Catholicism in German Culture.* Notre Dame, Ind.: Univ. of Notre Dame Press.

———. 1997. *Romano Guardini: A Precursor of Vatican II.* Notre Dame, Ind.: Univ. of Notre Dame Press.

———. 1999. "Karl Adam, National Socialism, and Christian Tradition." *Theological Studies* 60: 432–56.

Krüger, Frau (Nauen). 1939. To Mayor Urban (Nauen), Apr. 18. NE 703/770, Domstiftarchiv Brandenburg.

Lächele, Rainer. 1994. *Ein Volk, ein Reich, ein Glaube: Die "Deutschen Christen" in Württemburg 1925–1960.* Stuttgart, Germany: Calwer.

Lagebericht. 1935. Feb. Reichskanzlei R43/II/175: 289, Bundesarchiv, Berlin.

Lamb, Matthew. 1982. *Solidarity with Victims. Toward a Theology of Moral Transformation.* New York: Crossroad.

Lautenschläger, Gerhard. 1987. *Joseph Lortz (1887–1975), Weg, Umwelt und Werk eines katholischen Kirchenhistorikers.* Würzburg, Germany: Echter.

Lease, Gary. 1995. *"Odd Fellows" in the Politics of Religion: Modernism, National Socialism, and German Judaism.* New York: DeGruyter.

Lee, Robert. 1981. "Family and 'Modernization': The Peasant Family and Social Change in Nineteenth-Century Bavaria." In *The German Family: Essays on the Social History of the Family in Nineteenth- and Twentieth-Century Germany,* edited by Richard J. Evans and W. R. Lee, xxx–xl. London: Croom Helm.

Leonard, Oscar. 1937. "Anti-Semitism Disgraces Christianity." *B'nai B'rith Magazine* 51, no. 8: 283.

Lewin, Adolf. 1884. *Der Judenspiegel des Dr. Justus ins Licht der Wahrheit geruckt.* Magdeburg, Germany: D. L. Wolff.

Lewy, Guenther. 1964. *The Catholic Church and Nazi Germany.* New York: McGraw Hill.

Liebmann, Maximilian. 1988a. *Theodor Innitzer und der Anschluss.* Graz, Austria: Styria.

———. 1988b. "Bischof Hudal und der Nationalsozialismus: Rom und die Steiermark." *Geschichte und Gegenwart* 7: 263–80.

Littell, Franklin H. 1975. *The Crucifixion of the Jews: The Failure of Christians to Understand the Jewish Experience.* New York: Harper and Row.

Loge, Christian (Anton Orel). 1934. *Gibt es jüdische ritual Morde?* Graz, Austria: Styria.

Lortz, Joseph. 1933. *Katholischer Zugang zum Nationalsozialismus.* Münster, Germany: Aschendorff.

*L'Osservatore Romano.* 1943a. "Carità Civile." Dec. 3.

———. 1943b. "Motivazioni," Dec. 5.

Lowry, Lois. 1989. *Number the Stars.* New York: Houghton Mifflin.

Löwy, David. 1882. *Der Talmudjude von Rohling in der Schwungerichtsverhandlung vom 28. Oktober 1882.* Vienna: W. Banmüller.

Ludwig, Hartmut. 1971. "Karl Barth's Dienst der Versöhnung. Zur Geschichte des Stuttgarter Schuldbekenntnisses." In *Zur Geschichte des Kirchenkampfes. Gesammelte Aufsätze II,* edited by Heinz Brunotte and Ernst Wolf, 265–326. Göttingen, Germany: Vandenhoeck and Ruprecht.

Lux, Pastor (Groß Behnitz). 1933. To Superintendent Graßhoff (Nauen), May 8. NE 101/647, Domstiftarchiv Brandenburg.

Mallmann, Klaus-Michael, and Gerhard Paul. 1993. "Resistenz oder loyale Widerwilligkeit? Anmerkungen zu einem umstrittenen Begriff." *Zeitschrift für Geschichtswissenschaft* 99: 113–16.

Maritain, Jacques. 1936. *Freedom in the Modern World.* Translated by Richard O'Sullivan. New York: Charles Scribner's Sons.

May, Rollo. 1966. *Symbols in Religion and Literature.* New York: Brazillee.

Meier, Kurt. 1992. *Kreuz und Hakenkreuz. Die evangelische Kirche im Dritten Reich.* Munich: Deutscher Taschenbuch Verlag.

Metz, Johannes. 1979. "Ökumene nach Auschwitz." In *Gott nach Auschwitz*, edited by E. Kogon et al. Freiburg, Germany: Herder.

Michaelis, Meir. 1978. *Mussolini and the Jews. German-Italian Relations and the Jewish Questions in Italy, 1922–1945.* Oxford, U.K.: Oxford Univ. Press.

Minow, Martha. 1998. *Between Vengeance and Forgiveness: Facing History After Genocide and Mass Violence.* Boston, Mass.: Beacon Press.

Moltmann, Jürgen. 1974. *The Crucified God.* New York: Harper and Row.

Moore, Bob. 1997. *Victims and Survivors: The Nazi Persecution of Jews in the Netherlands 1940–1945.* London: Arnold.

Mooser, J. 1979. "Gleichheit und Ungleichheit in der ländlichen Gemeinde: Sozialstruktur und Kommunalverfassung im Östlichen Westfalen vom späten 18. bis in die Mitte des 19. Jahrhunderts." *Archiv für Sozialgeschichte* 19: 231–62.

Mosse, George. 1966. *Nazi Culture: A Documentary History.* New York: Random House.

———. 1977. *The Nationalization of the Masses: Political Symbolism and Mass Movements in Germany from the Napoleonic Wars through the Third Reich.* New York: New American Library.

Mouw, Richard J. 1997. "To the Jew First: Witnessing to the Jews Is Non-Negotiable." *Christianity Today* 41: 15–25.

Muench, Aloysius. 1946–1947. Muench Diaries 37/1–4, Oct. 24, 1946, to Apr. 9, 1947. Catholic Univ. of America archives, Washington, D.C.

Mussinghoff, Heinz. 1979. *Theologische Fakultäten im Spannungsfeld von Staat und Kirche.* Mainz, Germany: Matthias Grünewald.

Nauen District Church Office. 1931–35. To district pastors (various). NE 70/736, Domstiftarchiv Brandenburg.

———. 1935–38. To district pastors (various). NE 71/737, Domstiftarchiv Brandenburg.

———. 1936a. "Einführung von Konfirmandenrüstzeiten," Mar. 18. NE 125/744, Domstiftarchiv Brandenburg.

———. 1936b. To the Brandenburg Consistory (Annual Report for 1934–35), Sept. 30. NE 125/744, Domstiftarchiv Brandenburg.

———. 1937. To the Brandenburg Consistory (Annual Report for 1936), Feb. 11. NE 126/750, Domstiftarchiv Brandenburg.

———. 1938. To the Brandenburg Consistory (Annual Report for 1937), Mar. 18. NE 129/900, Domstiftarchiv Brandenburg.

———. 1939–44. To district pastors (various). NE 72/738, Domstiftarchiv Brandenburg.

———. 1939a. To the Brandenburg Consistory (Annual Report for 1938), May 11. NE 130/840, Domstiftarchiv Brandenburg.

———. 1939b. "Vakanzliste Nauen," Sept. 3. NE 142/944, Domstiftarchiv Brandenburg.

———. 1940. To the Brandenburg Consistory (Annual Report for 1939), July 22. NE 127/751, Domstiftarchiv Brandenburg.

———. 1941. To the Brandenburg Consistory (Annual Report for 1940), Mar. 5. NE 128/752, Domstiftarchiv Brandenburg.

———. 1942. To the Brandenburg Consistory (Annual Report for 1941), Mar. 10. NE 131/803, Domstiftarchiv Brandenburg.

———. 1943. To the Brandenburg Consistory (Annual Report for 1942), Mar. 9. NE 131/803, Domstiftarchiv Brandenburg.

———. 1944. To the Brandenburg Consistory (Annual Report for 1943), Mar. 7. NE 132/759, Domstiftarchiv Brandenburg.

Nauen District Synod Executive. 1940a. "Minutes," Aug. 23. 14/10559, Evangelisches Zentralarchiv Berlin, and 59/646, Domstiftarchiv Brandenburg.

———. 1940b. To the Brandenburg Consistory, Aug. 29. 14/10559 Evangelisches Zentralarchiv Berlin.

Nauen parishioners. 1940a. To the Prussian Supreme Church Council, in protest against the election of Pastor Gustav Gille, May 31. NE 141/835, Domstiftarchiv Brandenburg.

———. 1940b. To the Brandenburg Consistory, July 17. NE 143/948, Evangelisches Zentralarchiv Berlin.

Nicosia, Francis, and Lawrence Stokes, eds. 1990. *Germans Against Nazism: Nonconformity, Opposition, and Resistance in the Third Reich. Essays in Honor of Peter Hoffmann.* New York: Berg.

Niebuhr, Reinhold. 1964. *The Nature and Destiny of Man.* Vol. 1: *Human Nature.* New York: Charles Scribner's Sons.

Niemöller, Martin. 1946. *Die deutsche Schuld, Not und Hoffnung.* Zollikon-Zürich, Switzerland: Evangelischer Verlag.

———. 1938. *Here Stand I!* Translated by Jane Lymburn. Chicago: Willett, Clark and Co.

Noakes, Jeremy, and Geoffrey Pridham, eds. 1984. *Nazism 1919–1945. A History in Documents and Eyewitness Account.* New York: Schocken.

Norden, Günther van. 1985. "Zwischen Kooperation und Teilwiderstand: Die Rolle der Kirchen und Konfessionen—Ein Überblick über Forschungspositionen." In *Der Widerstand gegen den Nationalsozialismus. Die deutsche Gesellschaft und der Widerstand gegen Hitler,* edited by Jürgen Schmädeke and Peter Steinbach, 227–39. Munich: Piper.

Novick, Peter. 1998. *The Holocaust in American Life.* Boston, Mass.: Beacon Press.

Nowak, Kurt. 1987. "Evangelische Kirche und Widerstand im Dritten Reich. Kirchenhistorische und gesellschaftsgeschichtliche Perspektiven." *Geschichtswissenschaft und Unterricht* 6: 352–64.

O'Meara, Thomas. 1982. *Romantic Idealism and Roman Catholicism.* Notre Dame, Ind.: Univ. of Notre Dame Press.

———. 1991. *Church and Culture: German Catholic Theology, 1860–1914.* Notre Dame, Ind.: Univ. of Notre Dame Press.

———. 1998. "The Witness of Engelbert Krebs." In *Continuity and Plurality in Catholic Theology,* edited by Anthony J. Cernera, 127–53. Fairfield, Conn.: Sacred Heart Univ. Press.

Oesterreicher, Johannes. 1935. "Hominem non habeo." *Die Erfüllung* 1, no. 6: 3–13.

———. 1935b. "Zum Ritualmordbuch von Christian Loge." *Die Erfüllung* 1, no. 2: 43–47.

———. 1935c. "Ein Zeuge für Christian Loge?" *Die Erfüllung* 1, no. 5: 37–42.

———. 1934/35. "Michael Kardinal Faulhaber: Judentum, Christentum, Germanentum." *Die Erfüllung* 1, no. 1: 51.

———. 1936a. "R. N. Coudenhove-Kalergi, *Judenhass von heute.* Graf. H. Coudenhove-Kalergi, *Das Wesen des Antisemitismus.* Vienna: Paneuropa." *Die Erfüllung* 2, no. 4: 212–13.

———. 1936b. "Die Entleerung der Religion." *Die Erfüllung* 2, no. 2: 89–92.

———. 1936c. "*Kirche im Kampf,* herausgegeben von Prof. Clemens Holzmeister." *Die Erfüllung* 2, no. 4: 204–8.

———. 1936d. "Bischof Dr. Alois Hudal, Die Grundlagen des Nationalsozialismus." *Die Erfüllung* 2, no. 4: 200–203.

———. 1936e. "Das Minderheitsrecht für die Juden." *Die Erfüllung* 2, no. 1: 38–43.

Oliner, Samuel P., and Pearl M. Oliner. 1988. *The Altruistic Personality: Rescuers of Jews in Nazi Europe.* New York: Free Press.

Osborne, Francis D'arcy. 1945. To secretary for foreign affairs, Feb. 22. Public Record Office, FO 371/60 803, London. Document reprinted in *Veröffentlichungen der Kommission für Zeitgeschichte,* series A, 38, 904.

Ossenkop, Curate (Fehrbellin). 1939. To the Brandenburg Consistory, in protest against the election of Pastor Andrich, June 11. NE 703/770 and NE 143/948, Domstiftarchiv Brandenburg.

Ott, Hugo. 1984. "Conrad Gröber (1872–1948)." In *Zeitgeschichte in Lebensbildern.* Vol. 6, edited by Jürgen Aretz et al., 64–75. Mainz, Germany: Matthias Grünewald.

———. 1993. *Martin Heidegger: A Political Life.* Translated by Allan Blunden. New York: Basic Books.

Paldiel, Mordecai. 1993. *The Path of the Righteous: Gentile Rescuers of Jews During the Holocaust.* Hoboken, N.J.: KTAV.

———. 1996. *Sheltering the Jews: Stories of Holocaust Rescuers.* Minneapolis, Minn.: Fortress Press.

Parish Council of Groß and Klein Behnitz. 1938. To the Brandenburg Consistory, Mar. 9. 14/10318, Evangelisches Zentralarchiv Berlin.

Parkes, James. 1934. *The Conflict of the Church and the Synagogue*. London: Soncino Press.

Passelecq, Georges, and Bernard Suchecky. 1997. *The Hidden Encyclical of Pius XI*. Translated by Steven Rendall. New York: Harcourt Brace.

Pauley, Bruce E. "Political Antisemitism in Interwar Vienna." In *Jews, Antisemitism, and Culture in Vienna*, edited by Ivan Oxaal et al., 152–73. London: Routledge and Kegan Paul.

———. 1992. *From Prejudice to Persecution*. Chapel Hill: Univ. of North Carolina Press.1987.

Pawlikowski, John T. 1996. "The Holocaust: Its Impact on Christian Thought and Ethics." In *New Perspectives on the Holocaust: A Guide for Teachers and Scholars*, edited by Rochelle L. Millen et al., 344–61. New York and London: New York Univ. Press.

———. 1995. "Judaism and Catholic Morality: The View of the Encyclical." In *Veritatis Splendor: American Responses*, edited by Michael E. Allsopp and John J. O'Keefe, 177–93. Kansas City, Mo.: Sheed and Ward.

———. 1998. "Christology After the Holocaust." *Encounter* 59, no. 3 (1998): 345–68.

Peck, William Jay. 1973. "From Cain to the Death Camps: An Essay on Bonhoeffer and Judaism." *Union Seminary Quarterly Review* 28, no. 2: 158–76.

Peterson, Edward N. 1969. *The Limits of Hitler's Power*. Princeton, N.J.: Princeton Univ. Press.

Pfarralmanach für die Kirchenprovinz Berlin-Brandenburg. 1937/1939. Domstiftarchiv Brandenburg.

Phayer, Michael. 2000. *The Catholic Church and the Holocaust, 1930–1965*. Bloomington: Indiana Univ. Press.

Pierard, Richard V. 1978. "Why Did Protestants Welcome Hitler?" *Fides et Historia* 10: 8–29.

Pius XII. 1944. To Konrad Preysing. Mar. 21. Korrespondenz V/16–4. Diocesan archives, Berlin, Germany.

Poley, Hans. 1993. *Return to the Hiding Place*. Elgin, Ill.: Life Journey Books.

Pollefeyt, Didier. 1997. "Auschwitz or How Good People Can Do Evil: An Ethical Interpretation of the Perpetrators and Victims of the Holocaust in Light of the French Thinker Tzvetan Todorov." In *Confronting the Holocaust: A Mandate for the Twenty-first Century*, edited by G. Jan Colijn and Marcia Sachs Littell, 91–118. Lanham, Md.: Univ. Press of America.

Posth, Pastor Herbert (Berge). 1935. "Berge." *Evang. Sonntagsblatt für die Kirchenprovinz Brandenburg*, Mar. 3.

———. 1938. To the Brandenburg Consistory, Oct. 20. Ri 6/26, Domstiftarchiv Brandenburg.

Pottmeyer, Hermann J. 1997. "Kingdom of God, Church, Society: The Contemporary Relevance of Johann Baptist Hirscher, Theologian of Reform." In *The Legacy of the Tübingen School,* edited by Donald J. Dietrich and Michael J. Himes, 145–55. New York: Crossroad.

Power, David N. 1983. "Response: Liturgy, Memory, and the Absence of God." *Worship* 57: 328.

Power, David N., and F. Kabasele Lumbala, eds. 1993. *The Spectre of Mass Death.* Maryknoll, N.Y.: Orbis.

Prager, Moshe. 1947. *Hurban Yisrael Be'eiropah.* Ein Harod, Austria: Hotsa'at Hakibutz Hameuhad.

"Predigt gehalten bei der Probeaufstellung am 21. Jan. 1940 in Nauen durch P. Gille." 1940. 14/10559, Evangelisches Zentralarchiv Berlin.

Pridham, Geoffrey. 1973. *Hitler's Rise to Power: The Nazi Movement in Bavaria, 1923–1933.* New York: Harper and Row.

Priester, Curate. 1936. To Pastor Posth (Berge), Sept. 10. 14/10859, Evangelisches Zentralarchiv Berlin.

Pugnator (pseudonym). 1936a *Kampf der Jungend für Sozialreform,* as cited by Hovorka (1936).

Rahner, Karl. 1994. *Theologische und philosophische Zeitfragen im katholischen deutschen Raum (1943),* edited by Hubert Wolf. Ostfildern, Germany: Schwabenverlag.

Rasmussen, Larry, with Renate Bethge. 1990. *Bonhoeffer's Significance for North Americans.* Minneapolis, Minn.: Fortress Press.

Rausch, David A. 1984. *A Legacy of Hatred: Why Christians Must Not Forget the Holocaust.* Chicago: Moody Press.

———. 1991. *Communities in Conflict: Evangelicals and Jews.* Philadelphia, Pa.: Trinity Press International.

———. 1993. *Fundamentalist Evangelicals and Anti-Semitism.* Valley Forge, Pa.: Trinity Press International.

Reichsministerium des Innern. 1940. "Polizeiverordnung über die Kenntlichmachung im Reich eingesezter Zivilarbeiter und arbeiterinnen polnischen Volkstums vom 8. Marz 1940." *Reichsgesetzblatt: Teil I, Jahrgang 1940, Erstes halbjahr.* Berlin: Reichsverlagsamt.

Reichsschrifttumskammer. 1935, 1938, 1939. *Liste des schädlichen und unerwünschten Schrifttums.* Berlin: Reichsschrifttumskammer and Leipzig: E. Hedrich.

Reimann, Viktor. 1967. *Innitzer.* Vienna: Molden.

Ritter, Gaston (Arbogast Recterer). 1933. *Das Judentum und die Schatten des Antichrist.* Graz, Austria: Styria.

Rittner, Carol, et al., eds. 2000. *The Holocaust and the Christian World: Reflections on the Past, Challenge for the Future.* New York: Continuum.

Robertson, Edwin H. 1967a. *Dietrich Bonhoeffer.* Richmond, Va.: John Knox.

———. 1967b. *Christians Against Hitler.* London: SCM Press.

———. 1989. "A Study of Dietrich Bonhoeffer and the Jews, January-April 1933." In *Remembering for the Future.* Vol. 1, edited by Yehuda Bauer, 121–29. Oxford, U.K.: Pergamon.

Rohling, August. 1872. *Der Talmudjude.* Münster, Germany: A. Russell.

———. 1883. *Meine Antworten an die Rabbiner.* Prague, Czechoslovakia: Cyrillo-Methodische.

Rosenbaum, Stanley R. 1981. "Dietrich Bonhoeffer: A Jewish View." *Journal of Ecumenical Studies* 18, no. 2: 301–7.

———. 1937. To Reich Justizministerium. Aug. 25. R3001 III g17 558/38, Bundesarchiv, Berlin.

Rubenstein, Richard. 1966. *Auschwitz: Radical Theology and Contemporary Judaism.* Indianapolis, Ind.: Bobbs-Merrill.

———. 1983. *The Age of Triage: Fear and Hope in an Overcrowded World.* Boston, Mass.: Beacon Press.

Ruether, Rosemary R. 1974. *Faith and Fratricide: The Christian Theological Roots of Anti-Semitism.* New York: Seabury Press.

Ruster, Thomas. 1994. *Die verlorene Nützlichkeit der Religion, Katholizismus und Moderne in der Weimarer Republik.* Paderborn, Germany: Schöningh.

———. 2000. *Der verwechselbare Gott. Theologie nach der Entflechtung von Christentum und Religion.* Freiburg, Germany: Herder.

Schatz, Klaus. 1986. *Zwischen Säkularisation und Zweitem Vatikanum.* Frankfurt am Main, Germany: Josef Knecht.

Scherzberg, Lucia. 2001. *Kirchenreform mit Hilfe des Nationalsozialismus: Karl Adam als Kontextueller Theologe.* Darmstadt, Germany: Wissenschaftliche Buchgesellschaft.

Schmädeke, Jürgen, and Peter Steinbach, eds. 1985. *Der Widerstand gegen den Nationalsozialismus. Die deutsche Gesellschaft und der Widerstand gegen Hitler.* Munich: Piper.

Schmaus, Michael. 1933. *Begegnungen zwischen katholischem Christentum und nationalsozialistischer Weltanschauung.* Münster, Germany: Aschendorff.

Schmiechen-Ackermann, Detlef. 1998. "Katholische Diaspora zwischen Rückzug und Selbstbehauptung in der NS-Zeit." *Geschichte in Wissenschaft und Unterricht* 49: 462–76.

Schoeneveld, Jacobus. 1989. "The Dutch Protestant Churches: A Changing Attitude Towards the Jewish People in the Twentieth Century." *Dutch Jewish History* 2.

Scholder, Klaus. 1972 and 1985. *Die Kirchen und das Dritte Reich.* 2 vols. Berlin: Siedler Verlag.

———. 1986. *Die Kirchen und das Dritte Reich.* Vol. 1: *Vorgeschichte und Zeit der Illusionen 1918–1934.* Frankfurt am Main, Germany: Ullstein Verlag.

————. 1988. *The Churches and the Third Reich.* 2 vols. Philadelphia, Pa.: Fortress Press.

————. 1989. "Modern German History and Protestant Theology." In *A Requiem for Hitler and Other New Perspectives on the German Church Struggle,* edited by Klaus Scholder, 35–60. London: SCM Press.

Schopper, Hans. 1941. *Presse im Kampf.* Brunn, Czechoslovakia: R. M. Röhrer.

Schröder, Military Chaplain. 1942. To Interim Superintendent Simon-Oranienburg, Aug. 10. 14/10556, Evangelisches Zentralarchiv Berlin.

————. 1943. To Interim Superintendent Simon-Oranienburg, Jan. 12. 14/10556, Evangelisches Zentralarchiv Berlin.

Schubert, Kurt. 1977. "Der Weg zur Katastrophe." *Studia Judaica Austriaca,* no. 1: 31–66.

Schwaiger, Georg. 1984. "Görres, Joseph von." *Theologische Realenzyklopädie* 13: 550–52.

Schwarzchild, Stephen S. 1960. "Survey of Current Theological Literature: 'Liberal' Religion (Protestant)." *Judaism* 9: 366–71.

Scrivener, Jane. 1945. *Inside Rome with the Germans.* New York: Macmillan.

Senior, C. P. Donald. 1983. "Enemy Love: The Challenge of Peace." *The Bible Today* 21 (1983): 163–69.

Siegele-Wenschkewitz, Lenore. 1974. *Nationalsozialismus und Kirche. Religionspolitik vom Partei und Staat bis 1935.* Düsseldorf, Germany: Droste.

Siems, Pastor Friedrich (Nauen). 1940. To the Brandenburg Consistory, Oct. 11. 14/10559, Evangelisches Zentralarchiv Berlin.

Sigmund, Paul. 1994. "Democracy." In *The New Dictionary of Catholic Social Thought,* edited by Judith A. Dwyer, 269–75. Collegeville, Minn.: Liturgical Press.

Smith, Helmut Walser. 1995. *German Nationalism and Religious Conflict.* Princeton, N.J.: Princeton Univ. Press.

Smith, Ronald Gregor, and Wolf-Dieter Zimmerman, eds. 1966. *I Knew Dietrich Bonhoeffer.* New York: Harper and Row.

Smith, Tom W. 1999. "The Religious Right and Anti-Semitism." *Review of Religious Research* 40, no. 3.

Söhlmann, Fritz, ed. 1946. *Treysa 1945: Die Konferenz der evangelischen Kirchenführer 27.–31. August 1945.* Lüneburg, Germany: In Heliand Verlag.

Spotts, Frederic. 1973. *The Churches and Politics in Germany.* Middletown, Conn.: Wesleyan Univ. Press.

Staatsarchiv München, Munich, Germany.

Staatsarchiv Würzburg, Würzburg, Germany.

Stapel, Wilhelm. 1933. *Die Kirche Christi und der Staat Hitlers.* Hamburg, Germany: Rowohlt Verlag.

Stasiewski, Bernhard. 1971. "Zur Geschichte der katholisch-theologischen Fakultäten und der philosophisch-theologischen Hochschulen in Deutschland 1933–1945." In *Die Kirche im Wandel der Zeit,* edited by Franz Groner, 169–85. Cologne, Germany: J. P. Bachem.

———. 1984. "Die katholisch-theologischen Fakultäten und philosophisch-theologischen Hochschulen von 1933 bis 1945: Ein Überblick." In *Seminar und Hochschule in Eichstätt unter dem Nationalismus,* edited by Hermann Holzbauer, 23–48. Eichstätt, Germany: Universitätsbibliothek.

"Statistische Übersichten über äußerungen des kirchlichen Lebens im Kirchenkreis, 1929–1944." Undated. NE 96/754, Domstiftarchiv Brandenburg.

Staub, Ervin. 1989. *The Roots of Evil: The Origins of Genocide and Other Group Violence.* New York: Cambridge Univ. Press.

Steinert, Marlis G. 1977. *Hitler's War and the Germans: Public Mood and Attitude During the Second World War.* Edited and translated by Thomas E. J. de Witt. Athens, Ohio: Ohio Univ. Press.

Tal, Uriel. 1975. *Christians and Jews in Germany: Religion, Politics, and Ideology in the Second Reich, 1870–1914.* Ithaca, N.Y.: Cornell Univ. Press.

Talmon, J. L. 1973. "European History—Seedbed of the Holocaust." *Midstream* 19, no. 5 (May): 22–24.

Tec, Nechama. 1986. *When Light Pierced the Darkness.* New York: Oxford Univ. Press.

Teluskin, Joseph. 1994. *Jewish Wisdom: Ethical, Spiritual, and Historical Lessons from the Great Works and Thinkers.* New York: William Morrow.

ten Boom, Corrie. 1954. *A Prisoner and Yet.* Fort Washington, Pa.: Christian Literature Crusade.

———. 1975. *Corrie ten Boom's Prison Letters.* Old Tappan, N.J.: Fleming H. Revell.

———. 1978a. *Father ten Boom: God's Man.* Old Tappan, N.J.: Fleming H. Revell.

ten Boom, Corrie, with Jamie Buckingham. 1978b. *Tramp for the Lord.* New York: Jove Books.

ten Boom, Corrie, with C. C. Carlson. 1976. *In My Father's House: The Years Before "The Hiding Place."* Carmel, Calif.: Guideposts.

ten Boom, Corrie, with John and Elizabeth Sherrill. 1971. *The Hiding Place.* Old Tappan, N.J.: Fleming H. Revell.

———. 1996. *The Hiding Place: The Twenty-fifth Anniversary Edition.* Grand Rapids, Mich.: Chosen Books.

Tenfelde, Klaus. 1985. "Soziale Grundlagen von Resistenz und Widerstand." In *Der Widerstand gegen den Nationalsozialismus: Die deutsche Gesellschaft und der Widerstand gegen Hitler,* edited by Jürgen Schmadecke and Peter Steinbach, 799–809. Munich: Piper.

Tiefel, Hans. 1972. "The German Lutheran Church and the Rise of National Socialism." *Church History* 41: 326–36.

Tittman, Harold. 1945. To the state department, June 4. RG 59, box 28, National Archives, Washington, D.C.

Tomaszewski, Irene, and Tecia Werbowski. 1994. *Zegota*. Montreal: Price-Patterson.

Troost, Edith, et al. Undated. "Ich erhebe Einspruch gegen die Lehre von Herrn Pfarrer Gille aus Raguhn aus folgenden Gründen ..." 14/10559, Evangelisches Zentralarchiv Berlin.

Unidentified Nauener. 1933. To Lic. Kummel (Stahnsdorf, Westhavelland), July 27. NE 120/596, Domstiftarchiv Brandenburg.

Urban, Mayor (Nauen). 1941a. To the Brandenburg Consistory, Jan. 20. 14/10559, Evangelisches Zentralarchiv Berlin.

———. 1941b. To the Brandenburg Consistory, June 23. 14/10559, Evangelisches Zentralarchiv Berlin.

———. 1942. To the Brandenburg Consistory, Apr. 27. 14/10556, Evangelisches Zentralarchiv Berlin.

van der Leeuw, Gerardus, 1973. *Sacred and Profane Beauty: The Holy in Art*. New York: Holt, Rinehart and Winston.

Volk, Ludwig, ed. 1978. *Akten Kardinal Michael von Faulhabers, 1917–1945*. Vol. 2: *1935–1945*. Mainz, Germany: Mathias-Grünewald.

———. 1980. "Der Widerstand der katholischen Kirche." In *Gegner des Nationalsozialismus Wissenschaftler und Widerstandskämpfer auf der Suche nach historischen Wirklichkeit*, edited by Christoph Kleßmann and Falk Pingel, 126–39. Frankfurt, Germany: Campus.

———. 1987. *Katholische Kirche und Nationalsozialismus. Ausgewählte Aufsätze*. Mainz, Germany: Matthias-Grünewald.

Vollnhals, Clemens, ed. 1988. *Die evangelische Kirche nach dem Zusammenbruch: Berichte ausländischer Beobachter aus dem Jahre 1945*. Göttingen, Germany: Vandenhoeck and Ruprecht.

von Borsig, Dr. Ernst. 1938. To the Brandenburg Consistory, Mar. 14. 14/10318, Evangelisches Zentralarchiv Berlin.

von Kellenbach, Katharina. N.d. "Discourses of Forgiveness in German Families and the Perpetrators of the Holocaust." St. Mary's College of Maryland website, smem.edu/ Users/kvonkellenbach/forgive.htm.

Vorgrimler, Herbert. 1966. *Karl Rahner: His Life, Thought, and Works*. Translated by Edward Quinn. Glen Rock, N.J.: Paulist Press.

Watson, Jean. 1982. *Watchmaker's Daughter: The Life of Corrie ten Boom for Young People*. Old Tappan, N.J.: Fleming H. Revell.

Weinzierl, Erika. 1969. *Zu wenig Gerechte*, 95–112. Graz, Austria: Styria.

———. 1981. "The Beginning of John M. Oesterreicher's Work." In *Standing Before God*, edited by Asher Finkel and Lawrence Frizzell, 13–19. New York: KTAV.

———. 1985. "Oesterreichische Katholiker und die Juden." In *Ecclesia Semper Reformanda,* edited by Erika Weinzierl, 359–74. Vienna: Geyer.

Weiss, John. 1996. *Ideology of Death: Why the Holocaust Happened in Germany.* Chicago: Ivan R. Dee.

Welch, David. 1993. *The Third Reich: Politics and Propaganda.* London: Routledge.

White, Kathleen. 1983. *Corrie ten Boom.* Minneapolis, Minn.: Bethany House.

Wickert, Christl, ed. 1995. *Frauen gegen die Diktatur: Widerstand und Verfolgung in nationalsozialistischen Deutschland.* Berlin: Edition Hentrich.

Wiesenthal, Simon. 1997. *The Sunflower: On the Possibilities and Limits of Forgiveness.* New York: Schocken.

Williamson, Clark W. 1982. *Has God Rejected His People? Anti-Judaism in the Christian Church.* Nashville, Tenn.: Abingdon.

Willis, Robert E. 1987. "Bonhoeffer and Barth on Jewish Suffering: Reflections on the Relationship Between Theology and Moral Sensibility." *Journal of Ecumenical Studies* 24, no. 4: 598–615.

Winzen, Damasus. 1933a. "Gedanken zu einer 'Theologie des Reiches.' " *Catholica* 2: 97–116.

———. 1933b. "Zur Theologie des Reichsgedankens." *Werkblätter von Neudeutschland Älterenbund* 6: 74–80.

"Wir Endesunterzeichneten erheben hiermit Einspruch gegen Lehre, Gaben und Wandel des Herrn Hilfspredigers Gille." 1940. Feb. 19. 14/10559, Evangelisches Zentralarchiv Berlin and 59/646, Domstiftarchiv Brandenburg.

Witetschek, Helmut, ed. 1967. *Die kirchliche Lage in Bayern nach den Regierungspräsidentenberichten 1933–1943.* Regierungsbezirk ober-und Mittel Franken. Mainz, Germany: Matthias-Grünewald.

———. 1971. *Die kirchliche Lage in Bayern nach den Regierungspräsidentenberichten 1933–1943.* Regierungsbezirk Schwaben. Mainz, Germany: Matthias-Grünewald.

Wright, J.R.C. 1974. *"Above Parties": The Political Attitudes of the German Protestant Church Leadership 1918–1933.* Oxford, U.K.: Oxford Univ. Press.

———. 1977. "The German Protestant Church and the Nazi Party in the Period of the Seizure of Power 1932–33." In *Renaissance and Renewal in Christian History,* edited by Derek Baker, 393–418. Oxford, U.K.: Oxford Univ. Press.

Wunderlich, Frieda. 1961. *Farm Labor in Germany 1810–1945: Its Historical Development Within the Framework of Agricultural and Social Policy.* Princeton, N.J.: Princeton Univ. Press.

Young, Douglas. 1997. "Our Jewish Roots." *Bridges for Peace.* www.bridgesforpeace.com

Zabel, James. 1976. *Nazism and the Pastors: A Study of the Ideas of Three "Deutsche Christen" Groups.* American Academy of Religion Dissertation Series, ed. H. Ganse Little, no. 14. Missoula, Mont.: Scholars Press.

Zahn, Gordon. 1962. *German Catholics and Hitler's War.* New York: Sheed and Ward.

Zeller, Stephen. 1936. "Auseinandersetzungen um die Judenfrage in Oesterreich." *Schönere Zukunft* 11, no. 27: 703–6.

Zeman, Z.A.B. 1973. *Nazi Propaganda.* 2d ed. London: Oxford Univ. Press.

Zerner, Ruth. 1975. "Dietrich Bonhoeffer and the Jews: Thoughts and Actions, 1933–1945." *Jewish Social Studies* 37, nos. 3–4: 235–50.

————. 1983. "German Protestant Responses to Nazi Persecution of the Jews." In *Perspectives on the Holocaust,* edited by Randolph L. Braham, 235–50. Boston, Mass.: Luwer-Nijhoff.

————. 1994. "Martin Niemöller: Activist as Bystander: The Oft-Quoted Reflection." In *Jewish-Christian Encounters over the Centuries,* edited by Marvin Perry and Frederick M. Schweitzer, 327–38. New York: Peter Lang.

Ziegel, Pastor (Bredow). 1933. To Superintendent Graßhoff (Nauen). STN 1322, NE 101/647, Domstiftarchiv Brandenburg.

Ziegler, Walter, ed. 1973. *Band IV. Regierungsbezirk Niederbayern und Oberpfalz.* Vol. 4 of *Die kirchliche Lage in Bayern nach den Regierungspräsidentenberichten 1933–1943.* Mainz, Germany: Matthias-Grünewald.

# Index